HOW TO SURVIVE AND SUCCEED IN A SMALL FINANCIAL PLANNING PRACTICE

Andrew M. Rich, CFP

Reston Publishing Company, Inc., Reston, Virginia
A Prentice-Hall Company

Library of Congress Cataloging in Publication Data

Rich, Andrew M.
  How to survive and succeed in a small financial
planning practice.

  Includes index.
  1. Investment advisers.   I. Title.
HG4621.R53 1984   362.6'2   83–24453
ISBN 0-8359-2932-9
ISBN 0-8359-2931-0 (pbk.)

10   9   8   7   6   5   4

PRINTED IN THE UNITED STATES OF AMERICA

For years I have suffered from being a workaholic. At times, I am simply unable to stop. I guess the disease is, in my case, a result of being a lazy child and an even lazier teenager.

A workaholic most certainly needs help. And I have been fortunate to receive the best help available while both building my financial planning practice and writing this book.

My wife Beverly has worked with me as an equal partner, turning this book from thought to reality. She is an exceptionally talented woman, as I have learned, who has a fluid command of the English language. Her editorial ability and her constructive criticism have been invaluable to me.

My only concern is that we now suffer from the same disease. I'm afraid this book has turned her into a workaholic, too. Whether this book succeeds or fails, she has been more than an inspiration. She is my partner in life, in business, and in this book. She is my treasure box of jewels.

To Beverly, my wealth.

CONTENTS

FOREWORD

Fifteen to twenty years ago, the practice of personal financial planning was a mere concept in the minds of some individuals. There were a few brave forerunners of today's significant number of financial planners who were beginning to put in place some of the precepts of conceptual financial planning. But for the most part, the economic problems of individuals and families in the early 1960s were being met by practitioners who were oriented toward a single product and viewed their clients' goals as singular and unrelated. Through the diligence of that handful of pioneers, personal financial planning has gained recognition to the point that today, in 1984, it is recognized as an emerging profession in the financial services industry.

The major thrust of personal financial planning is that an individual's and family's economic problems and concerns are not singular and unrelated. They are complex, integrated problems. The job of the personal financial planner is to gather the necessary data from the client, both quantitative and qualitative, and put it together along with the client's goals, objectives and desires, into a unified, integrated, holistic plan. The personal financial planner indicates that an individual's retirement needs are not just retirement needs, but should be integrated into an overall retirement, insurance, tax, investment, and estate planning program. Insurance needs are not just insurance needs, but should be looked at against the tapestry of modern economic life. The same is true of an individual's or family's investment situation and their tax planning and management problems. In fact, it is true for all aspects of their personal financial situation.

All living things go through a life process. This is also true of the personal financial planning profession. Its birth took place in the late 1960s and early 1970s with the formation of the International Association of Financial Planning and the College for Financial Planning. In the ten to fifteen years since its birth, the field of personal financial planning has gone through the trials and tribulations of infancy and early childhood. People may not agree with me, but today I see personal financial planning as going through a troublesome adolescence while reaching for maturity. This emerging profession of personal financial planning is faced with many of the problems we would expect from a restless, dynamic adolescent. We may use other professions as our model, but personal financial planning is still sufficiently unique to have characteristics and problems all its own.

Several years ago Rich White, former editor of *The Financial Planner* magazine, referred to financial planning as a "cottage industry." At first, I did not grasp the insights Rich expressed. But, as I had a chance to review and study the business, I think Rich was quite insightful. Personal financial planning has been and continues today to be strongly influenced by the "cottage" professional. The majority of personal financial planners have in the past entered the business as sole enterpreneurs— independent business people out to service their clients.

Andy's book is specifically geared toward meeting the needs of those individuals who are contemplating entering the profession as sole entrepreneurial practitioners. I have known Andy for some time, and I believe that he is in a relatively unique situation to provide insights to the many newcomers interested in entering the profession. If we were to use the College for Financial Planning as a yardstick, it is safe to say that interest in personal financial planning as a career has never been higher. The timing of Andy's book is especially appropriate as more and more people within the financial services business and outside the financial services business contemplate financial planning as a means of establishing themselves as career professionals and as a means of best servicing their clients.

As I mentioned above, Andy is uniquely positioned to speak to those individuals who are contemplating entering and also to those who have just entered financial planning as sole practitioners or as owners of small financial planning businesses. He has, like many, entered the business indirectly as you will see when he speaks of his own emergence as a personal financial planner.

Putting together the small, independent financial planning practice is akin to building a home. You need a good set of blueprints to serve as a guide, a sound foundation upon which to build the practice, and a good mix of products and services to firmly hold the practice together. Once the decision is made to start an independent practice, a myriad of questions must be answered. How should one be compensated? What market does one want to serve? What products and/or services does one want to offer? How does one establish a client base? How does one market the practice? What should one include in the basic office? Andy discusses each of those questions and more in his new book. He weighs the pros and cons of each in great detail and offers advice on products, services, and business practices, but leaves it up to the individual reader as to which direction to follow; for example, he weighs the pros and cons of load products versus no-load products. He also explains the part due diligence plays in financial planning. He discusses how to attract and keep clients and how to develop good client relationships. He describes how to set up a sound business practice, how to establish an office, and how to specialize in one of two important financial planning areas—insurance or securities. In addition, he explains the importance of developing relationships with other professionals in the financial services field—in accounting, banking, insurance, and law. He provides checklists of what to look for in each field in developing a team of experts with whom the independent financial planner should work. Andy also profiles four independent financial planners, whom he considers have made it to the top of the profession.

I believe that one may judge the emergence of a discipline by examining the literature surrounding that discipline. When I started teaching economics several years ago, one of the courses I taught was Urban Economics. When I first began teaching that course, there were very few textbooks available in the field.

By the time I moved on to other interests, seven or eight years later, there was a wide variety of texts available—the literature surrounding urban economics and urban problems had grown. I find some definite similarities between that situation and the field of personal financial planning. Five or six years ago, there was only one recognized book in the field—Venita VanCaspel's *Money Dynamics*. Venita's book, which has gone through several revisions, remains a standard in the field; but it has been joined by Loren Dunton's book, *Your Book of Financial Planning*; Judith Zabalaoui's new book, *How to Use Your Business or Profession as a Tax Shelter*; Jim Barry's book; Beverly Tanner's book; and several others. In addition, there is a growing volume of literature from professional academicians interested in the field of personal financial planning. As far as I know, Andy's book is the first book written specifically to those individuals who are interested in surviving and succeeding in a small financial planning practice.

Andy would be the first to admit that there are many pitfalls in surviving and succeeding in a small financial planning practice. For those individuals who are interested in a future career in personal financial planning, Andy's book can ease the pitfalls. One of the things that has impressed me about those individuals who have been in the field of personal financial planning for some time is that they are very sharing individuals. They are willing to assist other individuals who are in the business but having problems. Andy, in taking time to write this book, is a concrete example of an individual who is willing to share his successes and his failures with his comrades.

As one planner indicated, "Financial planning is not a destination. It is a trip. It is a journey." I think the same can be said of examining financial planning as a life's work. Andy's book might be the first good road map for new entrants or recent entrants into the profession.

WILLIAM L. ANTHES, PH.D.

President
The College for Financial Planning
Denver, Colorado

PREFACE

As I travel through financial planning circles, everyone seems to ask the same questions: How do I start my own financial planning practice? How should I operate it? And how can I make it succeed? More and more, among insurance agents, stockbrokers, registered representatives, accountants, attorneys, and others, there is a growing awareness that financial planning is here to stay and will be around for a long, long time.

How to Survive and Succeed in a Small Financial Planning Practice was written for all the people on the fringes of financial planning, who would like to enter but cannot seem to find the entrance, at least from a practical sense. There appears to be a critical need among financial planners to understand specifically how to set up and conduct a successful financial planning practice. Even if a person is technically proficient as a planner in terms of conceptual theory, he or she might not have the foggiest notion of how to operate a planning practice. It is one thing to be a skillful financial planner, planning proficiently for your clients. It is quite another to be a small businessperson able to conduct an independent practice. In fact, I would venture to say that today, many aspects of practice management are even more complex and confusing to the planner than is financial planning itself.

This book will not teach you to be a conceptual financial planner. Your academic training must come from other sources, many of which are explored in this book. My intent is to instruct you on the steps to take to become a capable financial planner, in terms of the other aspects of your practice. It is a practical book, a "how-to" book, a book about the nuts and bolts of conducting your practice.

I have therefore selected those concepts and ideas that I feel are most important for the practicing financial planner to understand—and to use. I have devoted many pages to the areas of services and products to provide; compensation; regulation, ethics; change (both in your practice and the field as a whole); education; professional organizations; due diligence; personal determination; cooperation with peers and other professionals; an office; equipment, computers; and people—especially people. You must never forget that you have been hired by people to do a job for people. Financial planning is a people business.

It is unfortunate that one cannot think of everything, although I have sincerely tried. I have also tried not only to *tell* you "how-to" but also to *show* you, by repeatedly using examples of techniques that I use in my practice, and techniques that other planners use. Your financial planning peers set the tone for this industry, and for that reason you must not limit yourself to my ideas alone. You should have a menu of examples to choose from. Select the methods that will fit the style of your practice. And you must be comfortable with these ideas. Don't try to force them on yourself.

Admittedly, there are times when this book preaches a bit too much. There are also times when the subject matter or the underlying philosophy appears redundant. I can assure you this was intentional. It was deliberate and not an oversight. My purpose was to record my message solidly in your mind. I felt that if I failed to get my point across, this might place your practice in jeopardy of dismal failure. And my book is not about failure. It is about success—your success.

Some readers will not like what I am about to say, but it is too critical to your survival to be omitted. It is my belief that many areas of the financial services business are dead in their present forms, and it is only a matter of time before they are buried for good. The life insurance agency is one. This is a dying profession. Today, the life agent must offer clients a lot more than just life insurance. Competition is fierce, and commission margins are being narrowed by the public's growing awareness of lower premiums and better investment alternatives. It has even been said that someday the salaried life insurance salesperson will replace the commission agent. I believe that this will happen much sooner than most of us expect. One company has even started to market no-load life insurance, and before long other companies will follow suit. And what about the stockbroker? Squeezed by the discount brokers and soon by the banks, stockbrokers face a serious challenge to their livelihood. In the years ahead, the financial services industry will go through a period of revolution whereby today's financial service practitioner will in no way resemble tomorrow's. There will be purges, but there will also be much opportunity for those equipped to meet tomorrow's requirements. Tomorrow's financial service practitioner will have to offer more to the public than just one or two products. Thus I suggest that these persons look to financial planning as a source of salvation if they wish to remain in this business. Am I saying that all life insurance agents and stockbrokers face erosion of their jobs? No, of course not. The good ones will always survive. But many will not. The effects of these changes will be too much work, too much frustration for too little money. We have to be realistic. If companies hoped to introduce better products, they will have no choice but to reduce the load, the commission.

It took eight months of long, hard hours to write this book. I have, on occasion, persisted long after my brain and my body told me that it was time to quit. Whatever kept me writing, kept me thinking, is not easy for me to understand. Will power was a strong ally. I once thought the hardest work of my life was getting up at four in the morning at Fort Dix, New Jersey, listening to the bellow of my drill sergeant's voice. But not anymore. Writing is hard physical work, a tortuous profession where your head frequently goes numb and you plead to the unknown for assistance.

Yet, as tired as I am, the experience has been invaluable to me. I have met, interviewed, and become friends with many of the most respected and successful financial planners, educators, and experts today. They are wonderful, highly motivated people. They have shared with me a wealth of personal information that has proven vital to this book and to my own personal career. I am indebted to them all. Furthermore, I have also had the opportunity to share ideas with many other financial planners and professionals, and this, I feel, will make me a far better financial planner in the years ahead.

Primarily, I have written *How to Survive and Succeed in a Small Financial Planning Practice* for the small independent financial planning practitioner, not the large planning firm. However, managers of these large multioffice firms may find this book helpful in terms of new concepts that can be implemented into the firm's style of doing business. But I am convinced that the backbone of this industry will be the small financial planning practice, not the large firm.

However, no matter what the size or level of your operation, you must never ignore or forget the benefits of "networking." We are all financial planners, with a unique opportunity to help each other become even better planners. By sharing ideas we can improve our individual practices, large or small, and thereby advance the profession in which we share a common bond. I suggest to you that to ensure your long-term survival in this industry, you begin to perceive the planner across the street or down the hall as a professional associate, a source of help, and not as your competitor. It can be done, and is, in fact, now being done throughout the industry.

We are all in this brand-new business of financial planning together. We must therefore chart the unexplored waters of this industry as a group, not alone. If you go it alone, the sharks are sure to get you.

ANDREW M. RICH, CFP

ACKNOWLEDGMENTS

No one can write a book of this scope alone. One must seek help, and help is what I got. And I cannot be thankful enough to each and every person who contributed to this writing.

Special thanks to:

Beverly R. Rich, my wife, partner, my "in-house" editorial staff.

Betsey R. Mohlenbrok, my sister-in-law and administrative assistant, who provided invaluable guidance, research, editorial skill, and suggestion.

David Alschuler, President, Life Planning, Inc., Mineola, New York; Dr. William L. Anthes, President, The College for Financial Planning, Denver, Colorado; William Bartlett, CLU, Director of Membership and Promotion, The National Association of Life Underwriters, Washington, D.C.; Victor A. Bary, Assistant Professor of Psychology, The American College, Bryn Mawr, Pennsylvania; James A. Barry, Jr., CFP, President, Asset Management Corporation, Boca Raton, Florida; Dr. Robert F. Bohn, Director of MBA/MS Degrees in Financial Services, Golden Gate University, San Francisco, California; Dr. Jerry Boswell, Director of Academic Programs, The College for Financial Planning, Denver, Colorado; Douglas J. Boyle, Trust Financial Services Officer, Barclay's Bank of New York, Farmingdale, New York; Gailann Bruen, Gailann Bruen Associates, Morristown, New Jersey; Daniel G. Burton, CFP, Executive Vice

President, Innovative Monetary Designs, Rockville Centre, New York; Charlotte J. Carpenter, Director of Conventions and Meetings, International Association for Financial Planning, Inc., Atlanta, Georgia; Forrest Wallace Cato, former editor, *The Financial Planner*, Atlanta, Georgia; Anthony Chiarello, Sales Representative, Radio Shack Computer Center, Bethpage, New York; Mary E. Clark, The Institute of Certified Financial Planners, Denver, Colorado; Dr. Robert W. Cooper, Dean, Solomon S. Huebner School, The American College, Bryn Mawr, Pennsylvania; Loren Dunton, President, The National Center for Financial Education, Inc., San Francisco, California; Howard Erstein, Esq., Garden City, New York; Elise Feldman, CPC, Steven A. Adler, Inc., New York, New York; Cynthia Foreman, Academic Associate, The College for Financial Planning, Denver, Colorado; Professor Larry D. Gaunt, Georgia State University, Atlanta, Georgia; Daryl R. Glockner, Esq., McHenry & Gerver, Mineola, New York; Bill Gregory, Associate Editor, *The Financial Planner*, Atlanta, Georgia; Norman Gross, President, Diamond Portfolio Ltd., New York, New York; Hubert L. Harris, Executive Director, The International Association for Financial Planning, Inc., Atlanta, Georgia; William C. Heath, CFP, William C. Heath & Associates, Inc., Houston, Texas; Ron Hogarth, President, Delaware Valley Chapter, International Association for Financial Planning, Inc., Trenton, New Jersey; Marcia Horn, Investment Company Institute, Washington, D.C.; Charles G. Hughes, CFP, C.G. Hughes & Company, Bayshore, New York; Dr. Dale S. Johnson, Assistant Professor of Financial Counseling, The American College, Bryn Mawr, Pennsylvania; Dick R. Jones, CFP, Esq.; Waddell & Reed, Wichita, Kansas; Dr. Donald Kagin, President, Kagin's Numismatic Investment Corporation, San Francisco, California; Maudese B. King, Chief, Branch of Registrations and Examinations, Securities and Exchange Commission, Washington, D.C.; Nelson Kjos, CFP, President, Nelson Kjos & Company, Inc., Southfield, Michigan; David Knight, Academic Associate, The College for Financial Planning, Denver, Colorado; Lawrence A. Krause, CFP, Lawrence A. Krause & Associates, Inc., San Francisco, California; Dr. Robert T. LeClair, Dean, Graduate School of Financial Services, The American College, Bryn Mawr, Pennsylvania; Mary Louise Lehnhoff, Adjunct Faculty Coordinator, The College for Financial Planning, Denver, Colorado; Dr. Richard E. Lincoln, Dean, Examinations, The American College, Bryn Mawr, Pennsylvania; Charles H. Maher, Jr., CFP, Denver, Colorado; Jan McAlpine, Marketing Representative, Leonard Financial Planning Systems, Inc., Raleigh, North Carolina; Mary P. Merrill, CFP, Budget Counseling Services, Madison, Wisconsin; Henry I. Montgomery, CFP, President, Planners Financial Services, Inc., Minneapolis, Minnesota; Charles Padget, Esq., Regional Counsel, Securities and Exchange Commission, New York, New York;

Joseph G. O'Neill, Jr., Investment Advisor, Charlotte, North Carolina; Donald Platz, Operations Principal, First Eastern Equity Corporation, Armonk, New York; Dianna Rampy, Executive Director, The Institute of Certified Financial Planners, Denver, Colorado; William C. Riechert, President, Nassau Life Underwriters, Hempstead, New York; Virginia R. Richard, Esq. Kane, Dalsimer, Kane, Sullivan, & Kurucz, New York, New York; Mark Jeffrey Rosen, President, *The Financial Insider*, Boston, Massachusetts; Eileen M. Sharkey, CFP, Denver, Colorado; Richard M. Silverstein, CFP, Silverstein & Alexander, Inc., Los Angeles, California; Robert Smith, Secur-All Agency, Inc., Woodbury, New York; Edward C. Sunday, Director, Financial Services Center, Houston, Texas; Dr. Fred Tillman, Georgia State University, Atlanta, Georgia; Mike Viscousis, CFP, Money Tree Software, Corvallis, Oregon; Robert J. Underwood, CFP, Underwood Financial Planning, Inc., Birmingham, Alabama; D. Richard Wells, CFP, CLU, CMA, President, International Financial Data Systems, Inc., Atlanta, Georgia; Philip J. Williams, Director of Financial Management Programs, New York University, New York, New York.

And extra-special thanks to:

David C. Rich and Nancy L. Rich, for coping patiently with their mother and father during the long months of writing this book, and for providing expert technical assistance with television, movie, and toy information.

1

AN OVERVIEW OF THE FINANCIAL PLANNER

The growth of the financial planning industry in the last few years has been miraculous, to say the least. And chances are you haven't seen anything yet. We are in the dawn of a new profession. In the years ahead, the demand for financial planners should vastly exceed the supply, making financial planning one of the most lucrative and glamorous professions of the eighties and perhaps the nineties. As a result, the planner of today has the opportunity to build a substantial practice within a few short years. There are very few rules, and no established system of apprenticeship as required by so many other professions. Potential clients are everywhere—in every occupation, in every income bracket, in every city and state.

But you must understand that the opportunity is *now*. Starting your own practice now, before everyone else discovers that he or she wants to be a financial planner, is essential.

A financial planning practice, or any business for that matter, cannot be built of dreams. The requirement is nothing short of hard work and determination. This is one boat ride where you will have to do most of the rowing yourself. There is no magic carpet. There is no instant success formula. And there certainly is no assurance that you will succeed! It won't be easy—yes, I *can* guarantee you that. But if you do persist, there is a far greater probability that the end will justify the means. In other words, you have a much greater chance for success than failure if you are really willing to work to make it happen. *You must make it happen.* It will not happen by itself.

SOME BACKGROUND

Financial planning is a recent phenomenon. A decade ago very few people actually thought about it, certainly not the way it is thought of today. For the most part, financial planning was an insurance policy, a bank account, and perhaps a mutual fund or some other fixed-income or equity investment. But then the world began to change. The inflation rate, which had averaged under 2% for the years 1948–1965, began its ascent toward double digits, reaching over 13% in 1979 and 12% in 1980. Almost an entire population—the consumer, the creditor, those surviving on a fixed income—was squeezed by the shrinking dollar. During this time, the war in the Mideast began to affect the farmer in Des Moines, Iowa, the dentist in Houston, Texas, the motorist on the New Jersey Turnpike, and the oil sheik in Kuwait. In the mid-seventies fuel oil was in short supply and, like any product in a free-market economy, the price of oil began to climb; but in this case, the brakes of equilibrium failed to hold it. In 1970 the price of a barrel of oil was under $10 per barrel, whereas in 1980 the price was over $30, only to retreat again by late 1982. And interest rates—we certainly cannot ignore them, can we? For years Americans could bank on the safety and stability of AAA bonds. And they did—the bankers; the pension funds; the insurance companies; the widow in Topeka, Kansas. As both short-term and long-term interest rates rose toward the stratosphere, the market prices of triple A bonds fell into free-fall. In the early eighties, with Henry Kaufmann, the guru of interest rates, predicting a 25% prime rate, the bank rate for short-term funds was about par with the local bookmaker. All the rules, all the tradition, now became subject to many questions. New ideas were needed and the policymakers fled back to the campus to learn new ideas. But they found only the old ideas from professors who refused to acknowledge that a change had taken place. The need for a break with tradition had come.

The financial planner is a nontraditional advisor. Generally, he or she is a person of vast ideas, independent thought, unique solutions, and sensitivity. The financial planner also is a person of unusual depth with the ability to tie a multitude of loose strings into a tight knot. The need for the financial planner is based directly on the complexity inherent in our society and interrelationships among elements that comprise our personal lives. Life insurance, taxation, investments, pensions, retirement, education, and postmortem planning can no longer be treated as separate, independent items. Planning must be done as a whole. The experienced financial planner will look at the whole picture and judge how each piece should fit into the puzzle, rather than working with loose pieces that may never fit together. It is a marvelous business. There is money to be made, people to help, new ideas and concepts to discover. You are on the threshold of a brand new field—a field not polluted by ancient concepts.

The field of financial planning allows ordinary financial service practitioners to broaden their horizons and make their work a lot more flexible and interesting. If you simply sell insurance or securities, you should consider expanding to where the action, and the challenge, really are—in financial planning. You can always continue to sell insurance if you desire, but as a financial planner you could have a lot more to offer your clients. As a result, clients will seek you out as someone special, as the one person they can come to for *all* their financial problems, secure in knowing that you are providing them with *realistic solutions*. When people are sick, they go to see a doctor. But when a person or entity is financially sick, who can they go to? A life insurance salesperson? A stockbroker? An accountant? Yes, but only if they are so sick in just one area that they need a specialist. Generally, they don't know where their problem is. So what they really need is a general practitioner, a country doctor—a financial planner.

The financial planner might also be a specialist in certain areas. Many planners are. For example, I specialize in taxes. Some planners have extensive insurance backgrounds; others have been stockbrokers, investment analysts, or bankers for many years; and still others might be attorneys. Should a client have an extensive problem in an area unfamiliar to the planner, an experienced planner would arrange for the client to see a specialist to handle the problem. Thus the concept of "networking" among small financial planners is essential. The small planner does not have experts on staff as does the large firm, only professional associates that he or she can trust. There should not be *competition* among small financial planners, only *association*.

Looking back, the early financial planner was generally a life insurance salesperson, a mutual fund salesperson, or perhaps both. As with any profession, some took their clients' interests to heart and others thought only of lining their own pockets. The same is true today. Financial planners still practice on these two levels. Thus—the reason for this book! But no matter how noble the intention of the early financial planner, the rules of the game changed in the process, and a great many clients suffered as a result. If the early financial planner was convinced that whole life insurance was the proper route to take for protecting a family in the event of a death and providing for education and retirement, the planner was probably right. The investment return from a good participating insurance contract, figuring that most of the dividends were not taxable, was as good as the return from a bank

where the interest was subject to tax. Furthermore, the insurance contract offered protection, whereas, at best, the bank offered a toaster or
a coffee pot. As interest rates began to soar, however, the true distinction
between financial planner and insurance salesperson became quite clear.
The insurance salesperson was borrowing against the cash value of the
policy in order to purchase more whole-life insurance; the financial planner, on the other hand, was borrowing against the cash value of the
policy to purchase high-interest-bearing certificates of deposits, Treasury
bills, tax-deferred annuities, and other inflationary investments. The
same was also true of the mutual funds salesperson. Fifteen years ago,
if the client was looking for a conservative investment, a most suitable
investment would have been an income fund where the portfolio con-
sisted primarily of high-grade bonds. The funds generally offered a
return superior to that offered by the banks. Furthermore, severe price
fluctuation was not even a consideration. But that is exactly what happened. As interest rates headed skyward, the net asset value of the
funds nose-dived. Once again, the conservative client, whom the registered representative had tried to protect, became victimized by events
beyond anyone's control. On the other hand, those mutual fund salespersons who preached growth funds in the sixties are probably looking
like heroes today, provided that in the early seventies they had the
courage to convince their clients to hold on to the investment—or even
buy more—when the stock market headed south and stayed there for
quite some time.

Today the financial planner is faced with volatility unprecedented
in American history. The planners of today must be smarter, more alert,
trained in greater depth, and quicker than their predecessors. They
must be tuned into the vast quantity of alternatives and conditioned to
tie together a neat little package for their clients. Education is no longer
an option; it is a necessity.

LOREN DUNTON'S CONTRIBUTIONS TO
FINANCIAL PLANNING

Loren Dunton has been called the father of modern financial planning
by many in the profession. His contributions to financial planning over
the last 15 years have been remarkable, to say the least, considering that
he has never practiced as a financial planner. He is the founder of the
College for Financial Planning, the International Association for Financial Planning, and is presently spearheading a third great organization
called the National Center for Financial Education. There is perhaps
nobody more devoted to the true concept of financial planning than
Loren. He is a one-man strike force of ideas and energy. Through his

achievements Loren has opened the door of opportunity for today's planner.

In 1968–1969, Loren set up the Society for Financial Counseling with two divisions, the International Association of Financial Counselors and the College for Financial Counseling, which later, through the moral suasion of the Securities and Exchange Commission, were changed to the International Association for Financial Planning (IAFP) and the College for Financial Planning. Ironically, the Society began as a result of a trip around the world that Loren took with his family in the mid-sixties. He discovered that the rest of the world was very critical of the American free-enterprise system. If the system was so good, why did Americans turn to socialism (Social Security) to take care of their retired people? When he returned he did extensive research and found that although we did an outstanding job of getting people to spend their money through Chambers of Commerce, retail merchants associations, sales and marketing executives, and Madison Avenue, we did a very poor job of getting people to put money aside for the future.

Once the organization began to develop, the two divisions split into separate entities. The College remained in Denver and the IAFP moved to Atlanta in 1975. Loren edited and published *The Financial Planner* magazine for the first three years of its existence.

Loren Dunton, perhaps more than anyone, understands the importance of financial planning education. "In order to continue gaining recognition as a professional, it is essential that the financial planner become more and more educated and have a good continuing education program." Loren is not surprised that the College and the Certified Financial Planner (CFP) designation have grown to where they are today, and he is convinced that the surface has not even been scratched.

However, he also believes that financial planning education has a long way to go. There are still areas where both the training and the planner are weak. "What bothers me the most is the number of financial plans sitting in drawers unimplemented. It is the obligation of the financial planner to implement for the client." He therefore advises that the financial planner practice more salesmanship, more psychology, and more motivation. In fact, Loren believes that motivational and sales training should be incorporated into financial planner education. "There are a lot of financial planners who are very poor at motivating their prospects to become clients, and they feel that once they have done the financial planning their job is finished. To do a good job for the public, it is essential to know how to *motivate* the client to have a better financial future."

Loren's definition of a financial planner is simple, yet to the point: A financial planner is someone who helps people do financial planning. The relationship with the client corresponds to that in the medical profession except that the financial planner offers financial help instead of physical help. The key role in the future will be played by the generalist—the Certified Financial Planner. Loren advises the small financial planner not to make the mistake of copying the big companies. "Do what the big company did when it was small, to become big." He also advises doing research on planners you admire to find out what they did when they were small. Forget what they are doing now.

It is vital for the financial planner to be ethical. "There are certain salespersons or financial planners who pride themselves on the fact that they could sell anything. Well, I pride myself on the fact that I couldn't really sell something that I didn't believe in. The ring of sincerity, the salesperson who is being sincere exerts so much more power. I feel people have a built-in radar—people can really detect the insincere salesperson."

How someone could be so close to the financial planning field and never be a practitioner is truly amazing. But Loren's motivation was recognizing the need for financial planning, not the need to be one himself; neither his father nor his grandfather nor Loren himself had ever engaged in financial planning. "I could see how costly it had been to all of us. We had all been sold a bill of goods by insurance salespersons, stockbrokers and bankers. We have all bought the wrong thing at the wrong time. Nobody helped us to do financial planning. When I think about how much better my life could have been, their lives could have been, had they the services of even a faintly objective financial planner to motivate them into doing something about financial planning. . . . My father left nothing, no insurance, no real estate."

The goal of Loren's new organization, the National Center for Financial Education, is to increase the number of people able to retire in a sound financial position without depending on government subsidy or Social Security. "We must make people realize that Social Security will never take care of them in their retirement years. We must also convince them to spend less and put aside more for their future." The organization is the final step in Loren's three-step master plan. The Society and the College have already come into their own, but the National Center still needs Loren to nurse it. There is no one, in my opinion, better qualified.

The objective of the National Center for Financial Education will be to enroll individual members and corporate sponsors. The member will then, through the quarterly magazine and seminars, be exposed to motivational counseling for spending money less foolishly. Financial planners may also find it advantageous to expose their clients to the National Center, since the Center will be stressing the importance of the financial advisor rather than a "do it yourself" philosophy.

According to Loren, the Center is "an organization for the public, as opposed to a professional association; it plans to use the latest media techniques to get its message across. It will be furnishing free financial columns to newspapers, a television program to cable television stations, educational speakers to service clubs, and using a comic-book approach, to get its message into the elementary and secondary schools.

"The NCFE plans to assist the banking, insurance, securities, real estate and financial planning industries in their efforts to get the public to do a more intelligent job of saving, investing, insuring and planning for the future. As the objective voice to the public, it will also offer its help to associations and educational institutions in the financial services industry.

"Getting people to put more aside for the future and competing successfully with the many forces encouraging people to *spend* now, will take a coordinated effort by everyone in the banking, securities, insurance, real estate and financial planning professions," Loren feels.

"It is obvious that working separately to get people to save, invest, insure and plan for the future hasn't been effective and this country is way behind others. In England people put aside 12.4% of their disposable dollars for their future. In France, 13.3%, and in Japan, a whopping 19.4%. In this country," he said, "we put aside only 5% or 6%. It makes our free enterprise system look bad when we need Social Security and other government programs to take care of our retired people!"

The successful financial planner, according to Loren, has "high drive." The planner is also dedicated to what he or she is doing rather than just making money. A crusading zeal is almost vital.

As I sit here and write about the financial planning field, I think about the College for Financial Planning and the International Association for Financial Planning (discussed later), with its 13,000 members and its prestige that reaches out to all corners of the globe, commanding the respect of presidents, governors, and members of Congress. Both the College and the International Association for Financial Planning have meant so much to the development of my own practice and, I am sure, to the practices of many others. All this would not have been possible had it not been for the contributions made by Loren Dunton the man, and his ideas. Financial planners, from the beginner to the most successful, owe Loren a great vote of thanks. He certainly stands out as a person who has helped to professionalize the financial planning field. And he has not finished yet.

THE FINANCIAL PLANNING PROCESS

The role of the financial planner is to take an objective look at the client's complete financial situation, explore the goals and objectives of the client, help decide which alternatives are best, and provide solutions that are functional and in the best interest of the client. This is the *planning stage*. In other words, you draw the map and plot the way. Perhaps in the future, the map will have to be redefined as you discover or build new roads. However, to make the program work, there must be a second step to the process. This is the *action stage*. For unless you can get your client to follow the map, the plan, for all intents and purposes, is useless. You must therefore be more than a planner; you must be an implementer of your own ideas.

Since this is a book about financial planner practice management, I will not tell you what you should put into your clients' programs. There are excellent schools, which are discussed later in this book, that have designed courses for this very purpose. Besides, as you will find, or have found already, experience is a wonderful teacher. Above all, what I hope to stress in this book is the "how to" of planning a client's program, and conducting and developing your own practice. In the modern financial planning practice, the "how to" is just as important as the "what to."

Henry Montgomery's Philosophy of Financial Planning

"Bringing the future into the present for the client so he can still do something about it" is how Henry Montgomery, CFP, defines financial planning. He is a former board member of the International Association for Financial Planning and President of the Institute of Certified Financial Planners. He has done as much as any practitioner in the field to bring financial planning to its present stage. Through his hard work, dedication, and commitment to this profession, he has become one of the most respected planners in our industry. "Financial planning," Henry insists, "is not a plan, but a process. The plan is a snapshot of a particular point in time and that is just the very beginning. What the client needs is an ongoing relationship that helps him build an estate so that he can live better now—not when he dies. There is a great deal of confusion in the public's mind between estate planning and financial planning. There are many competent estate planners but they are not necessarily financial planners. Estate planning permits the transfer of an estate with minimum tax loss to another. And often you have to die first to create the estate, in order to have one to transfer. I think financial planning encompasses that, plus the creation of an estate while you are still living. I like to tell clients when I am working with them that I am working for the first husband and not the second. I want them living better *now* as a result of the work that I have done for them.

"Financial planning is a very popular buzzword today. There is a great necessity to avoid preconceived solutions or one- or two-product answers. It is a field filled with snake oil salesmen, like the medical profession 100 or 150 years ago. Yes, there were some doctors, but there were also an awful lot of would-be doctors and people who called themselves doctors. And, unfortunately, that is the field of financial planning today. There are relatively few competent practitioners compared to the number of people who call themselves financial planners. Furthermore, the public needs to be aware of this, and they need to protect themselves by using good common sense and not being afraid to ask questions."

Henry Montgomery advises financial planners that there is a way to achieve competency. It is not easy and there are no shortcuts or quickie courses in competency. Like financial planning, competency is an ongoing process. He recommends that the financial planner stay current through continuing education. He also advises planners to get involved in study groups, get involved with other professionals, and to work full time at being a planner. "The planner who shortcuts is not long for this profession. Your relationship with your client is everything. If you think you are a product salesman with the greatest delivery system of anyone in the financial services, I think you better go back to hardware or pumping gas, because that's not what financial planning is all about. Financial planning is a commitment to the client. It is a client service. If you happen to make money out of it, that's fine. But if you start out with the thought of making big money quickly, you're going to do nothing but hurt yourself. There are many people today who can see nothing but the dollar sign. If you service the client, the dollars will follow. But if you are looking for the dollars first, the clients won't follow."

Henry Montgomery has given much of his personal time to the development of this profession, much indeed. He views with great personal pleasure the goal of bringing financial planning out of the swamp so that it is a respected profession. "We are light years along the road today compared with where we were six or seven years ago. But we still have a tremendous way to go and always will have, because it is a knowledge business as well as an ethics business."

The Planning Stage

The initial process of the financial plan starts with the assumption that the financial planner will attempt to learn as much about the client as possible. It is the reverse of the selling process, where the salesperson wants to convince the customer of the merits of the product by detailing the facts and giving the benefits. The financial planner must learn to become a skilled questioner and an interested listener. In fact, listening is so important that it actually sets the tone for the rest of the planning process. Once your clients feel that you sincerely care about them, they will open up to you with the subjects most important to them—themselves and their families. And this is where you either make it as a planner, and as their friend and confidante, or you fail. Show sincere interest. Acknowledge their words—no matter whether you agree or disagree. Show respect. If you pay only partial attention to what the client is saying, if you interrupt constantly to voice your own philosophy, if you argue at this stage of the plan, your relationship with the client will quickly evaporate before it has really started.

The interview process can take from several hours to several days depending on the wealth and problems of the client. It is best to use a predesigned data-gathering and interview form, one with which you are comfortable. There are many on the market, so choose one that best suits your needs. If there are none that you like, develop your own. Under no circumstances should you leave your questions and answers to memory. You must walk away from the interview clearly understanding what your client's goals and objectives are. The client must walk away saying: "Why haven't I done this before?"

According to Dale S. Johnson, Assistant Professor of Financial Counseling at the American College and former Dean of the College for Financial Planning: "Gathering complete client information is the central, most important task in financial planning. This gives meaning to everything else that you do. Gathering this information enables you to counsel your client, which distinguishes financial planning from product vending, and carries through to the implementation of a plan using products that specifically match the client's circumstances. Without knowing your client's specific objectives you cannot do anything for that client except to sell a product, which, if it's not the right product, may create further problems for the client. Furthermore, the data-gathering process establishes the planner as professional rather than just a salesperson, and it lends credibility to the planner as a counselor working in the client's best interest. But above all, it establishes the vital personal facts of the client's financial situation."

Johnson stresses that if you do not thoroughly collect information from the client, covering especially those areas of the client's deepest sensitivity and feelings, you will not get the responses—both verbal and nonverbal—that will give you a sense of that client as a person, and enable you to shape and develop a plan. Although the client's financial and tax situation are crucial to the technical aspects of the plan, the really critical test is how the client can live with that plan. The most important thing is to work with your client, at a sustained level of energy and commitment to the plan. Consider this as simply part of an ongoing lifetime financial management process that requires periodic review and updating of the plan according to the client's changing circumstances. "Unless you find out at the very start who that client is, you will lose him."

As part of the data-gathering process, Johnson advises that one of the most important things a financial planner can do is to listen and observe the client's body language. He feels that body language is by far the richer, more expressive mode of communication. The financial planner has to be very sensitive to the implications of body language. Listen to and observe all verbal and nonverbal communication. Does the client get excited when he or she is talking about something? Or nervous? Or impatient? Pick up the signals. "The client and the financial planner must both be willing to get involved in the human communication process and to work it through, one on one, and thereby humanize the process of financial planning. Otherwise any possible solution to the client's problems is going to be arbitrary and almost certain to reflect prejudices of the planner, rather than reflect the real needs of the client."

Johnson has recently written an excellent article entitled, "Practical Communication Skills and Techniques in Financial Counseling," which appeared as a two-part article in the June 1982 and July 1982 issues of *The Financial Planner* magazine.

Once you have gathered the information, the next step is its analysis. This can be done with or without a computer. Either method has its own benefits and the planner must choose the preferred one. Remember, too, that you are free to change methods at any time. Change is part of a financial planner's life. Your analysis should include what you feel are deficiencies in the client's financial program, based on the parameters that you have set. Does your client need more life insurance? Does your client have disability income coverage or adequate hospitalization and major medical? Is there enough fire insurance on the home and business and liability coverage on the car? What other types of advisors will the client need to see? Do the clients' wills reflect their current wishes? Do assets need to be repositioned? Could a pension plan be helpful? You see how the financial planner weaves together all aspects of the client's life. Financial planning is an overall process, not a piecemeal process. After you have uncovered the deficiencies, what do you suggest as feasible solutions? You must take into consideration not only what a client needs, but also what a client can afford. Be aware that the solution to a financial planning problem is a highly subjective interpretation. There is no standard answer to a standard problem. What one planner suggests, another might criticize as being completely inefficient, and still another might consider it too much. Therefore, to be an independent financial planner, you must learn to develop your own solutions. In the end it will be you who must answer for your actions.

The last step of the planning stage involves the presentation of the problems and the solutions to the client. You have the freedom to present a detailed written case analysis, a shorter written case highlighting important concepts and leaving out the analysis, a computerized or word-processed plan, or an oral summation. The type of output depends naturally on you, the planner—your beliefs, and what you feel will work for your clients. The answers come through training and experience.

The Action Stage

Assume now that you have handed your client the plan, defined the problems, proposed solutions, and collected your fee. Are you finished? Only if the client hired you just for that purpose, and desires no more. Most clients, however, are looking for more than just verbal text; they are looking for you to do something about their problems. That is why they came to you in the first place. If they could solve their own problems, why would they need you?

The process whereby the planner turns ideas into action is called implementation. It involves action, not talk, not procrastination. Also, the action stage has nothing to do with the type of compensation you receive; there is absolutely no correlation between the two. The planner who receives only fees should provide guidance and assistance by selecting products that meet the client's goals and objectives; but at the same time, it is important that these products be no-load products or those that involve a commission to someone other than the planner. The planner who receives only commissions should be sure to sell products that meet the client's needs and will be of benefit. The planner who charges a fee as well as receiving a commission is free to do either. The point is that the end result of the action process is to place the plan into motion. But the financial planning process does not end here. It is incumbent on the planner to follow up the program and to make timely changes if necessary. The whole planning process could take years to complete, or perhaps a lifetime. It is a long-term business serving long-term needs.

I have given you a basic overview of the financial planning process. Future chapters cover each aspect of the process in much greater depth and detail. When you have completed this book, my intent is for you to walk away either satisfied that you are in the right profession already or unsatisfied because you are not yet a financial planner.

THE ROAD AHEAD

If there is any occupation where the streets are paved with gold, financial planning is that occupation. It can be rich in rewards, in terms of both money and self-satisfaction. It is one field in which you can achieve for your client and see the direct results. To see where the financial planning field is headed, all we need do is simply look around and observe what is happening. Insurance firms, security brokerage firms, mutual fund groups, and financial planning firms are merging into what we call "financial service organizations": Prudential and Bache, Shearson and American Express, Sears and Dean Witter, just to name a few. Each firm will target in on a particular market, some high income, some low income, some middle income. Some perhaps will try more than one market. But the intent is the same—one-stop financial services. To achieve this, the firm, large or small, must offer a competent level of planning. To offer this level of planning and retain clients, the firms need not salespersons but skilled financial planners—planners who respond to people's needs.

How this will be accomplished is still not clear. Whether the big firms or the small planner will be the victor only time will tell. But both *can* be winners if they service the needs of the client successfully. One thing is certain, however—there will be a tremendous need for financial planners for many, many years to come.

Although the small planner might at first appear to be at a disadvantage when compared to a large financial service organization, especially in terms of capital, marketing ability, sophistication, and products offered, the small planner has the one thing that the big organization can never achieve—identity and personality. And given time, a little experience, and the concept of "networking," the disadvantages of the smaller firm can easily be overcome.

But I am convinced that the key to your success as a small independent financial planner is *you*. Once you get into this business you will find that although your client is looking for "total financial services" under one roof, the client also wants to be recognized as a person, a very important person. Only you, the small planner, can provide *that* service.

To the giant financial service organizations, the client will always be a number. You can never convince me that the person down at the department store or brokerage house financial planning center will ever get as close to the client as you can. With you, the client has a name, a face. The client is a person and must always remain a person. Considering all this, who really has the advantage and who the disadvantage? As I have said, I can work with other planners, share fees, share costs. I can buy a computer and software to handle any numbers that I need to crunch. I can borrow funds to buy what I need. I can learn, with time, to market my products and my services effectively. And I can even get good products for my clients if I look hard and long enough. But people—I can never get people to like and to trust me unless, from the very start, I establish a person-to-person relationship, a relationship that must never falter through the years. The big firms, no matter how sophisticated, will have great difficulty achieving this. Sure they can always outservice your products or services, but they can never outservice you. In your lifetime you will probably never have a greater opportunity to become more successful than through the financial planning business.

The financial planner of today has already surpassed the financial planner of yesterday in terms of skills, product knowledge, and integrity. There is still, however, a long way to go in strengthening the profession. The reputation of tomorrow's financial planner is based on the integrity of today's financial planner. No matter which way you decide to run your practice, you must do it honestly. There is no compromise; there is no debate. There is only compliance if we hope to make financial planning a meaningful profession.

2

CHOOSING PRODUCTS, SERVICES, AND CLIENTS

SELECTING SERVICES AND PRODUCTS

A financial planner is only as good as the services and products that the planner offers. The prudent selection of these services and products, in terms of their quality and not quantity, is vital to the success or failure of the planner. If the planner offers low-quality financial services or products, the client may feel dissatisfied and cheated. Sooner or later, the client is bound to wake up to the deception and spread the word. That, of course, leaves the planner with the problem of finding new products, new clients, and overcoming a questionable reputation—not a very pleasant situation for someone who has invested many years developing a financial planning practice.

Start right. Do not take the quick route to making millions overnight. There is no shortcut in this trade. Hard work and good ethics are the keys that unlock the door to success. And once that door is open— and sooner or later it will be open if you are patient—the opportunity is endless.

The first step in starting your own financial planning practice is to invest many working hours deciding what you are going to market. The process begins by being completely honest with yourself regarding your capabilities, attitudes, beliefs, and desires. For example, if you don't like to sell products, then face that fact and don't sell products—sell services only. If you don't have the expertise to write an estate plan, then don't write one; recognize this shortcoming and search for an estate planner with whom you can closely work. There is great strength in recognizing one's weakness. Ask yourself just what services you are capable of providing to your clients. It takes a great deal of self-honesty to admit to personal inability and to filter out those services that you are not capable of offering. You are dealing with your ego and your own ego is never easy to deflate.

If you are not sure whether you are qualified to deal in a particular service, you are probably *not* qualified. The answer is to remain on the sidelines, study the subject in greater depth, converse with others who are truly proficient, and when you are convinced that you can be of benefit to your clients, then offer that service. And only then! Don't jump the gun. And don't jump into water over your head until you are sure that you can swim.

Products, too, are extremely important. What products will you want to recommend or sell? This is not as easy as it seems since there are a great many products from which to select, and, of course, we all know that everyone's product is the best. The point is that you shouldn't market any product until you are completely satisfied that it meets your highest standards.

Although the quantity of products that you offer your clients is important, it is actually the quality of the products that benefits the client in the long run. A small bowl of ripe apples is always better than a barrel of rotten ones. Persons who deal in rotten apples are not financial planners by any sense of the word. They are pirates who prey on a naive public. Unfortunately, however, the reality of being a small financial planner is that once in a while we deal in rotten apples out of lack of experience, especially in the early years, before we have gained the judgment and maturity to detect the rotten apples from the ripe ones. It is all part of the financial planner's learning process. You must have the instinctive ability to recognize that the rotten apple you sold or recommended will ultimately poison the whole system you are working so hard to build. Therefore, purging these apples swiftly, before the decay spreads, is part of the successful building and maturity process of the planner. Chapter 13 explains how to select only the finest, ripest apples for your clients.

As the years pass, you should gain a great deal of experience in terms of financial planning conceptual knowledge and product ability. When you feel confident that you are qualified to offer an additional service, you can always incorporate it into your business. Another means of adding a service to your practice is to build a relationship with another professional, such as an attorney, accountant, real estate broker, or other financial planner who can act as an extension of your firm. These other professionals, however, must be selected with a great deal of care, since their actions will be a direct mark on your ability and reputation. The selection of other professionals is a process of trial and error, and could take years to accomplish. Furthermore, you should develop the insight to select better products for your clients as your financial planning expertise grows, as the track records of products that you are familiar with begin to develop, and as the competition of the financial product market forces product creators to develop new and better products in order to survive. Experience will also give you the ability to judge who are the good product creators and who are bad.

Following is a list of most of the services and products that the planner can offer. As the years progress you may be creative enough to design and market innovative services and products of your own. You may even have some ideas now.

FINANCIAL SERVICES

FINANCIAL PLANNING (Case Approach). The planner presents the client with a written financial plan, designed around the client's goals and objectives. The plan generally will cover asset evaluation and restructure, income and estate tax planning, review of the client's risk management program, retirement and education planning, and an outline of the steps that the client must take to achieve his or her personal goals and objectives. Some planners write extensive scholarly works, whereas others write plans that are brief and to the point. Furthermore, some planners write plans on a word processor and/or may provide the client with vast schedules of computer projections and analyses, whereas other planners start from scratch with a pen and a yellow pad. How one writes a financial plan is a very personal decision. To date, there are no models or regulations to which you must adhere. The planner is free to choose the style and content most suited to him or her. The planner, in almost all cases, charges a fee for this plan.

FINANCIAL COUNSELING. Many clients today do not need a soup-to-nuts financial plan. A few hours or so of counseling would be adequate to meet their needs. Accordingly, a financial counselor would provide advice for a money problem similar to the way in which a psychologist would provide advice for an emotional problem. There would probably be a fee for this service unless the planner was providing a charitable service for a not-for-profit organization.

INVESTMENT MANAGEMENT.   The planner provides the service of managing the client's assets and investments. This may be achieved on either a discretionary basis, where the planner takes control of the investments through a power of attorney, or on a nondiscretionary basis, where the planner simply advises the client, who maintains the investment control. Once again, the planner will probably charge a fee for this service.

TAX PLANNING.   The planner provides the service of planning for reduction of the client's income tax and potential estate taxes. Although this is usually part of a case financial plan, the financial planner may market this as a separate fee service.

TAX PREPARATION.   Recognizing that the preparation of income tax is a key element in the client's financial program, planners may wish to provide this service as part of the full financial program or as a separate fee service. Tax preparation can help build a future client base for financial planning. This service can be especially important to a new financial planner who deals with middle-class clients. Also, the fees from tax preparation may help pay a great many of the bills while your practice is growing. Planners, however, should be qualified to prepare income taxes before they undertake this service. The use of a computer service to process the returns should be considered.

ACCOUNTING AND BOOKKEEPING.   A financial planner who plans to work in the business market might consider these services. If the planner decides not to provide this service, he or she may wish to hire a bookkeeper or junior accountant and then review the work. An alternative is that one of the principals of the small financial planning firm be an accountant.

CONSULTING.   Planners with strong backgrounds in one or several areas of financial planning may wish to provide a separate fee service for that skill. Areas that might be considered are pensions, real estate, management, and tangibles, to mention a few. Planners may also wish to consider providing services for other financial planners.

PRODUCTS

INVESTMENT SALES.   As part of a financial planning program or perhaps even as the main thrust of the business, the planner may choose to market investment products such as securities, mutual funds, and variable- and fixed-income annuities. Although most planners offer these products on a commission basis, a great many planners are beginning to offer these products on a no-load basis as part of a fee planning program.

LIFE AND HEALTH INSURANCE. The fact that these products are critical to a financial planning program requires the planner to give great thought to this area. The planner must first decide what type of insurance to market—term, permanent, disability income, medical expense, or all of these. Then there is the painful process of selecting those products most appropriate to the client's needs and the planner's personal insurance philosophy. In most states planners will need to obtain insurance licenses. A planner should also consider whether to write life insurance as an agent or to represent a particular insurance company as a general agent. Although a planner may be committed to a fee-only non-product practice, the planner must still have a thorough knowledge of insurance products in order to direct the client's program in a proper manner.

PROPERTY CASUALTY INSURANCE. This area is a world unto itself, comprising generally fire, theft, automobile, homeowners, business, and liability insurance. To practice in this area, a planner should be completely familiar with the market and the products, legally licensed, and prepared to undertake the enormous volume of paperwork associated with this field. Since this area tends to be highly complex, most financial planners avoid it, unless they are experienced as property casualty insurance agents or brokers. One danger the financial planner faces when practicing in this area is that, if the insurance company does not settle a claim satisfactorily in the client's terms, the client undoubtedly will hold the planner responsible; the planner then faces the loss of a client, no matter how many other wonderful services or benefits he or she has performed for the client. The financial planner must weigh this risk in relation to all the other services that he or she will provide.

TAX SHELTERS AND LIMITED PARTNERSHIPS. Since virtually any client's goal is to pay less in taxes now, this area is perhaps the most popular, and the most dangerous, to both the client and the planner. The planner must be extremely careful in the selection of tax shelter products for clients, since most potential client–planner problems generate from the selection of tax shelters with poor economics, a weak tax foundation, or unqualified or corrupt general partners. Furthermore, due to the lack of marketability of most shelters, careful consideration must be given to client suitability. Nevertheless, tax shelter sales is an extremely rewarding area for the planner—the commissions are high. However, most of the rotten apples discussed before stem from this area. As a planner develops, he or she may ultimately become a product creator of limited partnerships, leading to greater financial rewards, and more important, the ability to control the product in the best interest of the client.

TANGIBLE SALES.   Because the world we live in has become highly inflationary, tangible products such as gold, silver, platinum, diamonds, colored stones, rare coins, art, antiques, real estate, and collectibles have become very important sources of investments. Accordingly, many planners may wish to market tangible products to their clients. However, before jumping into the "black hole" of this field, study the particular market carefully and understand the products thoroughly. After that it will become critical to develop reputable product sources and relationships with experts with whom you can consult. You must always make certain that your clients are suited to the product and are not getting a raw deal.

Selecting the services and products that you will market to your clients is extremely difficult. It is best to begin in the few areas in which you are most knowledgeable and familiar. Even if it is only one area, it is a beginning. As time passes you may want to explore other service and product areas. I certainly suggest it. If you do not like an area or have no interest in it, you should work on developing good sources of referral for your clients. Be flexible. There is no substitute for trial and error.

In my own practice I started with income tax preparation. After a few years, while undergoing CFP training, I expanded to case financial planning, life insurance sales, and security products. Further down the road, I broadened to tax shelters and tangibles. Recently, however, I have retrenched in some of the product areas and have undertaken discretionary investment management on a fee basis, only to limit that and to broaden certain areas of product sales. In retrospect, every step of the way has been a series of trial and error. You will always be wondering what it would be like unless you really try it. It sometimes took me an exceptionally long time to work up the courage to undertake a particular service or product. Other times, I have jumped too fast, before understanding all the ramifications or doing proper product due diligence. But it is all part of the financial planner maturity process, which takes a lifetime to master. There is no substitute for exposure and experience. None whatsoever.

Of all the products that you may offer your clients, the principal product, for most planners, is unquestionably the case financial plan. The case financial plan is a written text that you present to your clients, telling them, in essence, how they stand and what they should do. Some planners give their clients a page or two; other planners keep it to about 10 pages or so; still others develop cases of 20, 30, 40, or 50 pages; and finally, some planners write books of 80, 90, or 100 pages or more. There is no standard format, no standard length, and no standard content that you are required to follow. In fact, the quality of the financial plan has nothing to do with its size, nor do the end results of the plan have anything to do with its quality. A financial plan is only part of the financial planning process—the strategic plan of action. The drive, the implementation, must also be achieved.

Nevertheless, the quality of your financial plans is perhaps the greatest reflection of your skill as a financial planner. What you write and how you plan to solve your client's problems (which is what a financial plan must do) depends, of course, on the particular client. I will not attempt to tell you how to write a plan or, in fact, what to put into your plan. That must be a product of your knowledge, your experience, your convictions, and your imagination. All I will attempt to do here is explain the "financial planning facts of life" to the inexperienced or would-be planner; you must accomplish the goal—helping your client—by writing a financial plan. Otherwise, there is absolutely no benefit to undertaking the plan in the first place. Achieving the right balance in the financial plan that you write is not as simple as it may appear, however. For one thing you must avoid "underkill," poor-quality plans that reflect stagnant thought processes on your part. You must also avoid "overkill," tremendously detailed plans that the client may not read past page two. The plan you write must achieve your objective (solving your client's problems) and must be interesting and readable enough for the client to understand and take seriously. You may need 200 pages to accomplish this task or you may need 3 pages. What is important, however, is to address the plan specifically to your client's needs and not dress up the plan with fillers. Give your clients the quality and the solutions they are paying for.

Financial planning is a field of change. The planner who wants to develop a successful practice must be receptive to change: product change, economic-condition change, tax-law change, client change. Most important, however, the personal preferences and desires of the planner change as he or she goes through the trial-and-error process of selecting services and products to offer clients.

TARGETING YOUR MARKET

The financial planner must have a clear idea of what services and products to offer clients. After all, the financial planning business is no different from any other business. You need clients to survive, cash flow to keep the doors open, and profit in order to eat. It is essential, therefore, to know to whom you will market these services and products.

The small financial planner cannot be all things to all people. The resources of a large planning firm are just not available to the small planner, nor does the small planner have the expertise, the stamina, or the time to compete with the larger firm. A large firm has attorneys, Certified Public Accountants, actuaries, Certified Financial Analysts, Chartered Life Underwriters, and Certified Financial Planners on staff who coordinate their skills to develop the best plan for the client. What resources does a small planner have? Only the professional relationships that he or she must build over the years.

Because of resources and time limitations, the small financial planner must generally target on one particular client market or perhaps a few specific client markets, but no more. The larger the spread of client types, the greater the need the planner has to seek outside advisory assistance. Trying to take on too many different types of clients may spread too thin a planner's time and energy. The result could be too much time spent on research rather than on dollar-producing activities, thus making the planner less effective to the majority of clients—not to mention the wear and tear and the mental strain placed on the planner.

Before starting a practice, try to imagine who your clients are going to be. This may not be easy. Select the type of client to whom you feel you can best relate. Your aim is to do a highly proficient job of planning without overstepping your limitations of time and resources.

With this in mind, take a deep breath, close your eyes, and try to envision who your typical client might be. Is the client old or young? Healthy or ill? Male or female? Is the client married, single, or divorced? How much money does the client earn? What is the client's earning potential? Where does the client work? Live? Vacation? What are the client's assets? And so forth. When the picture of your typical client is complete, snap a photograph in the back of your mind and open your eyes.

Now that you have a good idea of who your potential clients will be, concentrate your marketing efforts in this area. This becomes especially important if you are a one-person firm. Ultimately, through experimentation and experience, you may expand the scope of your market, shifting among various types of clients. A shift in the type of client that you plan for will depend on your level of comfort in dealing with that type of client, your willingness and ability to learn and broaden your conceptual and product knowledge, and the compensation you feel you should be earning relative to the hours you put in. For example, if you are working with middle-income clients and feel that you should be earning $100 an hour, you are either going to have to shift to more affluent clients or face the fact that a substantial portion of your market cannot afford to pay your fees—no matter how good they think you are or how much they like you. There is much truth to the old cliché, "You can't get blood from a stone."

I have discussed how to target your market in general terms, but to be effective, the approach must be more specific. Although there are numerous ways that client markets can be defined, I find there are three major ways to approach the subject: by income; by occupation or status; and by location.

TARGETING BY INCOME

In terms of one's financial problems, the degree of one's affluence has a direct functional relationship with the need for planning. Let's face it. The rich have problems quite unlike those of the poor, and the middle-class have problems that are different from both of the others. This in no way implies that the rich person's problems are more important than those of the poor or middle-class person—the problems are simply different. Let's take a look at these income target markets.

The Affluent-Client Market

Wealthier persons have more complicated financial problems than do persons of lower financial means. Large assets in the form of money, property, securities, tangibles, and so on, generate their own problems, due to the natural complexity of these assets, the human desire to preserve them, and the government's role of taking them away. It does not require much talent to recognize the fact that the more affluent person has a tremendous need for financial planning.

Accordingly, since the problems are more complex, the financial planner will need more sophisticated and in-depth training to meet the needs of the more affluent clients. Only experienced financial planners should attempt to operate in this market. Less experienced planners should concentrate on the less affluent markets, working their way up to this market as they gain more experience. It may take a few years, many years, or it may never happen. But the new financial planner should definitely not start out here.

Assuming, however, that the financial planner is capable of tackling this market, there is an abundance of clients seeking serious assistance, willing and able to pay substantial fees, and who are sources of valuable referrals when you do right by them. If you plan to practice in the affluent-client market, be prepared to spend a great deal of your time researching information and keeping abreast of the latest financial planning trends in the areas of investments, taxation, insurance, estate planning, and so forth. Continuous advanced training is an absolute necessity, and sorting through the masses of journals, periodicals, and looseleaf services reporting on timely topics is a daily ritual. Professional publications alone can cost the planner a few thousand dollars a year. Be prepared to pay it as these reference tools are an unavoidable expense. When dealing with the affluent client, you must keep in mind that this client generally is more educated and more financially sophisticated than less affluent clients, and accordingly, less receptive to a financial "snow job." Affluent clients are frequently in touch with their attorneys for one reason or another, so if you are going to work in this area, make the effort to deliver superior services and products.

The Middle-Income-Client Market

In the last several years, as tax laws have become more complex and investment markets have come to defy all laws of tradition, the middle-income client has become ever more lost in the sea of personal finance. The Tax Reform Act of 1976 replaced the old estate tax law with one that is completely different. No sooner was this law on the books than it was overhauled by a massive technical corrections act. In 1981, the Economic Recovery Act provided a sweeping change of the estate and gift tax laws, instituting great changes in the income tax laws. But did it stop there? Of course not. The Tax Equity and Fiscal Responsibility Act of 1982 added sweeping changes. Today, clients are faced with declining income tax rates, increasing unified credit, an indexed tax table, decreasing estate tax rates, accelerated recovery property, decreasing depletion, and ever-increasing problems as to what to do about all these changes. This confusion should spell problems for the client and a challenge for the financial planner. The middle-class client, who once could have settled for a tax return prepared at the end of the year, a life insurance policy or two, and a savings account, is now subject to the new parameters of this highly wacky world of universal life, variable life, whole life, complete life, annual term, term until Tuesday, money market, government money market, tax-exempt money market, and all the others. Furthermore, the two-income family has pushed the middle-class client into higher tax brackets and more complex planning needs.

Although the financial problems of middle-income clients are not as complex as those of the affluent client, they are certainly as abundant. While the wealthy generally have access to attorneys, accountants, and trust officers, middle-class clients generally have access to the stockbroker, registered representative, life insurance underwriter, property casualty broker, tax preparer, generalist attorney, neighbor, co-worker, bank clerk, or taxi driver—and it is hard to say who provides the best advice. One thing is certain, however; the advice and products tend to pull in many different directions, depending on beliefs, training, experience, and what may be in it for the advisor. Can you see why millions and millions of middle-class Americans need their personal financial programs fine-tuned by a skilled and trustworthy financial planner, a planner they can relate to for the rest of their lives? There are so many fish in the lake that the fish have no room to swim, but there are only a few fishermen on the bank. Come, cast your rod.

If you are thinking of working with middle-class clients, you must realize that these clients cannot pay the same fees that wealthy clients can pay. As a result, you will need to do more work to earn the same money as the planner who works strictly in the affluent market. Since there are more potential clients to whom to offer your services, the loss of a client or two along the way should not greatly disturb your practice. In the affluent-client market, the planner who has only 20 clients and loses 2 has lost 10% of his or her business. By comparison, the middle-class-client market offers the planner more diversity and greater independence.

As the years go by, not all of your clients will remain in the middle class. Some will see their economic level improve enormously. This is especially true for young professionals. What, then, does the planner do? Does the planner step into the more affluent market together with the client? Does the planner end the relationship with the client? Does the planner capitalize on a golden opportunity by selecting a limited number of the best clients with whom to work? Or is it time to think about becoming a large firm? These are difficult choices, but choices with which most planners will eventually have to deal. I hope it is evident to you as your practice develops that there are many, many bridges that you have the option of crossing. Some you will cross and others you won't; sometimes you will cross a bridge and then come back to the other side. The financial planning business is an "elastic" business, always stretching. It is a business of constant and continual change. You must be flexible.

The Less-Affluent-Client Market

Why would a planner work in this market? Let's be realistic; people with no money cannot pay big fees, and if you are working strictly on a commission basis, there won't be very much in it for you if you are doing right by the client. Why would a planner practice in a market that requires a lot of time for little compensation?

There are two obvious reasons. The first is that it is a safe place for the planner to begin, experimenting with methodology, and building the confidence to rise to the higher-level markets. Second, it is a self-satisfying and rewarding market where you can really help people who need help and have no other access to it. On occasion, I have practiced in this market and found the rewards extremely satisfying. I suggest that if you are going to work at all in this market, keep the variety and complexity of products short and simple so that you can achieve results.

TARGETING BY OCCUPATION

Another way a financial planner can target a client market is by occupation rather than by income level. This offers a unique opportunity for the planner to become a specialist for a select group of clients. The planner will have to work at developing specific skills that relate to the occupation rather than the general skills required for all types of clients. The planner must also be aware that targeting by select group generally requires a heavy degree of referrals from within that group plus referrals from other professional advisors. The following is a listing of occupations or groups around which you can build a practice. The list is by no means complete, so stretch your imagination as far as it will reach.

Physicians
Dentists
Executives
Salespersons
Celebrities
Attorneys
Athletes
Military personnel
Government workers
Teachers
Blue-collar workers
Single or divorced women
The two-person working family
The self-employed
Farmers
Ranchers
The small businessperson
The retired

TARGETING BY LOCATION

My practice is in Woodbury, Long Island, an affluent suburb of New York City. The range of clients that I have to select from is vast. My clients can be at almost any income level and they can have virtually any occupation. This wide range is likely to be available to any financial planner practicing in or around a large metropolitan area. However, what about the planner who practices in the smaller city or community? In that case, to restrict a practice to a select type of client or to a specific income level would be quite difficult, if not impossible. Accordingly, the planner would have only one choice and that is to target the practice by the location or the community in which the planner lives; otherwise, there just may not be enough clients to choose from. Planners who wish to open a practice in the small community should keep this in mind.

3

STRUCTURING COMPENSATION

The financial planner is in business to make money; there is no arguing that fact. There may be other reasons for choosing this business, such as the satisfaction of helping others, the diversification of working in a constantly changing field, or the gratification of showing a client legal ways of getting around the tax laws. But the overriding reason, in almost all cases, is to *make money*. A few financial planners might possess other motives, especially if they are already financially independent. However, these planners are rare, to say the least. Ask yourself: "What is my true motive for wanting to be an independent financial planner?" Be honest. If it is other than personal financial reward, I salute you. You are a rare person, indeed. If it is personal financial reward, I salute you, too. For you have the courage to become self-employed. It is a club certainly worth joining.

The small financial planning business is similar to most other small businesses. It requires *risk*. You are self-employed—an entrepreneur. The assurance of a weekly paycheck is gone forever. After all the bills are paid and all the salary checks are issued and the government gets its piece of the action, you get what's left over—if anything. Sometimes there's a lot; sometimes you have to dip into your own pocket. That's capitalism! If you find this difficult to swallow, running your own practice may not be for you. You may be better off with a nice weekly paycheck.

America is a land of opportunity—but only for those who seek it and are willing to take risks to achieve it. The financial planning business has a major advantage over many other forms of businesses—it is a service business and does not require a significant capital outlay to start. In fact, it does not really require any capital, just the serious determination to succeed. If you really had to, you could operate off a park bench. A little extreme, perhaps, but possible. In the long run a good financial planner operating off a park bench will go a lot further than a bad financial planner operating out of a plush penthouse office. The two magic ingredients are skill and determination. If you have them, you are on your way. If you don't, you had better develop them, because they are absolutely essential to your long-term survival.

Assuming that everything is "go," let's get to that dominant business motive of making money. How do you do it? There are three basic ways: fees; commissions; and fees and commissions. All three ways have advantages and disadvantages. Let's take a look at them.

FEES

The financial planner can operate on a fee-only basis. This method of compensation offers the planner the opportunity to be free of product influence. Since the planner is charging fees instead of relying on commissions, his or her motives should be to satisfy the client rather than the product promoter. Charging only fees offers the planner a much greater opportunity to be objective regarding the implementation of financial service products. However, the planner may encounter some difficulty implementing the products into the client's financial plan. Therefore, it becomes evident that the fee-only planner could thrive in the affluent-client market but starve in the lower-income markets, where financial planning may be only a matter of a few items and clients cannot afford to pay high fees.

The financial planner who charges a fee to a client must be registered with the Securities and Exchange Commission as a Registered Investment Advisor (a subject covered in Chapter 4). Securities and Exchange Commission registration, however, requires added expenses, time-consuming paperwork, and a special degree of trust regarding your client's account. Planners who are considering a fee-only practice are encouraged to listen to tapes on the subject released by both the College for Financial Planning and the International Association for Financial Planning. The most interesting and perhaps informed person on this subject is Robert J. Underwood, CFP, a fee-only planner from Birmingham, Alabama, who speaks about conducting a financial planning practice "as pure as the new driven snow." In a later chapter, I will talk further about Bob Underwood as a planner who has made it to the top through the fee-only practice.

A big advantage in using fees is that, under Section 212 of the Internal Revenue Code, most fees are tax deductible. This, in effect, offers clients the opportunity to allow the government to subsidize investment and/or tax advice; the higher their tax bracket, the more the government will pay. If used properly, the tax-deductibility feature becomes a highly effective marketing tool as well as a windfall to the client.

COMMISSION

This method of compensation is far different from the fee-only type of practice. Compensation is usually based on a percentage of what you sell. However, by using a variety of good-quality products and selling clients only what is best for them and not what generates the greatest commission, the planner can effectively use this method to the benefit of the client. Furthermore, this method can be highly effective where the client might be resistant to paying the planner fees, or where there is a limited product need.

The major advantage that I see in using this method is that after obtaining all the proper licenses and contracts to market products, the planner operates with the least amount of paperwork and regulation. A commission-only planner is not required to be a Registered Investment Advisor (although there is nothing to say the planner cannot be one). The commission-only planner usually operates under a Broker Dealer or Registered Representative exclusion of the Investment Advisors Act of 1940. The major disadvantage is that the commission-only planner has only one way to earn a living, and that is to sell. Therefore, the planner cannot spend time dealing with clients who are not good prospects for closing a sale. I have found from experience that proper financial planning does not necessarily require selling or implementing products into the client's program. This presents the following dilemma: Should you tell the client that he or she has no need for any of your products, thus costing yourself valuable time? Or should you go ahead and sell the client something anyway? Again, you must remember that the financial planner's prime reason for being in business is to make money. Since the two philosophies conflict, which is the right road to follow: the road that benefits the client or the road that benefits you? Think about this after you have not closed a sale in a few weeks.

But keep in mind that there are many excellent commission-only financial planners today who are quite successful, yet perform a proper and honest job for their clients. It can be done. This leads us to our third compensation method.

FEES AND COMMISSION

Charging both a fee and earning a commission is, in my opinion, the best of both worlds. Planners are guaranteed compensation for the use of their valuable time, either by a fee for providing a service, or by a commission from the sale of a product, or both. As a result, planners can be responsive to almost any type of client market. In effect, they can work comfortably in the upper-income market, where fees are predominent, or in the lower-income market, where products would be most beneficial. However, financial planners who operate under both a fee and a commission structure are most definitely faced with a conflict of interest, commonly referred to in the trade as "the wearing of two hats."

Under one hat, the planner is a planner—the designer and author of a financial plan for which he or she will charge a fee. Under the other hat, the planner is a salesperson selling a specific, recommended product for which a commission will be earned. Are the two hats totally different, or do they just seem different? Only the individual planner really knows. Is the written plan purely objective? Or is it simply a lead-on, a pretext that will lead to making a sale?

Conflict of interest? Yes! The two-hat approach can lead to a tremendous conflict of interest. But it does not have to—nor should it.

The objective of the fee and commission approach is to compensate the planner fully for the use of his or her valuable time. Fees are earned; they are compensation well deserved for providing the client with a superior-quality, objective financial plan. The amount of the fee after expenses should reward the planner with a net profit for the time invested in the plan, commensurate with the planner's level of expertise. I cannot agree with planners who provide written cases at break even, expecting to earn big commissions on the implementation of products. If planners are going to structure compensation on both a fee and a commission basis, they must take a true two-hat approach. Planning should be done with the intent to earn a profit; commissions from the sale of products must never be expected. If commissions do result, they are icing on the cake—a bonus to the planner for a job well done.

In my own practice, I work on both a fee and a commission basis. Currently, I charge an hourly fee for the time spent to develop a financial plan from start to finish. I either quote a maximum fee, which is guaranteed in writing, or, where possible, charge a specific fee, although sometimes I find great difficulty in projecting how many hours the case will require.

From the start I expect no compensation other than the fee derived for the initial financial plan. My client has the freedom to implement recommended financial products through any source desired. The objective is a no-strings-attached financial plan. Since a good percentage of my recommendations are for products without sales charges, I offer the client three basic choices after the plan has been completed: (1) the client implements the products independently (I usually provide the prospectus and application); (2) I implement the product at my standard hourly fee; or (3) we continue an ongoing client relationship through a quarterly tracking program. The client is then provided continuous service, including quarterly meetings, for a quarterly fee. The fee is based generally on the level of work and is adjusted annually. Some planners even take more responsibility and offer their clients a discretionary investment advisory service (managing the client's assets). However, discretionary investment management is a world unto itself, and planners should not undertake this task unless they really understand what they are doing from both an investment and a regulatory (Securities and Exchange Commission) standpoint. This subject is discussed in a later chapter.

Many planners recommend commission products to their clients. There is nothing wrong with that if you make the client aware that it is a no-strings-attached deal and that they are under no obligation to purchase the products from you. My policy is to encourage my clients to shop for better products. If they still want to purchase from me, fine. If not, I have already earned a fee for providing a service. Additionally, I always disclose to my client if I will be receiving a commission because (1) it adds credibility to the two-hat approach; (2) it makes good business sense to let your clients know that you are not doing things or making money behind their backs; and (3) it is required under the antifraud provisions of the Investment Advisors Act of 1940.

What is the future of compensation in the financial planning field? If my firm is any indication, it appears that fees are taking on added importance each day. However, interestingly enough, my commission income is also growing. I find that middle-class clients, who are the vast majority of my client base, are frequently resistant to a fee. But it is difficult to generalize about this. Some clients prefer fees, others prefer commissions. Freedom of choice has been an American institution for a long, long time. My policy is to let my client decide. I get paid either way.

FEES VERSUS COMMISSIONS: THE TAX ANGLE

The fees charged for the bulk of financial planning services are tax deductible for the client under Section 212 of the Internal Revenue Code. On the other hand, commissions are considered part of the purchasing cost (basis) and ultimately figure into the gain or the loss only when the investment is sold. For instance, client A purchases a load mutual fund from the financial planner, investing $10,000 at the share price. Since 8½% goes for sales commission, client A receives only $9150 of fund shares. The purchasing cost to client A is $850. Client B, on the other hand, purchases a no-load fund and pays the financial planner $200 for advice. Client B also invests $10,000 but receives $10,000 in shares. Furthermore, client B is in a 50% tax bracket and deducts the $200 investment advice fee as a miscellaneous deduction. The purchasing cost to client B is $100. The tax deductibility of most fees plays a critically important role in the marketing of financial planning services.

The method of compensation you choose to employ is a matter of personal preference. No one can tell you which to use; you must discover it for yourself. Try one method, try two methods, try all the methods. The right method, of course, is the one that works best for you.

A WORD ABOUT LOAD AND NO-LOAD PRODUCTS

As you probably know already, a load product contains a sales charge to the purchaser. A no-load, on the other hand, has no sales charges. The argument as to which is better suited for the client has been going on for years and I doubt that it will ever be settled, unless, of course, some regulatory agency mandates a solution. However, in the absence of regulation, the financial planner will sooner or later have to take a position as to how he or she will implement products into a client's plan. Since I am both a fee and a commission planner, and I use both load and no-load products, I have tried to handle this question as objectively as possible.

You can raise all the arguments in the world (and I'm sure I've heard them all), but obviously a no-load product is less expensive to the client. That's a fact. Given two equal products, the no-load will always be cheaper since the dollars that would have applied to the commission will instead provide the client with an additional investment or will be used to discount the price. Thus it would appear that a financial planner should always use a no-load product. However, it is not quite that simple. You must always remember that financial planners are in business for themselves and, like any other people in business, they deserve a fair return on what they have invested—their time and skill. Only a fool or a philanthropist works for nothing, and I assume that you are neither. In my practice I have taken the position that I will not work for nothing. If you expect to stay in this business, you won't either. You should be totally compensated for the time you have devoted to your client: by a fee, a commission, or both. That is certainly fair. Besides, I have yet to meet a no-load lawyer, a no-load accountant, or a no-load plumber.

When is it appropriate to use a load product rather than a no-load? The financial planner may use a load product if the purpose is to compensate for the time and services devoted to the client's case. When a client comes to you in need of your skills and expertise but does not wish to pay a fee, a load product would be most appropriate. In fact, even if you charged the client a fee for the formulation of a financial plan, a load product would be appropriate provided that (1) you gave the client the choice of buying the product elsewhere, and (2) you disclosed your commission to the client. The point is that you should not write a financial plan tailored to sell your client products now or at some future time. The plan you write must be objective and honest.

The argument, as I see it, is not really load versus no-load, but the proper use of load and no-load products. There are times for loads and times for no-loads. You—and only you—can settle this question within your own practice, depending, of course, on how your practice is structured and on your own personal beliefs. Then, too, there are the conflicting goals of making a profit while doing the best you can for your client.

In the case of mutual funds, I have yet to see a load fund that was cheaper than a no-load at original purchase. Be realistic. When a client only has 92 or 93% of the dollars spent going into the actual investment versus 100% for a no-load, how could the load be better? Generally, it can't. I am by no means implying that *all* no-load funds are better than all load funds. Nothing could be further from the truth. In fact, the 1982 *Forbes* magazine honor roll of best performing funds for the years 1970–1982 includes 10 load funds, five no-load funds, and one closed-end fund. A good load fund is always better than a bad no-load fund. What we try to do is compare apples to apples and fund to fund. A no-load fund that performs as well as a load fund is obviously a better investment for the client. When a mutual fund is selected for a client, the planner must look at the entire picture, not just a small segment. Among the factors to be considered in addition to load types are performance; beta; portfolio administration charges; exchange privilege; and the other funds available in the investment group. Flexibility is vital and a load fund is flexible only in relation to the fund for which it can be exchanged. For instance, if you select a load fund that offers no exchange privilege, the only way to switch the investment (should economic conditions warrant a switch) is to sell the fund at its net asset value, which means that the commission will be lost. A no-load fund, under the same circumstances, can be sold and changed to another fund group at net investment price, with no loss of commission. However, generally, a load fund in a large fund group can be switched to other funds within that group at a very nominal transfer charge. Fund mobility is certainly a major consideration.

The real proof of the quality of a mutual fund is its investment performance, not the sales charge. The sales charge is the purchasing cost; the performance (track record) is a measure of profit. There is absolutely no correlation between the two. The sole fact that a fund has a low or no sales charge does not make it a good fund, nor does a high sales charge make it bad. Where is it going, what it is going to do for your client, is important. The financial planner should examine the track record, both long term and recent. Is there a reason for a sudden change in performance? A change in management, perhaps? Talk to the fund managers. Ask questions about investment strategy, and so forth. A financial planner should choose a fund for quality and for no other reason. If you select a load fund, select a high-quality load; if you select a no-load, select a high-quality no-load. Only you can judge whether you should use a fund with a sales charge.

Another consideration the financial planner should not overlook is service. Service is very important to the financial planner. Does the fund group handle problems efficiently and professionally? From my experience, many groups have difficulty dealing with financial planners. Load groups, in general, probably do a better job from a service viewpoint since they rely primarily on sales.

Mutual funds are not the only products with which a financial planner deals. There are many others. Limited partnerships, like funds, have loads and no-loads. When examining a limited partnership the financial planner must look at the overall picture, not just the sales charge. Assuming that the partnership is a suitable investment, the overall payout should be analyzed. For example, you might find two equal partnerships in which one has no sales charges or general partner fees, but on the back end (profits distributed to the partners) the general partner retains 20 or 30%. The other partnership, however, has a 15% sales charge, plus a one-time partnership fee, but the general partner takes only 5% of the back-end profits. The partnership must be examined as a whole. The debate of load versus no-load could go on, investment after investment, and for other financial service products as well. Today, there is even no-load life insurance if you want it.

The answer to this debate must come from within. Just keep this in mind: Don't overload for your clients, but don't underload for yourself. Be fair to your client—and be fair to yourself.

4

THE WORLD OF THE INVESTMENT ADVISOR

SHOULD YOU BE A REGISTERED INVESTMENT ADVISOR?

The financial planner explores many different fields in the course of daily practice. In a single day the planner may cover investments, taxation, insurance, psychology, estate planning, management, accounting, sales, and perhaps a dozen or so other fields. There are not many other professions that can claim this degree of diversification. Perhaps this is why the financial planning profession is exciting, rewarding, and unusually challenging.

To practice effectively, the planner, in most cases, will require a handful of licenses and/or registrations with governmental agencies. The number of requirements depend on the scope, depth, and location of the planner's practice. One such registration on which the planner must place tremendous importance is with the Securities and Exchange Commission (SEC) as a Registered Investment Advisor. Any planner practicing must place a great deal of emphasis on this aspect of law, where the planner must be registered with the Commission.

Under the Investment Advisors Act of 1940 persons or entities who are in the business of providing investment advice to others must register with the SEC. There are, however, exceptions to this rule, which will be discussed later in the chapter. What we are concerned with here is how the Advisor's Act relates to the owner of a small financial planning business. Large financial planning concerns have battalions of SEC attorneys on staff and would have little reason to read this book. The small practitioner, on the other hand, usually has nobody to turn to and needs solid, straightforward advice in simple English, not legalese (a unique language that requires a paragraph to say yes or no). Therefore, rather than discuss SEC registration in reference to the various sections and subsections of the Investment Advisors Act of 1940, the presentation will be more general and, hopefully, more practical.

The general rule is that any person who holds himself or herself out to be a financial planner and charges a fee to the client must be registered with the SEC. This applies whether you provide investment advice on specific securities or just investment advice in general. The point to remember is that *if you charge a fee for your advice*, you must be a Registered Investment Advisor. Case closed! I can hardly conceive of a situation where a financial planner who charges a fee does not have to register. However, I do suppose that if a planner did not touch on the subject of investments, staying strictly within the fields of insurance, real estate, or tax consultation, perhaps a case for nonregistration might be valid. In that case, of course, the person wouldn't really be a financial planner, but rather a real estate broker or an insurance or tax consultant. Again, the situation may not be as clear-cut as it seems, especially if a fee is being charged for giving real estate investment advice. The point is that any questionable situation should be checked thoroughly with an attorney who handles SEC matters.

Fee planners are required to register regardless of the number of clients they have. There is no minimum number of clients. The rule is clear that if you hold yourself out to be a financial planner, you must be a Registered Investment Advisor. Yes, that means that even if you have only one client, you must register. The only exception to the rule is if you have fewer than 15 clients and *you do not hold yourself out* to the general public to be an investment advisor or financial planner. In other words, the investment advice must be incidental to your principal function, such as attorney or accountant. But practically speaking, anyone who would qualify for this exception to registration would not be a financial planner anyway. The vast majority of small financial planning practitioners *must* be registered.

The financial planner who works on a commission-only basis is another story. There are further exceptions to the Investment Advisors Act that exclude broker-dealers and registered representatives of broker-dealer firms. However, the law is not meant to give them total sanction from registration. For instance, a registered representative who only sells commission products for the broker-dealer firm is sheltered by the registered representative exclusion; but if this planner decides to present the client with a plan, the planner would probably be considered to be acting as an investment advisor, even if the client was not charged for this plan. The fact that the planner is receiving a commission based on a plan may be enough to require registration. If the planner did charge a fee, there would be no question that he or she would have to be registered.

The question of registration is undoubtedly a legal one and certainly beyond my expertise, or that of any nonlawyer, for that matter. Often there is a fine line regarding who is an investment advisor and who is not, although the law of probability states that you have a far better chance of being one if you are a financial planner. But in the business of financial planning, probability, assumptions, and guesswork are extremely dangerous, especially if a valid answer can be obtained quite easily. The first place to start is with a lawyer—and not just any lawyer.

Most attorneys, besides knowing that "SEC" stands for the Securities and Exchange Commission, know little else about SEC law. If you don't believe me, ask a few. You must seek out an attorney who specializes in SEC law, and this can be a most difficult and frustrating experience, since there are just not that many available. And when you do find one, the cost is often prohibitive—usually well into the thousands. But if you have a serious legal question, what alternative do you have? Let's see.

If you are typical of the small financial planner, the questions you may have regarding registration are quite routine. The answers are usually obtainable for the cost of a few long-distance phone calls. If you call your regional SEC office or the main office in Washington, DC, you will be able to talk to someone from the SEC, including attorneys, who can answer a great many of your questions. From my experience, I found that the SEC staff attorneys were most helpful, and in every case the answers they provided were correct. However, keep in mind that these are SEC government attorneys and not your own private attorney. The SEC attorney, although helpful, still receives his or her paycheck from the U.S. Department of Justice. Your attorney receives his or her fee from you, thereby representing your interests and not those of the government. My suggestion, however, is that you start first with the SEC, and if you find the procedures too difficult or not to your satisfaction, retain private counsel to process your registration. At the very minimum, you should have a conference with your own counsel regarding the legal aspects of your business even if you do not use an attorney to file for registration.

If you have a question that you feel should be a matter of

permanent record, such as a letter in your files stating whether you are required to register under the Act, what should you do? Certainly, if you are using private legal counsel you should request a legal opinion in writing from that attorney. If you are not using private legal counsel, write the Securities and Exchange Commission stating the facts of your situation and as much about your operation as possible. Ask them for an interpretive position, advising you whether you are required to register as an investment advisor under the Investment Advisors Act of 1940. Your request will then be reviewed by the office of the Chief Counsel in the Division of Investment Management and researched closely before the final decision is made. On the average, it should take about six to eight weeks for a reply. You should address your request to:

Chief Counsel's Office
Securities and Exchange Commission
450 Fifth Street
Washington, DC 20549

The subject of investment advisor registration is too important to rely on the verbal opinion of anyone, especially if the opinion is not to register.

To obtain further information on the subject of investment advisor registration, the College for Financial Planning in Denver, Colorado, and the International Association for Financial Planning in Atlanta, Georgia, have put out some excellent, up-to-date cassette tapes regarding this matter. In addition, the IAFP has published in *The Financial Planner*, its monthly magazine, many excellent articles regarding the Investment Advisors Act.

You have come this far and it would be unfair not to pass on the rest of the bad news. Ready? Registering with the SEC is only half the problem. The other half is registering with your State Security Commission and complying with your state security laws. Since all states have different laws, the use of an attorney familiar with the security laws in the states in which you wish to practice is highly recommended. Some states permit investment advisors to sell products, whereas other states do not. There are even some states in which the state security laws applying to Registered Investment Advisors are in conflict with the federal law. This, of course, is a very difficult problem and the solution is not easy.

If you are a financial planner who is not a Registered Investment Advisor but should be, you have a threefold problem. First, you are conducting your business in violation of the Investment Advisors Act of 1940. Second, clients can sue you for refund of their investments and, in some cases, for punitive damages. Third, your state can take further action against you for failure to comply with the state securities laws. All of these problems, together or separate, can be devastating to you and your career as a financial planner.

If you fail to register as required, the SEC has the right to seek an injunctive action. In other words, the SEC files suit in the U.S. District Court asking the court to direct you to cease rendering investment advice without being registered. Should the court enter a judgment for the SEC but you continue to practice without regard to the court order, the SEC may then ask the court to find you in criminal contempt and send you off to do your financial planning in a federal corrections institution.

But that is extreme. In the real world the SEC does not like to sue. Legal cases take time and are very costly to the government. According to Charles E. Padget, the Regional Counsel for the SEC in New York, the first step, assuming that no fraud is involved, would be that the financial planner is contacted by a SEC examiner and asked to come in for a chat to determine whether the financial planner really is an investment advisor according to the Act. If it is found that the planner should be registered, he or she will simply be advised to do so. "If the financial planner continues to break the law, we would have no option but to sue."

In a recent case in the Eastern District of New York, the SEC filed suit against a person alleging that the person is an unregistered investment advisor and in violation of the antifraud provisions of the Act. The SEC has asked the court to order this person to cease conducting investment advisor activities and return all monies to the clients, and to appoint an independent escrow agent to oversee the refund of these clients' funds. Although the preceding suit was filed against an unregistered investment advisor, not a financial planner per se, the SEC would make no distinction between the two.

According to the Act, the SEC has 45 days after the acceptance of an investment advisor's application to oppose the registration. Should the SEC have to go to the courts to enjoin an unregistered investment advisor from practicing, the advisor could still file for registration. However, the chances are that the SEC will then oppose the registration, or at best advise the examination staff to keep a watchful eye on the advisor.

REGISTERING AS AN INVESTMENT ADVISOR

Assuming now that you have decided to register as an investment advisor, what is your next step? Do you telephone the SEC and tell them to register you, or do you fill out a postcard and mail it to them? Sorry to say, it is not that simple. The wheels of bureaucracy do not turn that smoothly. The road is paved with cobblestones and mud. So roll up your sleeves and grab a pen with lots of ink. Welcome to paperwork city.

The application for registration as an investment advisor is made on Form ADV, a booklet about as thick as *Time* or *Newsweek*. If you are lucky you might get away with filling in only 30 pages. Or you can take a shorter route and throw the problem at your attorney. From that point on, you can sit back, let the attorney do all the work, and pay the charges. It is your decision—and your money. Otherwise, be prepared to do a lot of writing and a lot of thinking, especially the latter. Many of the questions that the SEC will require you to answer are paragraphs and sometimes pages in length. A copy of Form ADV with the instruction sheet has been provided in Appendix A.

A great many of the questions asked in Form ADV require considerable thought. Therefore, I suggest that the questions not be taken lightly. The answers, too, should not be instinctive. They are too important, much too important to brush over or to copy from a prototype. Furthermore, you should give careful consideration to the potential ramifications of your responses. For instance, let's start on page 1 with the simple question, "name of applicant." Easy enough? You have had years of practice writing your name. Why should this time be any more difficult? All right, go ahead. Write your name. Now, let me ask you this. Are you absolutely sure that you are the applicant? Give this question a little thought and my point will become obvious.

Does a Registered Investment Advisor necessarily have to be an individual? No. The advisor can also be a corporation, a separate legal entity. For instance, my firm, AMR Planning Services, Inc., is the investment advisor, and I am a mere employee. The reason I elected to be a corporate investment advisor is that, because I wear two hats (advisor and salesman), I wanted to legally separate the two functions. Many factors go into the ultimate decision in regard to selecting the investment advisor. Whether you are the advisor or your corporation is the advisor depends on the structure of your business, the services you perform, and the products you market. You must also take into consideration whether you will ultimately hire other financial planners in your firm.

There is much to be said for the corporate investment advisor and there is much to be said for the individual investment advisor. Either decision is correct—it is really a matter of personal preference, type of business, and the law of the state in which you wish to operate. My suggestion is that you speak to as many other planners as you can who have been through the painful process of SEC registration. Furthermore, if you are using an attorney to set up your practice and to advise you as to SEC and state securities regulations, one of the first questions you must ask is whether you should be a corporate or an individual invest-ment advisor. If your attorney cannot answer that, I would consider switching attorneys.

After struggling for days (or maybe weeks or months) through the two parts of Form ADV, you will find a special bonus at the end of your task: You will have the honor of attaching a $150 check which is a one-time nonrefundable filing fee. You will also need to prepare four copies of Form ADV, three for the SEC and one for your records. (Evi-dently, the Paperwork Reduction Act does not apply to the SEC.) Then be prepared for a number of rejections with pounds of paper bouncing back and forth between Washington and your office for several weeks. My first application, in fact, was returned for eight changes before it was officially accepted. As I remember, I was furious that the SEC had the nerve to reject my application, so I proceeded to call the Washington office to share my feelings of frustration. The woman who returned my call couldn't have been nicer. She explained to me exactly what was needed and why the SEC required that I make the changes. She also explained how I could expedite my registration. Furthermore, I had had some questions regarding requirements of the brochure rule (discussed in the next section of this chapter) and she gave me the name of an SEC attorney in the New York regional office who could help me. A few days later my revised application was on its way back to Washington.

About a month later another request for additional information arrived. This time, since I was heading down to Virginia anyway, I called the SEC and arranged to stop in. The amendment took 30 minutes, and they promised to expedite my registration once again. A week later it was approved.

According to the SEC, many of the investment advisor applications get rejected because Form ADV is not completed in its entirety. Many of the questions for one reason or another are answered, "Not appli-cable," especially in Form ADV, Part I, item 10, in which *every* question must be answered with a "yes" or "no" response. The SEC interprets the response "Not applicable" as meaning, "I'm too lazy to answer the question." But financial planners do appear to have more problems with some questions than with others. For example, on Part II, item 2 (on page 3), the planner must specify the type of client, such as companies, individuals, or to whomever the investment advice is geared. Also, Part II, item 3, must specifically indicate for which types of securities you will provide advice. And on Part II, item 1, you must specifically indicate the basis of your compensation, when your compensation is paid, and the amount charged. The SEC wants detailed facts. Many financial plan-ners make the mistake of answering Part II, items 4 and 12, as "Not applicable." Yet these questions must be answered or the application will be rejected. Also, Schedule D is frequently left out even though it must be completed for any officer or director of the firm. Furthermore, remember that your *original signature* must be on all copies of the execution page.

The whole process of registration should take less than 45 days. In fact, the SEC legally has only 45 days to act on an application or it must show cause for rejection. The time clock begins from the date on which the SEC determines that all information is in the application. A financial planner may request that the application for registration be expedited by submitting a cover letter with the application.

There is no question that registering as an investment advisor is a big pain. But let's look at it realistically—you have absolutely no choice. And besides, you only have to do it once.

However, be aware that although the law may require you to go through a tedious registration procedure, the staff of the SEC is eager to help you. All you have to do is ask. In fact, helping you makes it easier for the SEC to process your application through the examination phase of registration, as well as to expedite your registration. According to Henry Montgomery, CFP, former chairman of the IAFP and ICFP Regulatory Committee: "The SEC has had a very positive attitude regarding financial planners and wants to know what we are all about. In fact, they took this approach before they came out with their ideas on what we should and shouldn't do. This is the most sensible thing that I have ever seen a regulatory agency do."

Until the time that your application is processed, you are under the jurisdiction of the Washington office. You may obtain assistance by writing or calling:

> The Securities and Exchange Commission
> Office of Applications and Report Service
> 450 Fifth Street
> Washington, DC 20549
> (202) 272-3100

Once registered, you are under the jurisdiction of your regional office.

COMPLYING WITH THE SEC

What is an investment advisor? Every financial planner must know the answer to this question. The term "investment advisor" is defined in Section 202(a)(11) of the Investment Advisors Act of 1940:

any person who, for compensation, engages in the business of advising others, either directly or through publications or writings, as to the value of securities or as to the advisability of investing in, purchasing, or selling securities, or who, for compensation and as part of a regular business, issues or promulgates analyses or reports concerning securities.

When my initial investment advisor application was first rejected by the SEC, the following was included in their letter: "An investment advisor is a fiduciary who has a duty of undivided loyalty to his investment advisory clients and must deal fairly and honestly with them."

You can see that in both theory and practice, you owe your allegiance to your client and not to anyone else. Even if you feel a strong moral obligation to the broker-dealer or tax shelter promoter because they buy you a lobster and champagne for lunch once a week, the client, rich or poor, male or female, black or white, is the person you represent. And this—even in the face of losing a large commission check—must never be forgotten.

For some planners the idea of being a fiduciary may be an extension of the manner in which they already deal with their clients. Regardless of how you feel about a fiduciary relationship, one fact is perfectly clear—it is the law. And you must adhere to it, whether you like it or not.

Keeping this in mind, you might have a better outlook toward SEC rules and regulations. I grant you that the SEC rules and regulations are time consuming, bureaucratic, and costly to comply with, but I must agree with their intent. An investment advisor should be out in the open with clients, hiding nothing, and operating in a straightforward and honest manner. You owe this not only to your client, but to yourself. Furthermore, the Securities and Exchange Commission has the authority to take action to suspend operations, revoke registration, and/or ban an advisor from conducting business in the future.

The Brochure Rule

Even before a person has become your client, you must begin to comply with SEC regulations. Rule 204-3 requires the financial planner to deliver to the prospective client one of the following documents: either (1) a current copy of Part II of advisors' Form ADV or (2) a brochure containing information similar to Form ADV, Part II. Furthermore, the advisor must deliver or offer to deliver each year to the client a copy of the brochure or Form ADV, Part II.

In regard to a new client, the investment advisor must deliver the brochure at least 48 hours before entering into an investment advisory contract; or the advisor can deliver the brochure to the client at the time of the contract, as long as the contract provides that the client has five business days to terminate the contract.

Loyd Hall Black, Jr., legal counsel to the International Association for Financial Planning (whose tape "Simple Steps to Avoid Legal Problems in Your Financial Planning Practice," recorded at the 1982 IAFP New Orleans convention, should be familiar to all financial planners), advises that it makes very little business sense to enter into a contract, and then to inform the client that he or she has five days to terminate the contract. The better approach is to mail the client your brochure, making sure that the client receives it at least 48 hours prior to entering into the contract. Black also advises that you develop a consistent program for the delivery of your brochure.

For new advisors, the most practical approach is the use of Form ADV, Part II. All that is required is that you photocopy your SEC registration and you are in business. The procedure is quick and, more important, achieved at minimum expense to the advisor. The delivery of Form ADV, however, does little to enhance the marketing of the financial planner's products and services. Essentially, it is a dry document, but you might be surprised to learn that many clients actually read it. My guess is that clients are intrigued by this thick, ominous, official-looking document, and rather than tossing it in the garbage with the rest of the junk mail, they read it to make sure that you are legitimate.

On the other hand, a personalized brochure is much more effective from a marketing approach. It serves a dual purpose as both a sales and an informational tool. The only requirement is that it contain similar information to that found in the ADV, Part II. As a new financial planner, however, you should be cautioned against running out and printing up a thousand costly brochures. First, get your feet firmly planted on the ground before you purchase a brochure that could be quite expensive, considering the cost of printing, typesetting, photography, illustrations, graphic designing, and an attorney to check the content from a legal standpoint. An effective brochure can easily cost several thousand dollars. Another reason for not jumping the gun on brochures is that, as your practice develops, you will be making numerous changes, and these changes must be reflected in your SEC compliance material. Furthermore, as the style and complexity of your practice changes, so too will your brochure. My advice, therefore, is to work your way up to a brochure and avoid the costly mistake of being stocked with a closet full of obsolete booklets.

In my opinion there are four distinct phases that planners go through in developing their ultimate brochure. Phase I (the Beginner Brochure Phase) is simply a reproduction of Part II of Form ADV. Phase

II (the Intermediate Brochure Phase) is a basic brochure, either unillustrated or lightly illustrated, inexpensively produced with SEC compliance data and some marketing ideas integrated into the content. Phase III (the Advanced Brochure Phase) has greater depth, is graphically illustrated, moderately expensive, and may be either in color or in black and white. Phase IV (the Ultimate Brochure Phase) is a highly illustrated, very expensive brochure designed to attract the more sophisticated client. The emphasis of the brochure should be on the marketing of financial services.

The brochure that I use is a very simple, yet highly effective compliance and marketing tool. Right now I am in the Intermediate Brochure Phase (II), with seeds planted in my mind for the next phase. The format is in question-and-answer form and the brochure is entitled "Important Questions You Should Ask about AMR Planning Services." (A copy has been provided in Appendix B.) All questions and answers are designed to comply with the Securities and Exchange disclosure requirements, and to inform the client how I conduct my business. Until recently, the total cost of the brochure was the time involved putting it together (several months), a few pieces of typing paper, use of the office IBM Selectric typewriter, and the cost of printing 500 pieces of 11- by 17-inch paper folded into booklet form. The brochure cost less than $100, plus time, and I have the flexibility to change it as often as I like at minimal cost. But my newest technique, I feel, is even better. With the addition of a microcomputer system and word-processing program, I am able to modify the format of my brochure at will, changing fees and information when appropriate. The cost is only pennies per brochure, since I can run it off on my printer only as needed, and this eliminates the accumulation of outdated brochures.

The brochure that you use should be suitable for your type of practice, your client market, and certainly your expense budget. The best way to develop a brochure, I feel, is to start with the ADV Form, Part II, and over a period of several months or years develop a brochure by trial and error. It is also suggested that you speak to as many other planners as you can and collect their brochures in order to get new ideas. The best places to start are local chapter meetings and the national convention meetings of the International Association for Financial Planning, regional meetings of the Institute of Certified Financial Planners, and the Spring Conferment and educational program of the College for Financial Planning.

I have provided highlights of the Brochure Rule. However, I suggest that you review the Advisors Act thoroughly to become familiar with the other requirements that must be met. A copy of Release 1A-770, which pertains to financial planners, has been provided in Appendix C.

Disclosure of Commissions

Since the investment advisor is a fiduciary to the client, commissions and compensation received as a result of investment recommendations must be disclosed to the client. How far the investment advisor must go is a matter of interpretation. I have listened to advisory panels where legal counsel for the SEC has stated that all commissions from whatever source must be disclosed to the client. On the other hand, legal counsel representing practitioners has stated that the law relates only to securities and investment commissions. Thus the question arises: Legally, what commissions does the planner have to disclose? For instance, does the planner have to disclose term insurance commissions? Well, I preach in a later chapter that only attorneys should practice law. And I keep to that philosophy now—besides, I'm not sure of the answer anyway. Then again, I don't think that most attorneys know the answer either, or would agree with each other if they did know. My own feeling, nevertheless, is that in the spirit of being in a fiduciary relationship with the client, I disclose any commission of subsequent compensation no matter what the source. It is very important if you want to build a strong trust relationship with your client.

Furthermore, does SEC disclosure mean that the advisor has to send the client a letter each time the planner receives a commission? Again, I have heard conflicting legal interpretations on this issue. Continual disclosure of commissions, however, is more than a matter of trust; it is also a matter of practicality, something that bureaucrats living on salary have trouble understanding. So what do you do—inform the client in writing regarding each commission? Inform the client orally regarding each commission? Or is the offer to disclose the commission enough? In all honesty, if I knew that answer I would be an attorney practicing SEC law. Then, where do you find an answer? For the best interpretation I suggest that you start with your own attorney. After all, if the SEC decides to take action later, it will be your attorney who defends your position. If your attorney tells you to write a letter to each client regarding each commission, you had better do it—or find yourself another attorney.

My own procedure is, first, in my brochure I offer to disclose any commission that I personally received upon request of the client. This can be verbal or in writing—whatever the client wants. Second, if I sell any security product, such as a load mutual fund or a tax shelter, the sales charge is disclosed in the prospectus. If the client desires to know exactly what I earned, I send the following letter:

Dear Client:
    In compliance with SEC regulations, this is to advise you that I received a personal commission of $_____ from ABC Broker-Dealer for the sale of _____ units of XYZ Mutual Funds.

                                                        Sincerely,

I do not initiate written disclosure for sales of products that do not involve securities. I feel that my offer to disclose is enough. Since I write several term life insurance policies a month, written disclosure would be costly and impractical. Besides, I would seriously doubt the jurisdictional power of the SEC, since term life insurance is not marketed as an investment. On the other hand, a case for the disclosure of whole life commissions, variable life commissions, and universal life commissions may be made, especially if the Registered Investment Advisor markets the product as an investment.

The moral of the story is to verify what you must disclose with your attorney or directly with the SEC if you are not using an attorney. It is better to be safe now than accountable for your mistakes later. It is essential that a financial planner be up front with the client. The worst thing that could happen is that your client feels you are hiding certain forms of compensation you have received and thereby profiting at his or her expense. This insecurity on the part of the client, valid or not, can cause the whole client–planner relationship to dissolve. It's just not worth it!

Do not gamble with your future. As the years go by you will see that fees will play a bigger role in financial planning—and to place ongoing and continual fees in jeopardy is silly. You should, therefore, think of the disclosure requirements imposed by the SEC not as a threat to your privacy, but as a strong building block that will help you develop a positive and long-term client trust relationship.

Think of the disclosure of your compensation as your client's right.

Annual Reporting

The investment advisor is required to file an annual report with the SEC on Form ADV-S. The purpose of this report is primarily to let the SEC know that you are alive and well and not practicing with your clients' funds from the Brazilian jungle. Actually, you could be out of business for years and the SEC would never know it, since the average SEC audit is about every six years or so.

Form ADV-S is a very simple reporting form and should not take more than a few minutes to complete. It is required to be filed 90 days after the end of the advisor's fiscal year, and failure to file is a violation of Rule 204-1(c) under the Investment Advisors Act of 1940 which could result in action by the Commission to revoke your registration.

Certain advisors are required to file an annual balance sheet with the SEC. Any advisor who takes custody of client funds or charges fees more than six months in advance must submit a balance sheet with the Form ADV-S.

Books and Records

Any person or entity registered as an investment advisor should become familiar with Rule 204-2. This rule specifies what books and records the advisor must keep and for how long.

In respect to the financial planner, this rule requires that the planner keep every piece of paper relating to the client. This includes written financial plans and recommendations, all contracts and agreements, written disclosure of commissions, communication concerning receipt of the brochure and/or annual offer for a brochure, and all financial records. In effect, you are required to keep just about everything except your carbon paper and used typewriter ribbons.

Examinations

About every six years, give or take a few years, you can expect a visit from a representative of the SEC examination staff. The intent of an SEC examination is to see whether you are complying with all the rules and regulations. And the chances are that you are not! According to Mr. Padget, "It is a rare person who does not have a deficiency."

The examination has a twofold purpose: (1) to detect fraud and (2) to correct human mistakes. The vast majority of deficiencies are human mistakes and usually are corrected on the spot. Many of the mistakes involve improper paperwork procedures on the part of the advisor. Nonetheless, all the deficiencies are analyzed for three specific areas:

1. Does it involve fraud?
2. Is the integrity impaired by the deficiency?
3. Is the deficiency an error of omission or commission?

The advisor will then receive a deficiency letter which is really a directive to resolve the matter. It is likely that only in the case of repeated violations will the SEC take formal action.

The only way that an action can be commenced is by a formal vote of the Securities and Exchange Commission. A formal investigation cannot be commenced without the approval of the Commission. The Commission consists of five members, each having a five-year term with one member's term expiring each year. Each member must be appointed by the President with the approval of the Senate and no more than three of the Commission members can be members of the President's political party. The purpose of an SEC action is to restore the parties involved to equality and to prohibit violations. The SEC, in itself, does not punish and cannot sue for punitive damages. Only in a state court can a client sue an investment advisor for punitive damages.

Once again you are urged to learn everything that you can about SEC compliance. There are rules about contracts, cash referral fees, and others of which you should be aware. Read articles, listen to tapes, attend seminars, read the Advisors Act, talk to the SEC staff, confer with your own counsel, and talk to other financial planners who have registered.

But most important—for your sake and the sake of your client—comply!

5

BUILDING LONG-TERM CLIENTS

The main difference between the salesperson and the financial planner is in the relationship that each has with the client. In fact, you could say that the salesperson does not really have clients, but rather customers. There are customers whom the salesperson sees, customers whom the salesperson sometimes services, and customers who are absolutely useless (from a business viewpoint) unless they purchase products or recommend the salesperson to others.

A financial planner, on the other hand, has clients. Even if the planner is strictly on commission, it is the attitude toward the client that separates the planner from the salesperson. Financial planners working on commission do not sell products that their clients cannot use or products unsuited to their clients' needs. Commission is important since it might be the only source of revenue for the planner, but reputation is more important because the planner's livelihood depends on it.

The criterion that makes you a successful financial planner is not whether you only sell, only charge fees, or do both; it is the attitude that you have toward your clients. Are you doing right by them, or is your motive only to do right by yourself? The salesperson must continually prospect for new clients, day after day, list after list, call after call. Furthermore, he or she must continually press for new names—relatives, friends, associates. The same pitch, the same lines drag on endlessly. The bulk of the salesperson's time is spent prospecting, mak-

ing presentations, closing, and hoping that the customer will say, "Yes."
I am not implying in the least that financial product salespersons are
not financially successful. I am simply bringing to light the fact that the
salesperson and the financial planner have two opposing purposes in
dealing with the public.

The financial planner works with clients. The planner may prospect, make presentations, may close; but financial planning is the real
function. Generally, a great deal of time is spent per client, working
with each one on a continual basis. The planner frequently gets calls
from new people, since satisfied clients will actually prospect for the
planner. The financial planner, very much like the salesperson, is certainly concerned about making a living—and would be a very extraordinary person not to be—but the main concern is the client and the client's
needs. When faced with the problem of satisfying the client or the wallet,
the financial planner will *without question* choose the poorer route in
order to enhance a richer reputation. A true financial planner will inform
a client that a particular product is not needed, even at the expense of
a nice fat commission. A true salesperson will not.

At the very start of your practice, you will have to make a very big
decision. Do you want to be a true financial planner or do you want to
be a true salesperson? You cannot be both.

THE SUPER TRUST

What the planner must learn to implement into every client's program
is a "Super Trust." Is this Super Trust intervivos, testamentary, revoca-
ble, or irrevocable? Is this Super Trust used primarily to reduce income
taxes like a Clifford Trust, or is its main purpose to reduce the client's
estate taxes? None of these. What, then, is the purpose in setting up
the Super Trust?—To permanently bond the relationship between planner and client.

The Super Trust, you probably have guessed, is not a typical trust
as you may understand a trust to be. It is a unique trust that every
planner must set up with each client, no matter how wealthy the client
may or may not be. A Super Trust is a special bond that exists between
the client and the planner. It is a relationship of complete confidence
that the client feels for the planner and the respect that the planner feels
for the client. A client must know that you are trying your best. That's
what really counts. In many cases the client will continue a business
relationship even when the planner's investment performance has not
met expectations—or worse.

The establishing of a Super Trust is not by oral or written contract between the client and the planner. It generally takes a long time to establish—perhaps years. You must work at it. Over time, the client develops a special sense of trust toward the planner. The client is tuned in only to the planner and would not consider consulting with someone else. The planner becomes almost like a family member who advises the client. Establish 100 Super Trusts and not only do you have a business that is bound to succeed, but you also have 100 families as close personal friends.

The *key* to developing a successful financial planning practice is to establish this unique Super Trust relationship with your clients. Although it may take a considerable length of time, it is not that difficult to accomplish. In fact, all you really have to do is put your client's best interests ahead of your own financial gratification in each and every business transaction and event. The client comes first and you come second—without question. After a while your reward is that the client puts you first and no one else second. As I attend more and more seminars, especially those run by the College for Financial Planning or the Institute of Certified Financial Planners, I run into more and more planners who are building this very Super Trust relationship with their clients. Once a trust relationship is bonded between client and planner, it becomes airtight and there is no room for any other planner or salesperson to slip through that bond. You will know that an impervious bond has been established when your client is approached by a salesperson or another financial planner and replies, "You must speak to my financial advisor." I frequently get calls from insurance salespersons, stockbrokers, registered representatives, and tax shelter promoters who are referred to me by my clients. They generally want to know if they can be of assistance to my clients in one way or another. Unfortunately—for them, not me—they are years too late.

Don't let others set up a Super Trust before you do. Once they have, they are in with the client and you are out. When you begin working with a new client, the important thing to remember is to concentrate on establishing this Super Trust, not on earning large commissions.

THE PITFALLS OF QUICK COMMISSIONS

Unfortunately, in our business, new planners are often preoccupied with the quick and large commissions that can be made. This is normal, especially for those just starting out. I have been through it, too. And you will probably experience it if you haven't already. The temptation of those big bucks within your grasp is overwhelming. If fast dollars are your goal, there is probably nothing that I can say or do to convince you otherwise. You are in the magnetic field of the dollar and only you can get yourself out. The most I can say is that you are making a very big mistake.

Quick commissions usually do not last forever. Like most things they are cyclical, primarily because you run out of gas or burn out, the business cycle of the economy changes, products change, tax laws change, and most important, because clients change. By going after quick commissions you are sacrificing a long-term financial planning practice for the sake of short-term rewards. In the long run it is much more important to build a following of dedicated and loyal clients than a truck full of short-term dollars. Stick to the financial management theory of wealth maximization, not profit maximization. Your wealth is in your relationship with your clients. Give considerable thought to this approach.

THE HUMANISTIC APPROACH

People—this is what the financial planning business is all about. They come to you because they need your help. If they could plan their own financial future, they would not need you, would they? Another reason they may come to you is that you, in your wisdom, treat them as people. You listen when they go into detail about their lives, you don't yawn in their faces when they discuss their deepest problems, you never talk down to them, and you always show your concern. After all, these are your clients. They are people, not numbers. It is bad enough that the bureaucrats treat them like numbers. You cannot afford to—nor should you want to.

There is nothing more important to people than themselves and their families. When a client confides in you, and relates personal confidences that he or she would tell no one else, including family, it is your duty to listen and pay undivided attention. When I teach financial planner training I usually demonstrate the following technique: In an early class I ask one of my students to explain why he or she wants to be a financial planner, and why it is so important to this student. I listen attentively to the explanation, maintaining eye contact and nodding my approval. After, I say thank you, wish the student success, and ask another the same question. For the first several minutes I again maintain eye contact and give my attention, but once this student really begins to speak from the heart, I yawn and blink my eyes heavily. Then I turn away and stare out the window, breathing a few sighs of boredom.

Finally, before the student can finish, I interrupt, say thank you, and quickly begin to explain to the class why *I* became a CFP. The class is all smiles. But it is not so funny. Inattention, the lack of showing your clients that you really care about them, happens all too often in the real world.

The essence of financial planning is rapport between planner and client. A great part of the time the planner must listen to the client, absorb what is being said, analyze the situation, and diagnose the problems. I cannot think of anything more insulting than paying only partial attention to clients as they pour out their deepest concerns to you. Clients have told me financial matters that they would not tell their closest relatives. The financial planner must be more than a good listener, he or she must be a great listener. In the case of the salesperson, it is the customer who becomes the listener. The salesperson is primarily the talker, who must make that customer listen, convince the customer of a product's worthiness, and then close the sale. There is a clear difference between the role of the financial planner and the role of the salesperson—even if the financial planner wears two hats.

A technique you can use to set yourself apart from the salesperson is to call your client periodically. But doesn't a salesperson call the client? Of course—but usually just to sell something. Call your clients just to say hello, to see how everything is going, and to check that your suggestions are being implemented. If you are on a fee or fee-and-commission means of compensation, many of your suggestions may not involve commissions or any further compensation to you; therefore, the purpose of your call is to service the client and to show that you care. It is very important for the client to know that financial planning does not necessarily end once your fee has been paid. Explain to the client that you are calling to ensure that they are getting their money's worth. And once in a while invite them to lunch or dinner—on you, of course—for further counseling or financial planning therapy. A financial planner must be sincere. Place value on the relationship. And don't be too bashful to let clients know that you do.

Taking advantage of favorable provisions of the tax code could prove helpful. For the purpose of allowing businesspersons to deduct ordinary and necessary expenses for entertainment, Congress wrote Sections 162 and 274 of the Internal Revenue Code. Thus a financial planner can deduct the expense of taking clients to lunch, dinner, or to certain forms of entertainment. It is a marvelous way to let the government pay part of the cost of enhancing your relationship with your clients. But taking a client to lunch or dinner should be more than just a way to use government dollars; it should be a way to show clients that they are important to you. After all, what is your motive? Is it to show your client appreciation and concern, or is it to sell the client something? Surely there is a big difference, and your client should understand your motive without your having to explain.

Personally, I can think of no better way to relax and talk to clients about themselves, their families, their financial problems, their goals, and their satisfaction with the service they are getting. Clients are very concerned that *you* are concerned about the job you're doing for them. Many a Super Trust has been established over a friendly glass of wine.

Above all, remember that the financial planner has a financial family. The family members are your clients and they must be treated almost like a flesh-and-blood relative or a close friend.

THE PSYCHOLOGY OF DEALING WITH CLIENTS

Experienced financial planners will no doubt tell you that the wealth they have established over the years is measured by their client relationships. It does not show up as a dollar-and-cents asset on the planner's balance sheet. In fact, I would even say it is more important to be rich in client goodwill than in cash. Naturally, it is better to be rich in both. The real wealth of your business cannot be measured by bankers or credit analysts. They cannot measure the current or the quick ratio of your client goodwill nor can they measure net working capital. But—make no mistake—client goodwill is as tangible an asset as cash or office equipment. One typical financial planning firm might show assets of only a desk and a typewriter and still be a thriving financial planning firm, whereas another firm might show tens of thousands or even hundreds of thousands of dollars in assets and be headed down the tube.

Building client goodwill is directly related to understanding your clients psychologically. One planner who has developed a strong understanding of this is Gailann Bruen, a licensed marriage and divorce therapist in Morristown, New Jersey, who became convinced that the only real way to help her patients (and clients) was by including financial planning in her therapy. Gailann is a member of the American Association of Marriage and Family Therapists and has a M.S.W. degree from Columbia University. She has been in private practice since 1975. "One person after another kept coming in with problems that could be traced to money. Most of my clients were corporate people who had been shifted from other areas of the country and couldn't cope with the financial stress of living in the Northeast. I was frustrated. Being a good therapist didn't make you a financial planner."

Many of Gailann's early therapy clients were widowed and divorced women whom she described as "financially ignorant." The financial problem just added to the trauma. These women were absolutely devastated at having to learn about money in the midst of their life crisis. She saw financial planning as the key to being a good therapist. She decided to focus on these needs of her clients and become a financial planner as well.

She has presently completed four of the five parts of the CFP designation program and has worked hard to learn all she can about the financial planning field through reading and advanced training. She is quite skilled in the area of motivation and has been hired by New York University as an adjunct instructor of personal finance. In her own practice she wears two hats, that of the financial planner and that of the therapist, and often she must switch hats. However, she is very careful about doing this and will never solicit clients. "Clients may come into see me in regard to financial planning and before they leave [the office] the hostility in the marriage becomes clear."

Gailann pinpoints many reasons for financial problems. One of the biggest problems, she feels, is procrastination, which is more psychological in nature than the financial planner realizes. People are so overwhelmed by the massive variety of financial products that they are afraid to make the wrong investment decision. The result is that they do nothing, rather than make a mistake. She is convinced that before attempting to tackle the finances, the planner must deal with psychological stumbling blocks and pinpoint what can be done about them. "People," she says, "will subvert all the planning until that curtain or wall comes down." Although there are numerous reasons for financial problems, she offered five examples of how the psychological and the financial interrelate:

1. Some people are poverty conscious and security minded. These are mostly older people, first- and second-generation survivors of the Depression era, who are afraid to do anything constructive with their money. These are the clients who generally leave their money in 5½% time accounts or worse.

2. There are those who actually think that they don't deserve to be prosperous. For the most part, these are upper-income people whose internal finances are in shambles.

3. Some individuals sincerely believe that money is the root of all evil.

4. There are people who feel that you cannot be wealthy and happy at the same time.

5. Many people—and this could be the most common symptom—fear making financial errors.

Gailann points out that the financial planner should attempt to be

neither a therapist nor a psychologist. The planner should simply understand that the financial problems a client has may be a lot deeper than
they appear on the surface.

"Developing good client relations means that the planner must
begin where the client is. You must start with the client's most pressing
concern and stick to it no matter what. For example, if you are getting
information from a data sheet and the client keeps rambling off in
another direction about a different problem, then you must concentrate
on that problem. Otherwise, the rest of the planning process may be
useless. The planner cannot be on a rigid timetable. If the client is talking
about a problem, you can't skim by it simply because you feel the pressing need to get on to the balance sheet or the budget items. The roots
of your relationship start with listening and not just pretending to listen.
The tone of voice or the verbal messages may be a sign of a deeper
problem. Try to uncover the client's deeper problems. To be effective
you must turn off your own concerns and tune into the client.

"However, your method is most important. Don't probe. If the
client feels uncomfortable, back off until the client builds up confidence
in you, then tactfully return to the subject. The last thing in the world
you want to do when attempting to uncover a problem is to use a district
attorney approach. If you come on too strong you may destroy the
whole relationship that you are trying to build. One of the techniques
I use is mirroring. This means reflecting back what you see, what you
hear. I may say to my client, 'It seems like you are upset by . . . ,' or
'It appears that you have a question about . . . ,' or 'I understand your
priorities to be . . . Is that correct?' "

The client relationship starts during the first interview. In fact, it
may even begin over the telephone with the tone of your voice. "You
must be warm," Gailann insists; "You must take a humanistic approach
to money. Offer your client a cup of coffee or a soft drink. Make that
client feel as comfortable as possible. Remember that it takes a lot of
guts for the client just to walk in and say that he or she needs help."
Gailann's objective is to make it very clear to her clients that she is there
to help them accomplish what *they* want to do. She is a facilitator. Her
philosophy is that clients come to you in need of an authority figure
who will tell them what to do. The financial planner should help them
to clarify their goals, examine the different methods of reaching these
goals, and then carry them into the decision-making process. "You must
fit the plan to the client and not to the computer."

"However there is one thing that the financial planner must not
do. Under no circumstances should you be impatient, especially if they
ask very elementary questions. Impatience tells your clients that you
don't care about them—that you don't want to be bothered."

Gailann Bruen, of course, is not the only financial planner who believes in the total client approach. Most true financial planners do. The old-time financial planner who through the years has practiced this approach still has the same clients today . . . and their children . . . and their grandchildren. The planner who did not has a new set of clients . . . and will have a new set next year, and for each year to come.

As the years go by, the interrelationship between psychology and financial planning will become more evident. In my opinion, what will happen is that the importance of true financial planning will become increasingly apparent in the treatment of psychological and stress problems. More and more therapists, like Gailann Bruen, will awaken to some of the real causes of mental and divorce problems and either cross-train as financial planners or link up with planners who they feel can help their patients. In the years ahead financial planning may prove to be one of the new wonder drugs of psychotherapy.

6

BUILDING THROUGH CHANGE

Building a financial planning practice is somewhat like the making of a great wine. It takes time! As with wine, a financial planning practice must be aged. Yet, even before the winemaker ages the wine, there is a great deal of experimentation that must be done. The grapes must be picked at the proper level of acidity; the fermentation temperature must be established; the desired dryness or sweetness must be achieved. In all, it takes testing and retesting, change after change.

In fact, if you think about it, life is a big experiment. We are always striving to do better—to reach the highest plateau of our desires and dreams. Since the beginning of time people have always searched for better ways to do things. Think about all the things in your life that you were not satisfied with—your grades in school; your marriage; your career; your taxes. What did you do about it? Did you experiment? Did you make changes? Or did you accept the misery? A good novelist, for instance, takes years to write a book, page after page, chapter after chapter, only to edit, rewrite the pages, crumple them into paper balls, toss them into the wastebasket, and rewrite new thoughts on another day.

The financial planning business is no different. It is a business of change. If you are inflexible, resistant to change, you could be in the wrong profession. Hopefully, by telling you this, I can save you a great deal of time and pain.

What makes the financial planning business so subject to change? Well, it is a direct function of the state of the economy, the politics of tax legislation, the moods and opinions of the policymakers at the Internal Revenue Service, the client market and its needs, competitors, the big brothers at the SEC and the State Security Commissions, as well as dozens of other obvious and not so obvious factors. Change is the name of the game. Are you willing to make the continual changes needed along the way? You are in a most dynamic profession.

There is no perfect financial planning practice. It is a totally subjective field. In fact, it would take a great deal of searching to find two planning practices exactly the same. What works for one planner may not work for another. I am sure that the style of my own practice would not work for a great many other planners. So, what's the answer? Experiment!

In the early years try almost everything—at least everything that you find morally suitable. But if you object to selling certain products or providing certain services, do not feel that you must. My suggestion is that you try as many products and services as you can. That is important because you will never know if they are good unless you try them. And you may always wonder.

HOW MY OWN CAREER EVOLVED

My own practice began initially in the basement of my home as an income tax preparation service. This was a sideline of another career. My friends at work gave me the nickname of "H & R Rich." At first, my only goal was to pick up a little extra income and to get some practical experience in taxation while I worked toward my master's degree in taxation. The financial planning business was as foreign to me as the termite exterminating business. As the years went by, however, my tiny little tax business began to grow and the thought of changing my career as a Senior United States Customs Inspector twinkled in my brain. Would it be worth giving up my handcuffs, Smith & Wesson .38, flashy gold badge, $26,000 a year salary with another $20,000 in overtime, a pension in another 20 years at age 55 with a built-in cost-of-living adjustment, 26 days' vacation a year, paid sick leave, and limited responsibility? After all, the trade seemed fair, for in return I would get my own business with no guarantee that I would ever make a cent, no initial fringe benefits, an 80-hour workweek, and the responsibility of a family to support. Sounded like a good deal to me! Most of my companions at the Customs Service told me I had completely popped my cork and should check into New York's Bellevue Hospital for a complete psychiatric examination and a much needed rest. It is an unwritten law that no one quits government service, especially after 10 years. A few of my closest friends, however, supported me in my hours (years) of decision. That is when the seeds of the financial planning field began to germinate.

I knew that if I were to leave my comfortable position with the Customs Service, the tax business alone would not be enough to carry me financially. I had to be more than just a tax consultant. Surely I could be an acountant, too. I had the background, but I hated general accounting. I needed something else. But what? In true Hollywood fashion the words appeared before me—however, they weren't engraved on a tablet of stone, but in the April 1979 issue of *Money Magazine*. The article described the new and emerging field of financial planning, a growing trade association called the International Association for Financial Planning (IAFP), and a unique school, the College for Financial Planning, in Denver, Colorado. Since I had just finished my master's degree in taxation, and the education bug was still in my system, I decided to enroll in the CFP designation program given at the College. How hard could a correspondence course be after a 51-credit Master of Science program? I was in for quite a jolt. The CFP program turned out to be one of the most difficult of any that I had ever taken. It took only a few weeks after receiving my first textbooks and study guide to know that the field of financial planning offered everything I always wanted. During the next few months I studied and obtained my state insurance licenses (life, accident, and health) and my NASD license. Now my little business prepared taxes and sold insurance and mutual funds.

During the tax season of 1980 I added another 45 clients to my business and could barely function those months at Customs. My supervisors began to notice it, too. At tax season I showed up for work several times with an empty holster and a briefcase packed with 1040 forms. I was fortunate that most of my supervisors were clients, too, and were tolerant knowing that April 15 would come and go, and that I'd be back to my usual productive self. The time of the Big Decision was drawing near. The fact was that it would be physically impossible to remain at Customs and take on any new clients. And if my business was going to grow at all—if I was going to be the financial planner that I wanted so much to be—then I was going to have to quit Customs. Ironically, the Big Decision took about 15 seconds. It was very easy to make because my wife was so supportive of me. "So we don't eat for a few months," she said, jokingly. But I knew that I could count on her if the going got rough. And that, of course, meant all the world to me.

In the spring of 1980 I wrote my first financial planning case. I charged $275 for a 28-page plan that took about 30 hours to research and write. My next plan, a few weeks later, went for $320. Fees were based on where the dart landed on the corkboard. Since this was the big time, I formed a corporation (I always wanted to be a corporate president) and that summer registered "my corporation" with the Securities and Exchange Commission as an investment advisor. That September, while still employed by Customs, I rented an office. In December I unhooked my badge, took off my holster, and said "au revoir" to 10 years of my life.

The first problem I had was getting used to wearing suits to the office—for 10 years I had worn a uniform. So the end result was that I compromised with myself and switched to blue jeans. However, I must admit that once in a while, I sneak in a suit and tie if the need arises. But I'm not happy about it. Needless to say, in an emergency I can always go home and change, since my house is only 5 minutes from the office.

During my first tax season at the office I prepared 225 income tax returns, all manually, with the assistance of my wife and a secretary. It was the last year that I did manual tax returns, changing my method of operation to the use of a computer service. Since I had gotten so many leads during the tax season, immediately after April 15 I plunged into life insurance sales, case financial planning, and the sale of investment diamonds (my first major mistake, which will be discussed in a later chapter). In May I attended the College for Financial Planning Conferment in Denver and came home with my CFP designation, prouder of my CFP than of my master's degree in taxation. Once back from Denver, I was full of renewed energy and ready to tackle the financial planning world with the many new ideas that I had picked up from other planners.

In August 1981, convinced of my ability and determined to succeed, I decided to take the business full steam ahead and explore an area that had always been in the back of my mind but had been suppressed for fear of failure. Although my wife did not agree with me this time, I nonetheless undertook the awesome burden of discretionary money management. My first money management client had a tax-sheltered annuity of which a mutual fund salesman had managed to take $85,000 of client contributions and turn it into $62,000 over several years. I immediately moved the client into a no-load mutual fund group and switched the funds back and forth between the mutual funds in the group. My first-year performance was 20.4%. The second money management client came shortly thereafter, and then the third, and the fourth, and the fifth, and so on. By the end of 1982 I managed nearly 60 discretionary accounts, ranging from accounts as small as $1000 for clients in my forced savings program (a program that I have developed for clients with severe spending problems) to accounts approaching $200,000. But change once again swept over me. In 1983 I began to phase out of money management and into another system, called AMR Tracking, which for the most part is nondiscretionary.

The fall of 1981 saw other major changes. Thanks to my broker-dealer I became involved with oil and gas limited partnerships. I never took advantage of these investments before, because I found great difficulty doing proper due diligence. Also, I was not impressed by most of the public programs on the market. When my broker-dealer restructured their firm toward in-field developmental oil and gas drilling, I was satisfied with the level of due diligence and placed some of my clients' funds in their first project. I even purchased a small fractional unit for myself on the theory that if it was good enough for my clients, it was certainly good enough for me. Another major change that I made was to streamline my case financial plans, chopping a vast amount of the text and getting straight to the recommendations. My older plans included several pages of text that analyzed the client's portfolio, computed the after-tax return, analyzed appreciation, and dwelled on balance sheet ratios and income statement percentages. Now I simply use a meaningful statement like: "Your investment portfolio stinks!" The client gets my point rather quickly, and the message is a lot more effective than a dissertation on ratios and yields. In one of my earlier financial plans I wrote an 84-page masterpiece, handsomely bound, and charged the client $2500. Today the plan sits on a shelf in the client's office, gathering layers of dust. And except for a few superficial changes the client made, nothing was accomplished. The plans I write nowadays are generally no more than 20 pages and are concerned primarily with the implementation of my recommendations. Dealing with client procrastination has made me keenly aware that a financial plan is only as good as the end result—what actually gets done.

I have discussed the history of my own practice in order to demonstrate the value of continual change. Change is a necessity; it is the catalyst of any successful financial planning practice, and I cannot stress enough how important it is. On the financial planning highway that you will travel, the road is filled with detours, turns, forks, exit ramps, and junctions. The only way you will know where to enter and where to exit is by traveling that road. Some planners may find the road bumpy and congested, others may get lost, and still others may find it smooth and clear. You must be warned that the road signs are not clearly marked. Whether you succeed, whether you fail, or whether you stop for repairs and then go on is something you'll find out only if you try.

"Change is inevitable. In a progressive country change is constant."—Benjamin Disraeli.

THE STORY OF BILL HEATH'S CAREER

A change in career is certainly an important step in a person's life. In my case it was by choice. Today I could still be working for the Customs Service, assured of a comfortable paycheck for the rest of my life and assured, too, of unhappiness. Sometimes change is a matter of survival, of knowing that one career must end and another must begin. A decade ago, Bill Heath had one claim to fame. He could hit Bob Gibson, the St. Louis Cardinals' Hall of Fame pitcher, from one side of the Houston Astrodome to the other. Although Bill was never known as a hitter, the Astro catcher had Bob Gibson's number. "Of course, Bob Gibson didn't know who Bill Heath was, but I knew who Bob Gibson was." Bill once broke up a no-hitter of Gibson's and a shutout on another occasion. On the other hand, the New York Mets had a pitcher by the name of Jack Fisher. "Fisher could have thrown his glove out there and I couldn't hit him." The ability to hit Gibson was the highlight of Bill Heath's short major league career.

Bill began pro baseball in 1960 after graduating from the University of Southern California and playing on a national championship team. He played on the same team as Tom Seaver, Ron Fairly, Len Gabrielson, and Donny Buford. Those four made the big leagues fairly quickly. It took Bill, however, almost seven years in the minors to work his way into the Astro lineup.

His first chance at bat in the majors came in 1965 with the Chicago White Sox at the tail end of the season, the time of year when the rookies are brought up to crowd the bench. "In my first at bat in the big leagues I was scared to death. The first pitch was a blazer, inches from my nose and instead of backing off I stood there frozen. I finally grounded to second."

In the off-season Bill was sold to the Houston Astros, went to spring training with the club, and made the team, but a month later was sent down to Amarillo, Texas, because of a roster problem. But he was back within 10 days. His first hit in the majors was a pinch hit off Bill Hand of the Chicago Cubs. After the break for the All-Star game, he began to play regularly and wound up his rookie season batting .301.

But Bill Heath was a realist. The fact that he was in the major leagues didn't go to his head, nor did it alter his more important game plan in the game of life. "I knew I had limited ability because I was small and I wasn't the big bonus player that management has great aspirations for. I realized that this wouldn't last forever. I knew there would be a gigantic adjustment if I didn't do something in the off-season to bring up my standard of living. So I elected to get involved in accounting because I always liked numbers." While in the minors Bill started studying accounting through a university extension program. While the other players went to the movies, he would be in his room studying. Even when he went into the big leagues he continued to study, reading his texts of advanced accounting theory. But his schedule did not allow him the time to go back to school. In 1969 while with the Chicago Cubs, he became a conversation buddy of television announcer Jack Brickhouse. "On the plane when the Cubs traveled and most of the guys were sitting in the back playing pinochle and poker, I was usually sitting up front reading my text or studying or trying to do something constructive. Jack became quite impressed with me, that I was trying to make more out of myself than a broken-down ballplayer when it was all over with. Consequently, he would have me on his TV show quite a bit when the opportunity was there. But let's face it, who was interested in Bill Heath?"

In the off-season when ballplayers rest, hunt, fish, or play baseball in the Dominican Republic or Mexico, Bill took a seasonal job in the audit department of Haskins and Sells, an accounting firm. On September 19, 1969, while catching a no-hitter pitched by Ken Holtzman, he broke his finger. That was the last game he ever played in the major leagues. "It was the twilight of a mediocre career." In 1970 he began the season in Tacoma, Washington, and halfway through the season he was released. "In baseball terminology that means fired." He then had the opportunity to join a team in Buffalo, New York, but the thought of traveling around with a minor league team again for five or six years, hoping to work his way back to the big leagues, was too much. So Bill headed south, back to Houston, and hooked up with Price Waterhouse in the Big Eight league. He worked for two years on the audit staff.

From accounting, his next step was to sell office furniture. And ironically, he made a lot more money than ever before. The most he had ever made in the big leagues was $19,000. "In selling, I learned what servicing people's needs was all about." But Bill continued to do tax returns and write up work for small clients as well. They were always asking for advice, and bringing in more and more referrals. Three years later he had no choice but to open a full-time practice.

He started out as an accountant but he was perceptive and saw the need people had for a service beyond that level. "People wanted desperately to know what to do in the future. You don't make money looking over your shoulder. I discovered more and more the needs of the small business. These people needed to know what to do and how to plan."

Today William C. Heath & Associates, a Houston, Texas, financial planning firm, with four professionals and two support personnel on staff, specializes in strategic planning for small businesses and their owners. The firm is registered with the Securities and Exchange Commission as an investment advisor and is a fee-only planning firm. However, Bill Heath as an individual retains various insurance and securities licenses and can sell products. The firm charges an hourly fee for financial planning services with a minimum cost for any individual financial plan.

"I prefer to be a 'fee for service'," Bill says. "People are now beginning to be more aware of paying fees and are willing to pay them when you provide a real service. When we started out, our plans were $250. What we look for in providing for our clients is to identify where they are in today's marketplace. Then we coordinate this information with their objectives—where they want to be. We look to identify the strengths and weaknesses of the firm. It's my belief that the small businessman goes through the 'University of the IRS' where the tuition is 50% of what he earns. Basically he stands alone, confused and frustrated by payroll taxes, withholding, franchise taxes, sales taxes, etc. So education is necessary and what school provides it? The 'University of the IRS', of course. It is a very expensive education where they teach how to use their forms, their way. It costs an arm and a leg. But if this person is smart he will go out and surround himself with other good advisors. And although they may seem expensive initially, they will save him substantially, down the road."

Bill's academic career did not stop when he left baseball. Since then he has completed his M.B.A. degree from the University of Houston and his CFP designation from the College for Financial Planning. As a professional pursuing his master's degree, he made some interesting observations on the difference between the real world and academia. "Academia will take a problem and go to the nth degree with it. A businessman will take a problem and go far enough to get the job done. The difference between the nth degree and getting the job done is profit. It is, therefore, senseless to expend your resources to the nth degree because it pays nothing. And this is why academia has such a problem going out in the real world and making money. They are trying to go to the nth degree on everything while the businessman is saying, 'You're not listening—I don't need all that.' "

For Bill his whole planning business has been one of trial and error. There wasn't anyone out there telling him how to do it. Like most financial planning firms, his business grew through a process of change. In fact, his basic theory is: *ideas + change = innovation.* And putting this theory to use will keep you on the leading edge of the market. You must always seek new and better "ways to service your clients' needs. Quality—that is the way you stay in business. And quality is measured by results.

"I am not interested in producing a hundred plans a year. If I only produce one plan, and it's the best plan in Houston, then I have accomplished my objective. Every plan I write has to be better than the one before. It will get better if you continue your education, associate with other professionals, and exchange ideas with other planners. All our plans are written manually; we use internal forecasting through time-sharing with Control Data. I don't believe that you can automate recommendations."

The objective of William C. Heath & Associates is to be among the highest-quality providers of financial services in the Houston area. They are well on the road to becoming the planner's planner. "I live and die with that client and the decisions we make and how their business goes. In fact, I get very excited when their business is going well. You have to be part of the client's team, the client's organization. And when they are not doing well, you are not doing well."

To succeed, Bill says, the first thing you must do other than develop your skills is to do your own financial and business planning. Plan everything you will do in your firm, especially finances, location and alignment with other professionals. "A person's success is only determined by the skill level—the more skills you develop, the more success you will have. The problem is that people like to have skills, but they don't like to put forth the effort to develop these skills. A successful person will have a burning desire to achieve, the degree of desire being the point at which you sit down and quit. For example, in baseball, how many wind sprints are you willing to run before you quit? Or in financial planning—do you put forth the extra effort on weekends to develop and master the skill, or are you the kind that goes home and watches television?"

Bill sees credibility as a slow process and advises the planner to build up a network of credibility on two levels. The first level is with your clients. "Most of my clients deal with me because they believe that what I believe in is good for them." As a result, most of the firm's new clients are referrals. The firm's brochure cost $5000 to design and Bill's only regret is that he didn't do it long before. "But I was typical of the small businessman who only tends to see costs and not long-term benefits. Had I spent the money five years ago, we probably would have been much further along today than we are." The second level of building your credibility is with other professionals. Bill feels strongly that a planner not only needs to listen to his client, but also to professionals. "You must respect other professionals. Never embarrass them by presenting a new idea to the client in front of the other professional. Make sure that the other professional understands where you are coming from long in advance. For instance, if you are proposing an interest-free loan for the client, call up the professional first and ask to have a meeting to discuss an idea that will be of benefit to the client. The other professional should appreciate this opportunity to do his or her homework first. Remember, the financial planner cannot be all things to all people and you must always view yourself as a member of a team, as long as the ultimate objective of the team is to benefit the client. Dealing with ego—yours and that of the other professional—is very important."

Although Bill Heath was never a superstar on the diamond, he holds a respectable lifetime batting average of .260 in the major leagues. And there are probably still a few Bill Heath baseball cards floating around. But that was years ago in another profession. In Bill's new profession, financial planning, there's an excellent chance that someday he'll be a superstar, batting at the top of his league for his clients.

7

EDUCATION OF THE
FINANCIAL PLANNER

There are no formal legal requirements that you need to become a financial planner, other than perhaps SEC registration, which is open to almost anyone. Therefore, the industry is comprised of planners processing a myriad of qualifications, from the self-proclaimed planners to planners with master's degrees, law degrees, and doctorates. Admittedly, a person's level of education won't necessarily make him or her a good financial planner. There are many other factors, such as business ethics, personality, marketing ability, and determination, that play equally important roles. But a planner's education is generally a good indicator of theoretical skills.

Very few colleges today offer degrees in financial planning. The field is still very new. In fact, most colleges do not even offer courses in the area of financial planning or personal finance. The average college graduate has read Shakespeare, Milton, and Darwin, solved quadratic equations, translated a foreign language, and programmed a computer, yet cannot balance a checkbook. The average college graduate probably knows more about electrons and neutrons than about the money market. Even business administration majors, though well versed in conceptual theory, are often functionally inert.

Today, education is no longer an option. It is a requirement mandated by the needs of people living in a highly sophisticated and volatile economy. The goal of the financial planner is to be regarded as a client-oriented professional. It is unfortunate that few schools offer courses to train students to become functioning financial planners.

This chapter concentrates on some of the schools that have taken the lead in developing and implementing financial planner programs. Some of the programs are traditional college programs leading to degrees, including a doctorate in financial planning, while others are nontraditional programs leading to professional designations highly recognized in the financial planning community and the client marketplace. Needless to say, financial planner education is here to stay.

And because of the importance of financial planner education I have chosen to offer course descriptions within the framework of this chapter rather than in a separate appendix.

THE COLLEGE FOR FINANCIAL PLANNING

If any school stands out as a leader among educational institutions providing courses for financial planners, it is certainly the College for Financial Planning. This school was the first purely financial planning school that offered a financial planning program for practitioners long before the subject was popular. In other words, the College for Financial Planning was the first academic institution to respond to the future needs of a nation. Located in Denver, Colorado, it offers the Certified Financial Planner designation program.

Yes, I am associated with the College as a member of the adjunct faculty. And yes, I am biased. But I feel I have valid reason to stand behind my convictions. As I have stated, it was the first school ever to put together a program for financial planners. Since 1972 the program has progressively been improved. And today the CFP designation stands out as a must for future financial planners. The objectives of the college are to:

> Provide training to persons who are or will be offering financial counseling; investment and risk management advice; counseling related to retirement, tax or estate planning; or general personal financial planning or implementation

> Provide learning opportunities for such persons through programs of study, courses, textbooks, study guides, special reading materials, continuing education courses, seminars and classroom instruction by members of an adjunct faculty and affiliated colleges and universities

> Advance the knowledge, professionalism, public recognition and responsibility of those involved in the field of financial planning and counseling

Advance through its programs and influence of its activities the financial
well-being of the general public

CFP Bulletin, p. 4

The College for Financial Planning, established in 1972, is an independent, nonprofit educational institution. The program of education
offered by the College leads to a professional designation (CFP), not a
college degree. The trademark "CFP" has been registered with the U.S.
Patent and Trademark Office and "Certified Financial Planner" has been
accepted for registration. Although the school does not offer a degree,
the course of study nonetheless is recommended by the American Coun-
cil of Education for 15 semester hours of college credit at the upper-
division baccalaureate level. As of 1983 more than 4000 students have
graduated from the program and almost 15,000 are enrolled. Among the
many students and graduates are attorneys, Certified Public Accountants, and persons holding master's degrees and doctorates in the business area.

The scope of the College's program is to offer technical knowledge
and proficiency so that the practitioner will be equipped to analyze the
economic and tax positions of the client and delineate the client's economic objectives. The program trains the CFP candidate to write a comprehensive financial plan and to implement and monitor this plan in
the face of changing economic, financial, and personal conditions.

The Certified Financial Planner, by training, learns to serve the
interest of the client and not the planner. The CFP is bound by a professional code of ethics that:

Places the interest of the client first

Requires a high degree of personal integrity

Encourages a professional level of conduct in association with peers and
others involved in the practice of financial planning

Establishes individual responsibility for knowledge of the various laws
and regulations, not only in letter, but in spirit

Discourages sensational, exaggerated and unwarranted statements

Encourages prudent and responsible actions

CFP Bulletin, p. 26

Upon completion of the CFP program, planners are eligible for
regular membership in the Institute of Certified Financial Planners, an
organization that is separate and completely independent of the College
and is discussed in more depth in Chapter 8. One of the many responsibilities of an Institute member is to continue his or her professional
education in the areas of financial planning. The present requirement is

that the Institute member complete 30 contact hours of courses; this requirement, however, will probably be raised in the near future.

In order for you to become a Certified Financial Planner, the College offers three methods of study. You may use one or all of these methods to progress through the program.

Individual Study

The materials provided by the College for Financial Planning are designed for the individual study method. The student works from textbooks and a study guide for each of the six parts of the CFP course. However, self-study is not an easy method of learning since it involves tremendous discipline on the student's part, especially for those students who have been away from the academic community for any number of years. Since the emphasis of the College's program is on making the CFP candidate proficient in writing a case analysis, the self-study method may be especially difficult. The College's testing procedure is weighted heavily on the student's ability to read a financial planning case, analyze the facts, and present a realistic solution. As an adjunct faculty member of the College, I would recommend that a student supplement some or all of the self-study training with other methods of study.

Informal Group

Sometimes candidates are fortunate enough to know others in the program. Perhaps they work for the same company, or belong to the same professional or trade association, or have developed a new friendship as a result of the program. They can then get together to aid one another in studying the course material or to prepare for an examination. Sometimes this method can be more effective than it seems at first glance. The integration of professionals studying together can have tremendous results from both an academic viewpoint and a professional one. Informal study has led to the beginning of many close and successful business associations and even partnerships. For example, an informal study group may have a student who is an attorney, another in the life insurance business, another a stockbroker, another a pension specialist, another a generalist, another an accountant or tax consultant, and so on. Informal study may offer a lot more in terms of skill strengthening than even the course demands. No textbook in the world, no written theory, no study guide can ever substitute for the years of professional experience conveyed in an informal study group. Some of the best learning experiences have taken place in cocktail lounges or equally informal settings.

Formal Class

The College has adjunct faculty whose members teach the CFP courses in most major cities in the United States. Students can train through independent classes organized and taught by individual faculty members, or through the Affiliated College Program taught at various colleges and universities across the country. Currently, CFP courses are offered through the Affiliated College Program at the following schools:

Bentley College
Waltham, MA 02254

Brookhaven College
Farmers Branch, TX 75234

Broward Community College
Pompano Beach, FL 33063

California Lutheran College
Thousand Oaks, CA 91360

Charles Stewart Mott Community College
Flint, MI 48503

Cleveland State University
Cleveland, OH 44115

College of Mount Saint Vincent
Riverdale, NY 10471

Eastern Washington University
Cheney, WA 99004

Emory University
Atlanta, GA 30322

Fox Valley Technical Institute
Appleton, WI 54913

Franklin University
Columbus, OH 43215

George Washington University
Washington, DC 20052

George Washington University
Hampton, VA 23666

Golden Gate University, LA
Los Angeles, CA 90017

Golden Gate University, SF
San Francisco, CA 94105

Wm. Rainey Harper College
Palatine, IL 60067

Honolulu Community College
Honolulu, HI 96817

Indiana University
Indianapolis, IN 46202

Jersey City State College
Jersey City, NJ 07305

Loyola College
Baltimore, MD 21210

Metropolitan State College
Denver, CO 80204

Monmouth College
West Long Branch, NJ 07764

Roosevelt University
Chicago, IL 60605

San Diego State University
San Diego, CA 92182

Scott Community College
Bettendorf, IA 52722

Shoreline Community College
Seattle, WA 98133

St. John Fisher College
Rochester, NY 14618

St. Vincent College
Latrobe, PA 15650

University of Detroit
Detroit, MI 48226

University of Hartford
Hartford, CT 06117

University of Houston
Houston, TX 77002

University of Miami
Miami, FL 33124

University of Minnesota
Minneapolis, MN 55455

University of Missouri—KC
Kansas City, MO 64131

University of Southern California
Camarillo, CA 93010

University of Southern California
Los Angeles, CA 90007

University of Tampa
Tampa, FL 33606

University of Virginia
Roanoke, VA 24018

The CFP program consists of six separate parts that are taken sequentially by all candidates. The program was expanded from five parts as of June 1983. Each part is concluded by a comprehensive three-hour written examination. I had personally found the CFP examination to be about the toughest type of examination I have ever taken, including those in graduate school. There are numerous multiple-choice questions, a case study to read and analyze, financial statements to prepare and analyze, and essays to write. The test failure rate is currently about 25%. Examinations for each of the five courses are given every four months (April, August, December) at test centers throughout the United States and overseas. The following is a description of the CFP program as described in the 1983 College for Financial Planning Bulletin:

CFP I: INTRODUCTION TO FINANCIAL PLANNING

CFP I is an introductory course with four broad areas of emphasis. First, it introduces various concepts, theories, and approaches relevant to professional financial planning. Second, it emphasizes the importance of the client–planner counseling relationship, and provides instruction on how to gather and analyze client financial data and delineate client goals and objectives. Third, it introduces the basic concepts of case analysis and begins to explore a hypothetical client's case. Fourth, it provides a general overview of the spectrum of personal financial planning, that is, risk management, investments, taxation, retirement, and estate planning.

Textbooks: Hallman, G. Victor, and Jerry S. Rosenbloom. *Personal Financial Planning*, 3rd ed. New York: McGraw-Hill Book Company, 1983.

Clayton, Gary E., and Christopher B. Spivy. *The Time Value of Money.* Philadelphia: W.B. Saunders Company, 1978.

CFP II: RISK MANAGEMENT

Risk management focuses on the subject of transferring risks by use of insurance. The need for an organized and comprehensive plan of risk management is discussed first. Because risk is often transferred to an insurance carrier, the discussion flows into a consideration of the benefits of insurance. The insurance industry is examined as well as the rules and regulations governing it. The laws and requirements for insurance contracts are considered next. An insurance policy—a legal binding contract—should be understood by all parties concerned; therefore, guidelines for analyzing an insurance contract are presented.

The remainder of Part II explores the various fields of insurance—why each is necessary, how the contracts are written, what perils are insured against, etc. Part II concludes with a consideration of factors which may guide the client's and/or financial planner's choice of an insurer and an agent.

Textbook: Mehr, Robert I. *Fundamentals of Insurance.* Homewood, IL: Richard D. Irwin, Inc., 1983.

CFP III: INVESTMENTS

There is a wide variety of assets the client may include in his/her personal investment portfolio, and this unit of study discusses many of them. Understanding the nature of long-term assets, how they are bought and sold, how they are valued, and how they may be used in portfolio construction—is the thrust of CFP III: Investments. The breadth and depth of various investment theories and concepts of portfolio management, a survey of the major securities markets, major securities laws and regulations, and the relation of this whole field to personal financial planning are covered.

An integration of taxation concepts and theory relates tax planning strategies to the consequences of investment decisions and stresses the importance of tax management in investment planning. An appropriately complex case analysis is introduced and developed through the course.

Textbooks: Fabozzi, Frank J. *Readings in Investment Management.* Homewood, Ill.: Richard D. Irwin, Inc., 1983.
   Mayo, Herbert B. *Investments,* alternate ed. Hinsdale, IL: Dryden Press, 1983.

CFP IV: TAX PLANNING AND MANAGEMENT

CFP IV is a study of federal income taxation, gift and estate taxes, and other relevant topics in the planning and management of taxes for an individual's financial plan. Understanding current tax law, researching tax problems, and applying the client's particular tax situation within allowable constraints is the focus. Client situations (cases) are presented and the candidate is required to provide analyses and recommendations based upon applicable tax laws and regulations.

Textbooks: Swanson, Robert E., and Barbara M. Swanson. *Tax Shelters—A Guide for Investors and Their Advisors.* Homewood, IL: Dow Jones–Irwin, 1982.
   Sommerfeld, Ray M. *Federal Taxes and Management Decisions,* 3rd ed. Homewood, IL: Richard D. Irwin, Inc., 1981.
   U.S. Master Tax Guide. Chicago: Commerce Clearing House.

CFP V: EMPLOYEE BENEFITS AND RETIREMENT PLANNING
(Course description to be published by college in the next bulletin.)

CFP VI: ESTATE PLANNING
(Course description to be published by college in the next bulletin.)

Not everyone can enroll as a CFP candidate. An applicant must have a minimum of five enrollment credits in which the combination of credits must include one credit for professional experience. An applicant who does not meet the enrollment credit requirements for CFP candidate status may apply for Associate Financial Planner status (AFP) and, upon completion of the course and experience requirement, may petition the College to grant the CFP designation. The College has a policy of weighing experience heavily as an enrollment requirement. Enrollment credits are awarded for the following:

1. One credit for each full year (12 months) of *relevant* employment experience in personal financial planning or closely related applicable experience, as currently approved by the College.

   Relevant experience is defined as full-time (or equivalent part-time) employment in the practice of personal financial planning, whereby financial planning is done directly and personally for clients for compensation. Noncurrent experience will be excluded.

   The following types of experience are considered to be related and applicable to financial planning. Each application will be evaluated on a case-by-case basis by the Registrar.
   a. College/university professors teaching and/or conducting research in personal financial planning or a closely related field
   b. Manager/administrators in the financial services industry
   c. Professionals interacting directly with financial planners and engaging in similar client-related functions (e.g., attorneys, public accountants and bank trust officers)
2. One credit for each approved professional designation held. Those approved include Certified Public Accountant, Chartered Financial Analyst and Chartered Life Underwriter. Other professional designations will be considered when supporting material accompanies the application.
3. One-half credit for each full year of college attended. One year is defined as 24 semester or 36 quarter credit hours, whichever applies, at a regionally accredited college or university.
4. One credit for each full year (24 semester or 36 quarter hours) completed toward a graduate degree at a regionally accredited college or university.
5. One credit for one bachelor's and each graduate degree earned at a regionally accredited college or university.

CFP Bulletin, p. 1

The cost of the CFP program is currently $1195. Information and a current bulletin may be obtained by writing or calling:

The College for Financial Planning
9725 East Hampden Avenue
Denver, CO 80231
(303) 755-7101

THE AMERICAN COLLEGE

Traditionally, the American College, located in Bryn Mawr, Pennsylvania, has been recognized as the nation's foremost institute of life insurance education. However, tradition must sometimes make way for progress. The American College has broken with tradition by incorporating financial planning education into the curriculum and is no longer devoted solely to life insurance training. The two major financial planning programs offered are the Chartered Financial Consultant (ChFC) designation offered through the Solomon S. Huebner School, and the Master of Science in Financial Services degree offered through the Graduate School of Financial Services.

The American College was established in 1927 to serve the professional education and certification needs of persons directly or indirectly involved with the protection, accumulation, preservation, and distribution of the economic values of human life. It is a degree-granting institution, accredited by the Commission of Higher Education of the Middle States Association of Colleges and Schools. Over the years the school has carried out its mission through the Chartered Life Underwriter program (CLU), graduating more than 50,000 CLUs.

However, times change, and in 1981 the Board of Trustees officially broadened the aims of the College by introducing additional courses and programs beyond the scope of life insurance. The first Chartered Financial Consultant class graduated in October 1982. Although the American College offers numerous programs, including the CLU, ChFC, M.S. degree in Financial Services, advanced career studies program, and a new M.S. degree in Management, I will concentrate on the ChFC and M.S. degree in Financial Services since these are the courses most relevant to the small financial planner.

In January 1981, the American College, recognizing radical change in the financial services environment, broadened its horizon by including a program designed for those engaged in comprehensive financial planning. Furthermore, many life insurance agents, agencies, and companies had themselves broadened their scope by becoming financial planners and planning firms, so the College was compelled to meet the needs of this industry. Even those persons who preferred to remain solely life insurance oriented still needed even more comprehensive training just to remain competitive. Thus the thrust came externally, from the demanding requirements of the field personnel.

Although the Chartered Financial Consultant program is designed for self-study, students may enroll for classes organized by local CLU chapters. About 65% of the candidates proceed in the program through self-study, while 35% take classroom training. It is estimated that a student will take about four to five years to complete the designation.

Applicants for matriculation in the program must be high school graduates, or the equivalent, with good moral character. Although persons of any age may enroll in the program, the designation is not awarded to anyone under the age of 21 or to anyone with less than three years of satisfactory experience in activities related to financial services, although certain other experience may be substituted. Students must take 10 courses to complete the program. The following is a description of the program.

HS 320 FINANCIAL SERVICES: ENVIRONMENT AND PROFESSIONS
Consumers' needs for comprehensive financial counseling and planning; the financial planning process; effective communications skills and techniques in financial planning; gathering client information in the financial planning process; standards of professionalism and ethics; relationships among professionals in financial services; the financial services markets and institutions.

This introductory course sets the stage for the CLU and Chartered Financial Consultant programs by providing an overview of the environment in which financial services professionals assist clients in meeting their financial counseling needs. The financial planning process is presented as the framework for identifying client objectives and formulating and assessing plans to achieve them. Special emphasis is placed on effective information gathering and client counseling techniques.

STUDY MATERIALS:

1. *HS 320 Study Guide*. The American College.
2. *Readings in Financial Services: Environment and Professions*. The American College.
3. Polakoff, N. E., and Durkin, T. A. *Financial Institutions and Markets* (special edition). Boston: Houghton Mifflin Company.
4. *HS 320 Cassette Review Program*. The American College.

HS 321 INCOME TAXATION
The federal income tax system with particular reference to the taxation of life insurance and annuities. The income taxation of individuals, sole proprietorships, partnerships, corporations, trusts, and estates.

The way income tax laws apply to transactions of individuals and businesses is important to financial services professionals in planning that can result in avoidance, minimization, or deferral of taxation.

STUDY MATERIALS:

1. *HS 321 Study Guide.* The American College.
2. *Readings in Income Taxation.* The American College.
3. Parker, A. J., Leimberg, S. R., and Satinsky, M. J. *Stanley and Kilcullen's Federal Income Tax Law* (student edition). New York: Warren, Gorham, and Lamont, Inc.
4. *HS 321 Cassette Review Program.* The American College.

HS 322 ECONOMICS
Basic economic concepts with emphasis on such macroeconomic and microeconomic topics as the price system and the market economy, the circular flow of national income and product, stabilization policy, the determinants of national income, multiplier theory and fiscal policy, the supply of and demand for money, unemployment and inflation.

This course is designed to explain the basic economic principles and institutions, an understanding of which is necessary for an appreciation of alternative explanations of and alternative solutions for the more common economic problems found in private and government sectors.

STUDY MATERIALS:

1. *HS 322 Study Guide.* The American College.
2. Dolan, E. G. *Basic Macroeconomics* (2nd edition). New York: Holt, Rinehart and Winston.
3. *HS 322 Cassette Review Program.* The American College.

HS 323 FINANCIAL STATEMENT ANALYSIS/INDIVIDUAL INSURANCE BENEFITS
This is the first course in the CLU and Chartered Financial Consultant programs providing coverage of products, tools, and techniques. The initial assignments cover various topics related to personal and business financial statements, including the basic concepts of accounting, the format and contents of key financial statements, the techniques of financial statement analysis, and personal budgeting. A thorough understanding of the contents and analysis of financial statements is critical in assessing a client's financial condition.

The second section of the course describes various types of individual insurance coverages available for meeting life, health, and personal property and liability risks. These include individual life insurance policies, individual annuities, disability income policies, medical expense insurance, homeowners policies, and automobile insurance.

STUDY MATERIALS:

1. *HS 323 Study Guide.* The American College.
2. Montgomery, A. T. *Financial Accounting Information* (2nd edition). Reading, MA: Addison-Wesley Publishing Co., Inc.
3. Huebner, S. S., and Black, K. *Life Insurance* (10th edition). Englewood Cliffs, NJ: Prentice-Hall, Inc.
4. *HS 323 Cassette Review Program.* The American College.

HS 327 EMPLOYEE BENEFITS

Employee benefit plans for providing security with respect to the economic problems resulting from death, old age, unemployment, and disability. Social security and other governmental programs. Analysis of group insurance benefits, including contract provisions, plan design, and alternative funding methods. Also, basic features of pension plans, profit-sharing plans, other retirement plans, and deferred compensation arrangements.

The growth of social insurance, group insurance, and retirement plans underscores the significance of these areas. It is important that the students in financial planning understand the benefit provisions and the advantages and limitations associated with each of these methods for meeting economic security needs.

STUDY MATERIALS:

1. *HS 327 Study Guide.* The American College.
2. Rosenbloom, J. D., and Hallman, G. V. *Employee Benefit Planning* (1981 edition). Englewood Cliffs, NJ: Prentice-Hall, Inc.

HS 328 INVESTMENTS

Various aspects of investment principles and their application to personal finance. Yields, limited income securities, investment markets, valuation of common stock, real estate, debt and credit, mutual funds, variable annuities, tax-sheltered investments, and principles of personal portfolio management.

The significance of this course is highlighted by the growing importance of money management to individuals. Effective financial planning requires that investments be selected that meet personal objectives and are consistent with personal risk preferences.

STUDY MATERIALS:

1. *HS 328 Study Guide.* The American College.
2. Gitman, L. J., and Joehnk, M. D. *Fundamentals of Investing* (1981 edition). New York: Harper & Row Publishers, Inc.
3. *HS 328 Cassette Review Program.* The American College.

HS 329 WEALTH ACCUMULATION PLANNING

The principles of real estate investment and taxation including risk and return, the acquisition, ownership and disposition of property, principles of loan amortization and depreciation, capital gains and losses, installment sales, exchanges, cash flow analysis and applications, creative financing, and forms of real estate ownership. Fundamentals of tax sheltered and tax incentive investments with emphasis on the major tax, investment and organizational characteristics of real estate, oil and gas, agricultural, and equipment leasing limited partnerships. Planning for the living estate—a framework for accumulation and retirement planning including methods for preserving wealth, tax planning, time value and budgeting concepts, and special tools and strategies such as IRAs, Keoghs, tax-saving portfolio management techniques, gifts, trusts, and interest-free loans.

STUDY MATERIALS:

1. *HS 329 Study Guide.* The American College.
2. Allen, R. H. *Real Estate Investment and Taxation* (1981 edition). Cincinnati, OH: South-Western Publishing Company.
3. Drollinger, W. C. *Tax Shelters and Tax-free Income* (special edition, 1981). Orchard Lake, MI: Epic Publications.

HS 330 ESTATE AND GIFT TAX PLANNING

Estate and gift tax planning include the nature, valuation, transfer, administration and taxation of property. Particular emphasis will be given to a basic understanding of the unified estate and gift tax system. The course covers gratuitous transfers of property outright or in trust, wills, powers of appointment, federal estate and gift taxation, the marital deduction, uses of life insurance in estate planning, and other estate planning devices. Also covered is the estate planning process including the client interview, fact finding and development of appropriate personal estate plans using various estate planning devices.

STUDY MATERIALS:

1. *HS 330 Study Guide.* The American College.
2. *Readings in Estate and Gift Tax Planning.* The American College.
3. *HS 330 Cassette Review Program.* The American College.

HS 331 PLANNING FOR BUSINESS OWNERS AND PROFESSIONALS

Tax and legal aspects of organizing a business; problems in continuing a business after an owner's death and the insured buy–sell agreement; retirement of a business owner, including estate planning and "estate freezing" techniques; stock dividends, corporate recapitalizations, stock redemptions, and other techniques; lifetime disposition of a business interest—taxable and tax-free dispositions and the use of the installment sale and other methods; business uses of life and health insurance for the benefit of business owners; disability buy–sell agreements, key employee life and health insurance plans, and split-dollar life insurance plans; and business uses of property and liability insurance. The course also covers special problems of professional corporations.

STUDY MATERIALS:

1. *HS 331 Study Guide.* The American College.
2. White, E. H., and Chasman, H. *Business Insurance* (5th edition). Englewood Cliffs, NJ: Prentice-Hall, Inc.
3. *Readings in Planning for Business Owners and Professionals.* The American College.
4. *HS 331 Cassette Review Program.* The American College.

HS 332 FINANCIAL AND ESTATE PLANNING APPLICATIONS

A case course aimed at both integrating the various techniques, tools and products covered in the earlier courses in the Chartered Financial Consultant program with the financial planning process outlined in HS 320 and giving students practical application in analyzing and solving realistic financial problems of individuals and businesses. Cases range from simple fact patterns and basic documents to complex situations involving not only personal financial problems but also financial problems associated with businesses and business ownership. Clients used in the cases vary by age, income, family status (married with and without children, single, divorced), occupation (executive, professional, owner of a closely held business), and their objectives and related financial problems.

STUDY MATERIALS:

Casebook: Financial and Estate Planning Applications. The American College.

The standard tuition plan enables students to register for any two Huebner School courses during the academic year for $270. Students may take both courses in one semester or one in the fall, one in the spring. Those who wish to register for more than two courses may do so by paying $85 per course for each additional course registration.

For those students seeking education beyond the academic level of a professional designation, the American College offers a Master of Science in Financial Services degree. This program, like the Chartered Financial Consultant program, is basically self-study with a formal classroom option. The M.S. program, however, requires a two-week period of resident study at the Bryn Mawr campus. The difference between a conventional M.B.A. degree and the M.S. degree at the American College is that the American College's M.S. does not focus primarily on the management of the business enterprise. Instead, emphasis is placed on the professional's role of analyzing, planning, implementing, and coordinating complex financial programs for individuals, families, and corporate administrators. The curriculum is designed to broaden the students' knowledge; to improve their capacity for effective decision making in the areas of finance, economics, and insurance; and to help them realize their vital social responsibility of ensuring the financial well-being of their clients.

To be considered by the Graduate Admissions Committee, an applicant for the master's degree should possess either a bachelor's degree from an accredited collegiate institution, or a professional designation in the financial sciences, such as CLU, CPA, CPCU, or CFA (Chartered Financial Analyst). When this initial requirement has been met, the Graduate Admissions Committee reviews each application and determines admissibility of each applicant to the master's degree program.

Applicants for the master's degree who have not earned a bachelor's degree are required to take certain examinations offered by the College Level Examination Program (CLRP). These examinations are intended to substantiate an applicant's general education and knowledge gained through life experience. Examinations are required in the areas of humanities, natural sciences, and social sciences. The results of these examinations, which are held in confidence, may be considered by the Graduate Admissions Committee in evaluating the application.

A maximum of 12 credits may be transferred from educational institutions other than the American College. In general, credits will be accepted only from degree-granting institutions having regional or national accreditation. Credits must be earned at the graduate level in courses essentially similar to those presently offered by the American College. Credit may be accepted only for graduate courses taken within a seven-year period immediately preceding admission to the Graduate School.

The Master of Science in Financial Services degree requires 36 credits. Thirty credits are earned by taking courses in the Advanced Graduate curriculum as described in the American College 1982/83 Catalog. I have listed the names of these courses below:

GS 511: Advanced Estate Planning I
GS 512: Advanced Estate Planning II
GS 515: Employee Benefit Planning
GS 521: Advanced Pension Planning I
GS 522: Advanced Pension Planning II

GS 525: Business Tax Planning

GS 535: Financial Counseling

GS 545: Government Regulation of Business

GS 555: Legal Foundations of Business

GS 560: Risk Management of Property-Liability Exposures

GS 565: Financial Accounting

GS 575: Business Valuation

GS 580: Managing the Financial Services Enterprise

GS 585: Professionals and Organizational Behavior

GS 590: Human Resource Management

GS 600: Research Methods

GS 610: Economic Issues in Financial Security

GS 620: Human Relations and Ethics

GS 610 and GS 620 are mandatory and must be taken in residence at the American College.

Examinations for both the Chartered Financial Consultant designation and the Master of Science in Financial Services degree are given at examination centers located throughout the United States, Canada, and Puerto Rico. The examinations are given twice a year, in January and June, and it takes six weeks to receive results.

However, under a brand new program, "Examinations on Demand," students can take the exam almost any time they desire at a Control Data Corporation PLATO Learning Center Location using a computer terminal, and they will receive immediate results of their examination.

GOLDEN GATE UNIVERSITY— SAN FRANCISCO, CALIFORNIA

The CFP and the ChFC are excellent professional designation programs; however, the serious student of financial planning, the student who has a real thirst for knowledge and seeks to understand and uncover the depth of the profession, may desire a master's degree in financial planning.

A leader in this area, perhaps *the* leader among all the academic institutions, is Golden Gate University in San Francisco, California. For the reader who has not heard of Golden Gate, it is the third largest (about 11,000 students) independent accredited university in California, just behind the University of Southern California and Stanford. It does not have a football team to bring its name to national attention, but what it lacks on the gridiron it makes up for in its graduate financial planning program, housed in the Graduate School of Banking and Finance. If financial planning ever had an educational Rose Bowl, Golden Gate would most certainly be one of the teams playing, coached by Robert F. Bohn, the program director and a pioneer in financial planning education.

"We are tuned into industry," Bohn says. "We have an advisory board of key people in the financial planning profession. And we listen to what they have to say. Furthermore, we meet with our advisory board periodically to learn what the current needs are for a sophisticated professional to become a functioning financial planner. Then we incorporate these ideas into our curriculum, and the advisory board critiques our course proposals. In this way we are able to provide a whole new level of client-oriented financial planners. Golden Gate University has responded to the business community's need for professional education. We, therefore, have an excellent relationship with the business community."

Although Golden Gate has a full-time faculty, the financial planning area relies heavily on adjunct professors who currently practice in the financial planning field and who are competent academically. They have found that the practicing nontraditional professors, in general, do a much better job than the Ph.D.s. This is because the objective of the financial planning program is to prepare professionals to practice in the business community, and to do this, "you must use those people who are on the cutting edge to teach the class," explains Bohn. "Professionals who are active in the financial planning field can provide material to the student that is current and relevant in today's world. Unfortunately, the traditionally educated Ph.D. teaches yesterday's concept in today's environment. Unless, of course, that Ph.D. has kept current through business practice."

The philosophy of the University is to upgrade the skills of its students. The objective is to have a student come out of the financial planning program with a wide range of knowledge and insight with which to help a client. In fact, according to one of the school's policies, a student in financial planning can petition to have a basic course waived in an area in which the student is strong and to substitute a more advanced course. For example, a student with a tax background might not be required to take a basic tax course, but could instead substitute a more advanced course from the Master of Science in Taxation curriculum. According to Bohn, "It is not our intent to place hurdles before people." Since most students work, the school offers classes one day a week for 2 hours and 40 minutes, instead of three weekly 50-minute sessions. They prefer to make it easier on working students who might otherwise have to spend a great deal of time commuting. Golden Gate operates on a trimester basis.

The graduate program at Golden Gate is a two-track program leading to either a Master of Business Administration (M.B.A.) or a Master of Science (M.S.) in Financial Planning. The most significant difference between the M.B.A. and the M.S. curriculum in financial planning is that the M.B.A. is a broader, more general business program, dealing with concepts, tool subjects, and analytical skills essential for the mastery of more advanced and sophisticated professional course work; the M.S. program focuses more on actual financial planning. The following description was provided by Golden Gate University.

M.B.A. DEGREE IN FINANCIAL PLANNING

The Master of Business Administration in Financial Planning degree requires completion of 60 semester units in the graduate program, assuming no previous course work was completed elsewhere. Where comparable course work has already been completed, a student can petition for replacements or substitutions. GM 300 (Written Case Analysis) should be taken immediately after completing the "General Business Program" as a transition into the other 300-level classes. Each course carries three semester units of credit and is listed according to the generally recommended order of class sequencing:

GENERAL BUSINESS PROGRAM (30 Units):

GB 200 Mathematics for Management (first semester)

GB 201a Financial Accounting for Managers
Prer: GB 200 and 201a

GB 207 Computer Technology for Managers
Prer: GB 200

GB 203 Finance for Managers
Prer: 201b

GB 202 Economics for Managers
Prer: GB 200

GB 209 Statistical Analysis for Managers
Prer: GB 200

GB 204 Marketing Management

GB 205 Organizational Behavior and Management Principles

GB 212 Law of Contracts and Business Organizations

ADVANCED PROGRAM (30 Units):

FP 301 Personal Comprehensive Financial Planning (first semester)

GM 300 Written Case Analysis
Prer: GFB 203, 204, 205 (advised but not formal prerequisite)

GM 375 Personal Risk Management

GM 397 Federal Taxation
Prer: GB 201a

BF 311 Investments
Prer: GB 203

FP 300 Real Estate and Investment Analysis (or RE 300)

FP 303 Wills and Trusts
Prer: GM 397 (advised but not formal prerequisite)

FP 304 Company Retirement Planning, Buy and Sell Agreements

FP 305 Financial Planning Case Problems (last semester)

Elective course: One course (3 units) may be selected from any of
the courses in the 300 series. Refer to "Elective and Substitutional
Classes."

M.S. DEGREE IN FINANCIAL PLANNING

While the M.B.A. in Financial Planning degree provides a broader management scope, the Master of Science (M.S.) in Financial Planning degree
requires fewer "General Business Program" classes, but still requires
comparable "Advanced Program" course work. Also, note that the M.S.
in Financial Planning degree has an extra elective in the advanced course
work. Students with no previous business-related academic background
would complete a total of 48 units (16 classes), realizing that petitions
for replacements or substitutions of classes are possible where comparable course work has been completed. Although GB 207 (Computer
Technology for Managers) is not required, it is highly recommended for
the M.S. degree.

GENERAL BUSINESS PROGRAM (18 units):

GB 200 Mathematics for Management (first semester)

GB 201a Financial Accounting for Managers

GB 201b Managerial Accounting for Managers
Prer: GB 200 and 201a

GB 203 Finance for Managers
Prer: GB 201b

GB 202 Economics for Managers

GB 212 Law of Contracts and Business Organizations

ADVANCED PROGRAM (30 Units):

FP 301 Personal Comprehensive Financial Planning (first semester)

GM 375 Personal Risk Management

GM 397 Federal Taxation
Prer: GB 201a

BF 311 Investments
Prer: GB 203

FP 300 Real Estate and Investment Analysis (or RE 300)

FP 303 Wills and Trusts
Prer: GM 397 (advised but not formal prerequisite)

FP 304 Company Retirement Planning, Buy and Sell Agreements

FP 305 Financial Planning Case Problems (last semester)

Elective courses: Two courses (6 units) may be selected from any of the courses in the 300 series. Refer to "Elective and Substitutional Classes."

ELECTIVE AND SUBSTITUTIONAL CLASSES

The following is representative of the kinds of 300 series courses which are available at Golden Gate University as potential elective or substitutional classes that are particularly relevant to the financial planning field. Note that any 300-level class listed in the Graduate Bulletin, from any discipline, can be used as an elective. For detailed course descriptions and prerequisites, refer to the current Golden Gate University Bulletin (Graduate Programs).

BF 300 Financial Markets and Institutions

BF 317 Investment Portfolio Management

BF 321 Venture Capital and the Business Enterprise

BF 312 Business Development and Marketing Strategy

BF 322 Investment Banking

BF 323 Stock Market Analysis

BF 324 The Law and the Securities Market

RE 301 Financial Analysis for Real Estate Professionals

RE 302 Valuation of Real Estate

RE 303 Taxation of Real Estate

RE 304 Topics in Real Estate Law

RE 306 Developing Commercial Properties

RE 307 Developing Residential Properties

RE 310 Architecture and Design Factors in Real Estate Development

RE 316 Property Management

RI 300 Advanced Topics in Risk Management

RI 310 Actuarial Science and Underwriting

RI 330 Research, Development and Marketing

RI 341 Economic, Social and Political Issues in Risk and Insurance

One reason for the success of Golden Gate's financial planning program is the attitude that the institution takes toward its students. Students become personally involved. The school encourages feedback, which it uses to gauge future programs, instructors, and courses. In my opinion, the school's extraordinary success can be attributed to this attitude: the school does not treat students as typical students, but rather as clients.

In the years ahead, Dr. Bohn, a major force behind Golden Gate's success, would like to see the other educational institutions across the country become more in tune with financial planning. If this does not happen, he hopes the industry will take the time to identify the unique institutions, such as Golden Gate University, that offer students a higher professional level of education. Because most institutions today do not have financial planning courses and programs, many financial planning practitioners cannot get proper training and therefore practice at a less sophisticated level than they could be were these programs more abundant. Says Bohn: "Financial planning education will make the professional thought of in a more sophisticated manner."

Golden Gate University, the financial planner, has a deep interest in the needs and objectives of its students, the clients.

For further information about the program, contact:

Dr. Robert F. Bohn, Director
M.B.A./M.S./B.S. Degrees in Financial Planning
Golden Gate University
Graduate School of Banking and Finance
Suite 435
536 Mission Street
San Francisco, CA 94105
(415) 442-7221

GEORGIA STATE UNIVERSITY

Because it is symbolic of where the financial planning industry is going, I have saved the Georgia State University program—the ultimate in financial planner education—for last. You only have to look around to observe the complexities and the intense interaction of all the related financial disciplines. You could say that to really understand it requires becoming a Doctor of Financial Planning. And that's exactly how the directors of Georgia State felt, too. At last, the financial planning field will have doctors. We have arrived.

Georgia State University in Atlanta, Georgia, now offers a Ph.D. in Business Administration degree with a concentration within the risk and insurance field in financial and estate planning; it is headed by Fred

Tillman, CFP, who is also a practicing attorney in Georgia specializing in estate planning.

Doctoral candidates are required to complete 100 quarter-hours of study plus any background courses in which the candidate may be deficient. Furthermore, the candidate must complete the dissertation requirement involving one or two years of advanced research. Within the 100 quarter-hours requirement, the following breakdown will generally be observed:

Computer-based information systems	10 hours
Advanced microeconomics and macroeconomics theory	10 hours
Quantitative research methods and decision models	15 hours
Major field of concentration, including the following courses: life and health insurance, business insurance and taxation, social and group insurance, pensions, wills, trusts and estates, and estate planning, plus two advanced Ph.D. seminars	40 hours
Additional requirements based on student's background from the fields of taxation, finance, and real estate	25 hours

As you have probably observed, the emphasis is to make the Ph.D. proficient not only in financial planning but also in the quantitative area and in computer systems. The program should take several years to complete.

While working toward a Ph.D., the doctoral candidate may pick up an M.B.A. in Financial Planning along the way or enroll separately for the M.B.A. The Georgia State master's program is a coordinated program of interdisciplinary study designed to prepare students for entry into the financial services industry with the knowledge and skills to pursue a career in personal financial planning. The emphasis is placed on conceptual financial planning, and the student is instructed in the techniques for determining an individual's goals and objectives, then formulating and implementing a comprehensive plan for the accumulation, conservation, and transfer of personal wealth. The focus for study includes accounting, finance, insurance, investments, legal studies, management, quantitative methods, real estate, and taxation. A collateral objective of the program is to assist students in preparing for the Certified Financial Planner (CFP) and the Chartered Financial Counselor (ChFC) professional designations.

For further information regarding the Georgia State University master's or doctoral programs, you should contact:

Dr. Fred Tillman
College of Business Administration
Department of Insurance
Georgia State University
University Plaza
Atlanta, GA 30303

SUMMARY

After researching the material necessary for putting this book together, especially this chapter, I am firmly convinced that my philosophy regarding financial planning education is sound. For the most part, traditional academia, our colleges and universities, are in another world where financial planning is concerned. The courses and programs they offer, graduate and undergraduate, have little meaning in the real world of financial planning and business. Many of our business schools—even the best business schools—turn out graduates so incapable of dealing practically with personal finances that they might as well have majored in the fine arts for all the good their education does them. They have been taught theories by professors who were taught the exact same theories many years ago by their professors, who, in turn, had learned those same old theories from their professors. In the past few years I have communicated with several schools whose reaction to financial planning was to turn up their noses and look down on it as an unimportant, low-life field, not suitable or dignified enough for the college campus. One professor even told me that personal finance was beneath the undergraduate level. I, of course, beg to differ.

Unfortunately, many of our business graduates are incapable of preparing even a simple tax return; they have never heard of the gift or estate tax, do not understand the difference between whole life and term life, and think a tax shelter is something only a millionaire can afford. However, they can tell you the maximum output of widgets needed to reach the break-even point. It is really funny that we teach widgets to students but we don't teach life. And once they graduate and enter the working world, they find out to their dismay that the government will not accept payment of taxes in the form of widgets.

As a college educator I find it pathetic that college students, especially juniors and seniors, have great difficulty tuning into what's going on around them. Financial planning programs cannot succeed from a purely theoretical approach. It's like a home study course in medicine or dentistry. Accordingly, the schools and universities that teach or will begin to teach these programs must synchronize their courses from both a theoretical and practical approach.

New York University, where I am currently the faculty coordinator
of the Financial Planning Program in the School of Continuing Education, has taken such an approach. In the spring of 1983 the school will
offer courses for financial planners, leading to a diploma in financial
planning and full college credit for the completed course work. The first
semester went very well in what is the start of a complete financial
planning curriculum. The objectives of the program are to provide
instruction in the concepts and techniques necessary for the successful
performance of the financial planner, who will be called upon to evaluate
and recommend appropriate strategies designed to ensure a client's
financial stability, and to provide for retirement and estate planning.
The program has been designed by the school's administrators, faculty,
and industry leaders. And the continuing objective of the program,
according to Philip J. Williams, the program director, is to stay in touch
with the latest financial planning concepts. "This means utilizing the
most current publications and instructors who stay current with the
latest changes in the field."

As part of the NYU program, I am excited about seeing this program get off the ground. The school is making things happen, and this
is progressive education. Both the administration and faculty realize that
there is a great deal of work ahead to make this program successful. But
given time and proper leadership, the program should succeed—the
demand is certainly there. What excites me the most, however, is that
the school offers a course in financial planner practice management as
part of the diploma curriculum. This, to my knowledge, will be the first
course of its type offered by any university.

Make no mistake, financial planning education is here to stay—and
it is here to stay for a long time. In fact, it should be one of the hottest
subjects for the next decade and beyond. No longer can the accountant,
the banker, or the attorney look down on the financial planner as a
salesperson out to peddle products. Today's financial planner reaches
out to areas that many of these professionals have never even heard of.
*And ironically, many attorneys, bankers, and accountants are turning to finan-
cial planning as a way to better service their own clients.* The financial planning profession has become a melting pot of many other professions.
Attorneys, stockbrokers, insurance agents, accountants, bankers, tax
shelter people, and product representatives are all beginning to see the
need for sharpening their skills in order to enhance their professions;
and in many cases, they are giving up their old professions to become
pure financial planners.

And then there are the students sitting in college classrooms across
the land, fully aware that the financial planning revolution is here, but
not quite sure what financial planning is all about. Furthermore, they

are frustrated because their school's master plan does not call for a financial planning course to be offered for the next 12 years; or worse, the school offers a financial planning course taught by an old-line traditional professor fully versed in widgets.

If all the academic institutions in the country relied on profit to survive, a great many of them would be in "Chapter 11" tomorrow. Any business that expects to be profitable must be responsive to the needs of those it serves. It's simple. For example, if the country demands small cars, General Motors either produces them or closes down the assembly line until the public will buy whatever GM wishes to produce; otherwise, the car dealerships of America may be stuck with many unsold large automobiles. The rules are no different for academia. When the country is begging for financial planning programs and courses, the colleges must, for all those same business reasons, provide them.

I have no doubt that eventually academia will respond to this crushing need for financial planning education. Unfortunately, by the time academia gets around to this, it may be too late. Financial planning theory changes very rapidly. Why? Because it is a current solution to a current problem. The professors hired to teach these courses must be prepared to update their notes every semester or perhaps even more frequently. The schools' best bet is to go to the financial planning community itself and seek out devoted financial planners who have strong academic credentials and business knowledge. Here they can take an example from Golden Gate. Schools can no longer stay in a vacuum; they must reach out to the business world for help.

Some day I hope that the educational revolution will catch up to the financial planning revolution. There are a lot of bright and eager people in the financial planning profession as well as on the campuses who are certain to make this happen. We have seen what Golden Gate University in San Francisco has accomplished as a school "tuned into" financial planning. Georgia State in Atlanta has recently instituted the Ph.D. in financial planning. The University of Houston will soon offer a master's degree. New York University has begun. Brigham Young University in Provo, Utah, has had a B.B.A. in financial planning for years. And the nontraditional schools, such as the College for Financial Planning in Denver, Colorado, and the American College in Bryn Mawr, Pennsylvania, are doing an excellent job of carrying the ball, while the others still have a watch-and-wait policy. These schools, traditional or nontraditional, deserve a great deal of credit for being leaders in the field of financial planning education.

8

ORGANIZATIONS THAT YOU SHOULD KNOW ABOUT

Organizations are especially important to the financial planner. You cannot take on the world alone. The building of a successful practice requires interaction with others, education, information, publicity, legislation, as well as moral support from striving planners who are in the very same boat that you're in. So if you plan to isolate yourself from the rest of the financial planning community, your chances of success as an independent financial planner will probably be greatly hampered.

I have described below five organizations that I feel the small financial planner should know about. Of course, the decision to join or to use their services is entirely up to you. Each organization should be examined for the benefits that you will derive, the philosophy and the work of the organization in relation to your own philosophy, and the cost. You must also remember that it would be most impractical to join every organization that comes along. However, I do suggest you get involved in those organizations that you feel will benefit you the most. Remember, too, that some of the organizations that will appeal to you may have membership requirements, some educational, some vocational; if you do not meet these standards, you might not be able to join until you do.

Obviously, there are many more organizations than those discussed here. Your preferences will depend on your individual background and the type of planning practice you have or expect to have. For instance, if you are a Chartered Life Underwriter (CLU), you might wish to consider the American Society of CLUs in Bryn Mawr, Pennsylvania. There are other organizations for planners who specialize in pensions, investments, or accounting. Select organizations that you believe in. Make use of the organization and try to participate in it to some degree. If you join, it would be beneficial to be more than just a dues-paying member. Each organization that you choose should hold some purpose for you. Those that I will discuss here are more appropriate for the small, generalist financial planner.

A complete directory of financial services organizations can be found in *Horizon*, published by the International Association for Financial Planning.

THE INTERNATIONAL ASSOCIATION FOR FINANCIAL PLANNING (IAFP)

Founded in 1969 as part of the Society for Financial Counseling, this organization today has grown to over 13,000 members, with the goal of 25,000 by 1985. A nonprofit association, it is without question the oldest and largest organization representing the comprehensive financial planning community. The benefits of membership are numerous, from national regulatory and legislative representation to local chapter meetings where you can meet fellow planners in an informal setting, and in an atmosphere of cocktails and hors d'oeuvres learn the latest "what's happening" in financial planning. Every financial planner should belong to the IAFP, whether or not he or she sells products.

According to Hubert L. Harris, Jr., the Executive Director of the IAFP: "The Association promotes financial planners to potential users, the individuals and families faced with the financial needs of the future. In doing so the IAFP enhances the professional standards of those who practice financial planning."

The Association's philosophy, mission, and Code of Professional Ethics demand continuing education, a unified approach to the solution of the client's financial problems, a dialogue among the professions, and the preservation and enforcement of high ethical standards. An individual member must practice under the Code of Professional Ethics or face possible disciplinary action that may result in loss of membership.

THE CODE OF PROFESSIONAL ETHICS

Canon 1

Members should endeavor as professionals to place the public interest above their own.

Rules of Professional Conduct:

R1.1 A member has a duty to understand and abide by all Rules of Professional Conduct which are prescribed in the Code of Professional Ethics of the Association.

R1.2 A member shall not directly or indirectly condone any act which the member is prohibited from performing by the Rules of this Code.

Canon 2

Members should seek continually to maintain and improve their professional knowledge, skills, and competence.

Rules of Professional Conduct:

R2.1 A member shall keep informed on all matters that are essential to the maintenance of the member's professional competence in the area in which he/she specializes and/or claims expertise.

Canon 3

Members should obey all laws and regulations, and should avoid any conduct of activity which would cause unjust harm to others.

Rules of Professional Conduct:

R3.1 A member will be subject to disciplinary action for the violation of any law or regulation, to the extent that such violation suggests the likelihood of professional misconduct.

R3.2 A member shall not allow the pursuit of financial gain or other personal benefit to interfere with the exercise of sound professional judgment and skills.

R3.3 In the conduct of business or professional activities, a member shall not engage in any act or omission of a dishonest, deceitful, or fraudulent nature.

Canon 4

.Members should be diligent in the performance of their occupational duties.

Rules of Professional Conduct:

R4.1 A member shall competently and consistently discharge the member's occupational duties, to every employer, client, purchaser or user of the member's services, so long as those duties are consistent with what is in the client's best interests.

Canon 5

Members should establish and maintain honorable relationships with other professionals, with those whom the members serve in a professional capacity, and with all those who rely upon the members' professional judgments and skills.

Rules of Professional Conduct:

R5.1 A member has a duty to know and abide by the legal limitations imposed upon the scope of the members' professional activities.

R5.2 In rendering or proposing to render a professional service for another individual or an organization, a member shall not knowingly misrepresent or conceal any material limitation on the member's ability to provide the quantity or quality of service that will adequately meet the financial planning needs of the individual or organization in question.

R5.3 In marketing or attempting to market a product to another individual or an organization, a member shall not knowingly misrepresent or conceal any material limitations on the product's ability to meet the financial planning needs of the individual or organization in question.

R5.4 A member shall not disclose to another person any confidential information entrusted to or obtained by the member in the course of the member's business or professional activities, unless a disclosure of such information is required by law or is made to a person who necessarily must have the information in order to discharge legitimate occupational or professional duties.

R5.5 In the making of oral or written recommendations to clients, a member shall (a) distinguish clearly between fact and opinion, (b) base the recommendations on sound professional evaluations of the client's present and future needs, (c) place the needs and best interests of the client above the interests of the member or the member's employer or business associates, (d) support the recommendations with appropriate research and adequate documentation of facts, and (e) scrupulously avoid any statements which are likely to mislead the client regarding the projected future results of any recommendation.

R5.6 Before rendering any professional service, a member has a duty to disclose, to a prospective client, any actual or potential conflict of interest that is or should be known by the member and is likely to impair the member's objectivity as an advisor or provider of professional services to the prospective client in question.

R5.7 In the rendering of a professional service to a client, a member has the duty to maintain the type and degree of professional independence that (a) is required of practitioners in the member's occupation or (b) is otherwise in the public interest, given the specific nature of the service being rendered.

Canon 6

Members should assist in improving the public understanding of financial planning.

Rules of Professional Conduct:

R6.1 A member shall support efforts to provide laypersons with objective information concerning their financial planning needs, as well as the resources which are available to meet their needs.

R6.2 A member shall not misrepresent the benefits, costs or limitations of any financial planning service or product, whether the product or service is offered by the member or by another individual or firm.

Canon 7

Members should use the fact of membership in a manner consistent with the Association's Rules of Professional Conduct.

Rules of Professional Conduct:

R7.1 A member should not misrepresent the criteria for admission to Association membership, which criteria are: (1) a professional interest in financial planning; (2) sponsorship by a member of the Association, which member is in good standing and has been a member for at least one year; and (3) a written commitment to abide by the Bylaws and the Code of Professional Ethics of the Association.

R7.2 A member shall not misstate his/her authority to represent the Association. Specifically, a member shall not write, speak, or act in such a way as to lead another to believe that the member is officially representing the Association, unless the member has been duly authorized to do so by the officers, directors or Bylaws of the national Association.

R7.3 A member shall not use the fact of membership in the Association for commercial purposes but may use the fact of membership for the following noncommercial purposes: In resumes, prospectus, and in introductions if the speaker clearly states that the opinions and ideas presented are his/her own and not necessarily those of the IAFP.

R7.4 A member or prospective member applying for Association membership shall not misrepresent any credentials or affiliations with other organizations.

Canon 8

Members should assist in maintaining the integrity of the Code of Professional Ethics of the Association.

Rules of Professional Conduct:

R8.1 A member shall not sponsor as a candidate for Association membership any person who is known by the member to engage in business or professional practices which violate the Rules of this Code.

R8.2 A member possessing unprivileged information concerning an alleged violation of this Code shall, upon request, reveal such information to the body or other authority empowered by the Association to investigate or act upon the alleged violation.

The organization strives to solicit as members all who sincerely desire to do a better job for their clients, regardless of their method of compensation. IAFP membership is truly diverse, representing many different financial planning disciplines and a true cross section of the financial services industry. Members include registered investment advisors, stockbrokers, insurance agents and brokers, bankers, real estate brokers, accountants, attorneys, service and product suppliers, educators, financial writers, editors, and publishers.

For an annual fee of $95 the IAFP provides two different membership levels. On the national level, the IAFP Regulatory Committee is active in matters regarding the latest regulations and legislation affecting financial planners. And each month, in *The Financial Planner* magazine, there are several pages on the latest regulatory review. In addition, when vitally important regulations or legislation are introduced or still pending, each member who desires will receive an IAFP Regulatory Alert. This alert informs the member of the proposed legislation or regulation, advises when the IAFP will testify, asks for the member's comments, and urges the member to contact his or her congressional representatives. In fact, a recent National Board Meeting of the IAFP was held in Washington, DC, in order to make the presence of this organization felt and to establish closer liaisons and new avenues of dialogue between key officials of the federal government and the financial planning industry. And shortly, they plan to open a Washington office to deal with all the legislative problems applicable to financial planners.

However, according to IAFP Regulatory Committee Chairman William "Jerry" Ball, writing in the September 1982 *IAFP Forum*, "Board members cannot do the job alone," and he encourages all members of the IAFP to write their elected representatives in Congress to express their feelings on pending legislation. "The interest of clients and the financial planning industry as a whole are best served by the participation of as many people as possible." And that reason alone, if you get or want nothing else from the IAFP, is reason enough for joining.

But the chances of getting nothing out of the IAFP are remote indeed. The organization has one of the best continuing education programs, which is remarkable for a predominantly trade organization. On a national level, the IAFP provides two major programs a year. One is "Expanding Horizons," the annual convention, four days of educational programs and product exhibits by the latest marketers of financial services products, such as mutual funds, tax shelters, tangibles, market timing services, computers, software vendors, publishers, and educational institutions. The other is the midyear strategy conference; an intensive conference usually running for several days, it concentrates on advanced financial planning topics, including practice management—the "how to" of financial planning. In 1983 the IAFP had its first World Congress in Monte Carlo, and in April 1984 the second will be held in London, England.

Other benefits of membership include discounts on various publications and accessories that a financial planner might need; organized foreign tours for financial planners who want to review investments in other areas of the globe; and *The Financial Planner* magazine, the foremost publication of the financial planning profession and a major benefit in itself.

The Financial Planner, the official journal of the International Association for Financial Planning, is published monthly and has a paid circulation of about 17,000. In a recent in-depth readership study by Epsilon Data Management of Burlington, Massachusetts, 97% of those members surveyed indicated that *The Financial Planner* was their most regularly used service provided by the IAFP. In fact, 82% of the readers used the publication as a source of permanent reference.

In its 10-year history, *The Financial Planner* has evolved from a 48-page publication with very little paid circulation to a glossy 212-page issue (October 1982). It is a magazine of exceptional editorial quality written by professionals for professionals. Formerly under the direction of Forrest Wallace Cato and now, Jack Lang, former editor and publisher of *Atlanta Magazine*, *The Financial Planner* has developed into a highly regarded magazine whose devoted readers channel over $5 billion a year into the financial services market. In fact, according to the *Wall Street Journal*, the readers of *The Financial Planner* constitute a mini-Wall Street.

Another very important benefit of belonging to the IAFP is the interaction you will have with other professionals, both on a national level and in your own community. There are currently about 85 local IAFP chapters; most have meetings several times a year, working hard to put on programs of continuing education for their members. Elise Feldman, CPC, heads the Education Committee for the Metro New York IAFP Chapter. On the average she spends 10 hours of her own time each week working toward developing educational programs for chapter members. It is a most difficult task to do right, since not all programs can appeal to all members. Some need basic-level training, whereas others can handle a more advanced level of training. "Our objective is to provide a forum to our members to learn about new developments in the market place which will stimulate their creative thinking process and aid their clients in financial planning."

In 1982–1983 the Metro New York Chapter put the following programs together:

How to Put Together a Financial Planning Practice	One session
What Makes a Viable Real Estate Investment?	One session
Equity Investments	Three sessions
Where to Find Computer Software for Financial Planning	All day
Educational Forum	All day
New Products on the Horizon	All day
Due Diligence on Products	One session
TEFRA—the Practical Approach	One session

Recognizing that the term "financial planner" has become generic and possibly confusing, the IAFP has developed the Registry of Financial Planning Practitioners as a means of more clearly identifying individuals who represent themselves to the general public as financial planning professionals. The Registry was initiated in 1983; applicants must apply in writing, list references, participate in face-to-face interviews, and complete 30 hours a year of continuing education. Furthermore, individuals must re-register every two years, at which time updated documentation will be required to assure compliance with the standards set by the IAFP.

For further information regarding this organization, you may contact:

The International Association for Financial Planning, Inc.
5775 Peachtree Dunwoody Road
Suite 120-C
Atlanta, GA 30342
(404) 252-9600

THE INSTITUTE OF CERTIFIED FINANCIAL PLANNERS (ICFP)

This organization was established in 1973 by the first graduating class of Certified Financial Planners and is devoted to the interests of CFPs and their clients. The aim of the Institute is to voice the needs and concerns of the Certified Financial Planner to the industry, the decision makers, and the public. In regard to the public, the Institute strives to promote visibility for the CFP in order to build the confidence and trust of the general public, and thereby enhance the CFP's credibility. Furthermore, the Institute has a vital mission to promote professional growth, peer interaction, continuing education, dissemination of pertinent information, legislative and regulatory representation, and public awareness for its members.

There are three classes of members. Regular membership is open only to practicing CFPs who currently and continuously render financial planning services to the public as a primary business activity. Associate members are CFPs who do not practice full time or have not met the yearly continuing education requirements. Fees for regular and associate members are $100 per year. Students of the College for Financial Planning are granted provisional membership for $60 per year, and may become regular members once they have completed the CFP designation program.

All members must subscribe and adhere to the Code of Ethics and the Standards of Practice of the Institute.

THE ICFP CODE OF ETHICS

These principles are intended to aid the Certified Financial Planner individually and collectively in maintaining a high level of ethical conduct. They are not laws but standards by which a CFP may determine the propriety of conduct in relationships with clients, with colleagues, with members of allied professions, and with the public.

The honored ideals of the Institute of Certified Financial Planners states that the responsibility of the CFP extends not only to the individual but also to society. The CFP will participate in activities which improve the financial well-being of the client and the community.

A CFP should strive continually to improve one's skill and knowledge, and make available to clients and colleagues the benefits of professional attainments.

A CFP should practice a method of planning founded on a legal and practical basis and should not voluntarily associate with anyone who violates this principle.

A CFP may choose whom the CFP will serve. Having undertaken a client, the CFP may not neglect the client unless discharged. The CFP may discontinue service only after giving due notice.

A CFP should seek consultation in doubtful or difficult cases, and whenever it appears that the services of members of other professions would tend to provide a more complete and better quality or degree of advice.

A CFP may not reveal the confidences entrusted in the course of consultations, or the deficiencies the CFP may observe in a client or any client's affair unless the CFP is required to do so by law.

The members of the Institute of Certified Financial Planners should guard the public and themselves against any planner deficient in moral character or professional competence. CFPs should obey all laws, uphold the dignity and honor of the profession and accept its self-imposed disciplines. They should oppose, without hesitation, illegal or unethical conduct of fellow members.

The Institute offers many benefits to its members. Perhaps the most important of these is the advanced continuing education program conducted both regionally and nationally. Each summer the Institute conducts a long weekend retreat consisting of advanced financial planning education; this program is designed to enhance the spirit of the Certified Financial Planner and the professional quality of his or her work. In 1981 and 1982 the retreat was held at St. John's University in Collegeville, 80 miles north of Minneapolis, in the woods of Minnesota. The purpose of the retreat is to promote maximum education and interaction among the members of the Institute who attend. Furthermore, the instructors are among the most successful and knowledgeable financial planners in America today.

The bylaws of the ICFP empower its board of directors to adopt a continuing education requirement as a condition of membership. Presently, each member is required to complete at least 30 contact hours of continuing education each year in order to retain his or her regular membership status. Courses may be taken only in the following subject areas and only from educational organizations approved by the Institute:

Accounting
Business Administration
Business Development
Communications
Computer Science
Consumer Economics
Economics
Estate Planning
Family and Money Management
Finance
Human and Family Relationships
Investments
Law
Management
Marketing
Math and Statistics
Professional Development
Risk Management and Insurance

Specialized Tax Shelters

Taxation

Another benefit of the ICFP is the referral service. When a request for information is received, a list of CFPs in the inquirer's area is sent together with a brochure. According to Dianna Rampy, the Executive Director of the Institute, about 12,000 requests for CFPs are made each year.

The ICFP also offers a host of other benefits for its members, including professional liability insurance for which only regular Institute members are eligible, regional continuing education groups, a quarterly journal and newsletter, and an annual membership directory.

For further information about the Institute of Certified Financial Planners, you may contact:

Dianna Rampy, Executive Director
The Institute of Certified Financial Planners
3443 South Galena, Suite 190
Denver, CO 80231

SOCIETY FOR INDEPENDENT FINANCIAL ADVISORS (SIFA)

This is a small, select group of independent fee-only financial planners. There is an exclusive membership requirement that no members may have an insurance or security license. There are no dues and members share the cost and responsibility of all meeting arrangements.

In order to join you must be invited to attend one of the meetings, and if the group feels that you can contribute something to their organization, you will be invited to a second meeting. You are then asked to bring one of your cases so that you can share your knowledge and expertise with the group. At the end of the second meeting you will be informed as to whether you qualify for membership. SIFA is an organization for advanced fee-only planners, and inexperienced planners will generally not qualify for membership until they gain enough experience to offer a meaningful contribution.

One of the main advantages of being a SIFA member is that the organization concentrates heavily on product due diligence and organizes screening committees for various tax-sheltered investments. For example, if a SIFA member wants to place a client in an oil and gas venture, the member would first check with the chairman of the oil and gas screening committee for input, such as whether the investment is

fairly structured as to fees and other provisions of the partnership agreement. The same would be true of agriculture, cattle, or real estate
partnerships. The SIFA members also share their due diligence files to
save each other valuable time and expense.

In 1983 SIFA will sponsor a new organization for the beginning
fee-basis financial planner. Here the more experienced SIFA members
will try to assist the new fee-basis SIFA financial planners by helping to
prevent the same mistakes that they've made. This new organization
will enlighten those who are currently licensed to sell products but are
interested in how fee-only financial planning works. According to Bob
Underwood, CFP, SIFA president, there has been much interest in this
group, especially from CPA firms who are seriously considering the
financial planning profession.

For further information regarding SIFA, you may contact:

Robert J. Underwood, CFP
Underwood Financial Planning, Inc.
400 Century Park South, Suite 208
Birmingham, AL 35226
(205) 823-1120

THE NATIONAL ASSOCIATION OF LIFE UNDERWRITERS (NALU)

Even if the financial planner sells life insurance as a small part of the
business—or does not sell insurance at all—membership in the National
Association of Life Underwriters (NALU) should definitely be considered. A NALU member not only belongs to the national association
but also to a state association and local chapter as well. On all three
levels NALU works to assist and protect the life underwriter on the
legislative and regulatory fronts and provides continuing professional
education for the life insurance professional. Furthermore, on all levels,
it strives to maintain high visibility before the federal and state governments and the public in general.

A major task of NALU is to get heavily involved in legislation that
involves life insurance or touches upon the life insurance community.
As an organization NALU represents individual life underwriters and
not their companies, although speaking realistically, what is good for
the life underwriter is generally good for the company. NALU involves
itself directly with the legislative process. It takes a firm stand regarding
many of the bills before Congress. I have reviewed several of the more

recent positions that NALU has taken, and it appears that much of the legislation NALU supports would also benefit the financial planner—whether or not the planner sells life insurance. I therefore suggest that you pick up a recent copy of the *Life Association News*, the official publication of NALU, and review NALU's activities and positions in several legislative areas. These positions are openly reported each month in two sections of the magazine: "NALU on the Legislative Front" and "Washington in Focus."

Another major benefit of membership is that you will receive the monthly copy of *Life Association News*. This publication is an excellent source of information for the financial planner who wants to know the latest insurance products and concepts, their advantages and disadvantages. By reading many of these articles, whether or not you agree with the marketing of certain products, you are sure to become a much better financial planner. The magazine alone is worth the cost of the dues. For example, the April 1982 issue contained a special 37-page section on advanced underwriting, covering how to lay out a tax package for the small businessperson, deferred compensation, Retirement Life Reserves, Voluntary Employee Benefit Associations (VEBA), and Section 401(k) of the Internal Revenue Code. NALU also provides benefits in the continuing education area, especially in the 10 states where life underwriters must take continuing education courses to maintain their insurance licenses.

The state associations provide benefits similar to the national association except that they work on a more local level, providing the legislative lobbying arm of the life underwriter at the state capitol. The state association may be quite meaningful to you, since life insurance is regulated primarily on the state level. For instance, I belong to the New York State Association of Life Underwriters, which provides a voice in Albany; in addition, it is through this association that I can purchase professional liability insurance for my life insurance and mutual funds sales.

The last level is your local chapter, which generally provides interesting speakers, interaction among members, and a newsletter about what's happening in your community. If you—the financial planner—sell insurance products, your local chapter can serve as a better means of helping you service your clients. If you do not sell products or your practice is more generalized, your local chapter can serve as a place to meet life insurance professionals with whom you can either work and share commissions, or to whom you can send your clients for insurance, knowing that they will do the right thing for your clients.

For further information regarding NALU, contact:

William Bartlett, CLU
Director of Membership and Promotion
National Association of Life Underwriters
1922 F Street NW
Washington, DC 20006

THE INVESTMENT COMPANY INSTITUTE

The purpose of the Investment Company Institute, formerly the National Association of Investment Companies, founded in 1941, is to represent the mutual fund industry, its investment advisors, and its shareholders in matters of legislation, regulation, taxation, public information and advertising, statistics, and economic and marketing research. The Institute provides a clearinghouse where interested persons and communications media may turn for information regarding the mutual fund industry in the United States. It also serves as spokesman and fact finder in many areas affecting members, shareholders, and the investing public. Presently, the Institute represents about 800 mutual funds (both load and no-load), which make up 90% of the industry's total net assets.

The financial planner would not, as a general rule, be a member of the Institute, but may still derive benefits from some of the Institute's services, such as its brochures, publications, and films about mutual funds and financial planning concepts. The following is a list of the latest brochures and publications put out by the Institute:

Brochures:
  How Can I Have More Money in the Future Than I Have Today? (24 pages)
  How Will You Ever Scrape Up the Money When Your Child's Ready for College? (12 pages)
  Plan Tomorrow Today . . . with Your Own IRA (32 pages)
  Investment Responsibilities under ERISA: The Role of Mutual Funds (12 pages)
  Invest Today . . . for a Child's Tomorrow (16 pages)
  IRA: What Employers Need to Know (package)

Publications:
  Mutual Fund Fact Book (annually)
  Mutual Funds Forum (quarterly)
  Monthly Statistics (monthly)

For further information, contact:

Marcia Horn
Investment Company Institute
1775 K Street NW
Washington, DC 20006
(202) 293-7700

9

CAPTURING THE PUBLIC'S EYE

Just as automobiles need fuel to run, the financial planner needs clients to survive. Whether your financial planning practice is small or you run your firm from a multioffice complex on Manhattan's Park Avenue, clients are the main element of your business. Without them, you have no business. It therefore becomes important for the planner to be not only a skilled financial practitioner, but also a skilled marketer of products and services. If you have any thought of starting your own practice, you must develop skill at getting your name or your firm's name out into the world.

In May 1982 I conducted a round-table discussion at a conferment for the College for Financial Planning in Denver, Colorado. The question asked most frequently by those desiring to start their own practice was: "How does the new planner find clients?" Several of the more experienced planners in the group described how they obtained their clients. Although the methods were quite different, there was one common idea shared by all the planners—this idea was that they earned their clients. They worked hard in many different ways to prove to their clients that they deserved their business.

Financial planning clients do not come easily. There are many reasons for this, of course. First, before people will trust you with their personal confidences and hard-earned money, they must have trust *in you*—both in your ability as a planner and in your high moral standards as a person. And you won't win their trust at your first meeting with a simple handshake—it must develop with time. The reputation that you establish over the years is crucial to your ultimate success. Second, financial planning itself is new. The concept is still in the infant stages and most Americans are just beginning to hear of it. And even those people who have heard of it may not really understand what it is all about. Third, the concept of paying a fee may create a barrier for the client. Most people are just not accustomed to paying for something they have gotten free all those years—or at least thought was free. You must educate them to understand that paying a fee can be in their best interest, since you will act as an impartial advisor, free of the influence and temptation of commissions. And you must also justify these fees. You must show them that you are worth every cent they are investing in you. This may not be easy, since most plans will generally run several hundred or even several thousand dollars. Fourth, there is a natural tendency for people to procrastinate. This I call, "The First Law of I'll Do It Tomorrow," which, of course, translates to, "I will never get around to doing it." Although many persons may be thinking seriously about financial planning, few cross over that troublesome barrier of procrastination and really do it. It therefore becomes your job to convince them of the merits of taking positive action. Whether you are a fee-only, commission-only, or fee-and-commission planner, salesmanship is crucial.

If you charge fees, perhaps one of the best arguments a financial planner can use to sell a client on the concept of financial planning is to play up the benefits of Section 212 of the Internal Revenue Code. Section 212 reads as follows:

SEC. 212 EXPENSES FOR PRODUCTION OF INCOME
In the case of an individual, there shall be allowed as a deduction all the ordinary and necessary expenses paid or incurred during the taxable year—

1. For the production or collection of income;
2. For the management, conservation, or maintenance of property held for the production of income; or
3. In connection with the determination, collection, or refund of any tax

This means, in effect, that the client is actually using some tax dollars to pay the cost of a financial plan. Does this mean that the U.S. government is subsidizing a portion of the client's plan? Yes, that is exactly what it means. Let us analyze the psychology involved. For example, in a comparable situation, Section 44C allows a 10% tax credit for making certain energy improvements on a personal residence. As a tax preparer I can tell you for a fact that in a great many cases, the energy credit makes the difference between whether or not the improvement is actually made. And all we are talking about is a 10% credit. For the person who undertakes financial planning, there is usually a much greater benefit. The amount the client can save is the cost of the plan times the client's marginal tax bracket. Therefore, if a client is in a 50% tax bracket and pays $1000, he or she will save $500 in taxes. Yes, *50%* of the cost! Where in the Internal Revenue Code can you find tax benefits like this? The planner who charges fees should definitely stress Section 212. Usually, everyone wants to take advantage of a windfall *at the expense of the government*. It's human nature. In addition, if you could leverage a financial plan you might have a unique tax shelter, especially if the long-term benefits eventually prove fruitful.

One approach that I use to convince persons to use my continual tracking program or to undertake a financial plan is to calculate the real cost to the client after factoring in the Section 212 deduction. I then explain to the client that the cost of my service is a tax deduction if they itemize their taxes, and that investment and/or tax advice is one of the best bargains around for this reason. Of course, the higher the marginal tax bracket of the client, the more advantageous the deduction becomes. We are somewhat unique. Lawyers' fees are generally not tax deductible and doctors' fees are hampered by a 5% exclusion of adjusted gross income. Financial planner fees, on the other hand, rendered for tax and/or investment advice are fully deductible. Both the planner and the client should take advantage of this fact.

At this point I wish to caution planners that many of your potential clients will ask you how well you will be doing for them. This is a very common question indeed. A Registered Investment Advisor (and don't forget that if you're charging fees, you must be one) is never allowed to guarantee the performance of an investment. (You may, however, refer to your historical track record if you have established one.) In both your written brochure and contract you should reinforce the fact that you do not in any way guarantee investment performance. Simply let your clients decide whether they feel you will do a better job than they have been doing. Your clients know how poorly or how well they themselves have done in the past.

So where does a new financial planner just starting out in the business begin? You begin with patience, knowing that the road ahead is a long one.

But building a financial planning practice does not come just from patience. It comes from the active pursuit of getting out into the world and letting people know that you are alive. Here are five different ways of accomplishing this, each way requiring its own special talents and skills. I suggest that you start with what is most comfortable for you, and then experiment with other methods along the way. Keep in mind, above all, that you must capture the public's eye.

ADVERTISING

Marketing your services and products through advertising is not a unique skill. Businesses have been advertising products and services for years. And proper advertising techniques will certainly attract the public's attention. But advertising is a very personal form of publicity. Some planners feel comfortable with it, whereas others do not. Personally, I don't care for it, since it does not attract the type of client I seek. From experience, I have found that too many people who are not really serious about financial planning waste too much of my time. Furthermore, I am not comfortable having to give a sales pitch over and over again. Accordingly, I rely on my clients to do my advertising for me through recommendations. And for me it has worked. I have never really needed to advertise since I have been fortunate enough to work off my base of tax clients. But advertising can be a very effective way to get new clients if you feel comfortable using it and know how to use it correctly.

If you decide to advertise, you should keep *four* key points in mind. First, advertising can be expensive; newspaper ads, television and radio spots, flyers, telephone book ads, and direct mail are all quite costly. And, of course, there is no guarantee that you will ever break even. For the planner who has a limited amount of funds to work with, I don't suggest it. Advertising is probably not as effective a tool for the small planner as it is for the large firm that has substantial resources and a good advertising agency at its disposal. The small planner might do best to stay with lower-cost advertising targeted to a select clientele. Second, advertising requires time to be truly effective. The fact is that you cannot place a spot ad in a newspaper or on radio and really expect it to be effective. Successful advertisers, as you have no doubt seen, run their ads over and over and over again. A friend of mine who heads a large life insurance general agency said that it took him almost a year of repetitive advertising in *Newsday*, the largest newspaper on Long Island, New York, to achieve even a moderate response. Unless you are prepared to take on a long-term advertising campaign, your ads may not be successful. And long-term advertising is certainly not cheap. Third, if you are going to advertise and you are charging fees, I suggest that you stress the tax-deductibility feature. Fourth, if you are a Registered Investment Advisor, you must keep in mind that you are restricted in the type of advertising you can use. You may not advertise testimonials nor may you distort the truth or any part of the facts in any way.

Charles Hughes, Jr., CFP, from Bay Shore, New York, has had excellent response from advertising. His approach is not to overwhelm the reader, but to target in on the particular objective he is trying to accomplish. Charles concentrates in two areas: advertising for seminars and advertising for financial planning with coupons to be sent in for further information. In fact, at a seminar recently, more than 100 people turned out to see what financial planning was all about. "Determine what you want to accomplish through advertising and certainly don't expect to open any accounts," he advises. "Also be certain that you don't cross over into forbidden territory and use a trademark or a registered trade name."

One of Charles' ads, which generated an overwhelming turnout, ran on April 16, 1982. His intent was to bring people out to talk specifically about tax planning but within the framework of total financial

planning. Just look at his ad and you will know why it was so successful. You must keep in mind that Holtsville is the IRS Service Center for the New York Metropolitan area.

SPEAKING

Speaking is cheap, perfect for the small planner. All you have to do is get someone to let you speak and then someone to listen to you, although this may not be as easy as it seems. There are many groups looking for interesting speakers, especially on financial planning topics. What you have to learn, however, is to become an interesting, capable, and well-prepared speaker. Prepare seminars on your strongest subjects and be sincere with your audience, without putting too much emphasis on selling your products or services. Chances are that people are not there to listen to a sales pitch. An overly pushy attitude can ultimately do you more harm than good. What you could do is to blend your marketing techniques into your talk. For example, after speaking about a particular financial planning topic, or perhaps several topics, open the floor to questions. If someone asks a personal question (and I'm sure someone will), you can decline to answer, stating that you are only answering more general questions. Tell the audience that you will answer personal questions only on a professional basis, and that they can call you at your office. Then give your address and phone number, which you should also include on any handouts you provide to the audience. What you have done, in effect, is to maintain your professional dignity by showing that you are more concerned with the audience in general than with that one person who might bring you business. You have given a marketing pitch in response to an inquiry. Ironically, the chances are that the person who asked the personal question will never call, but several others in the audience will. Through experience I have found that the quiet ones, not the loud ones, turn out to be your best clients. At the end of your presentation try to get the moderator or group host to give a sales pitch for you. It always looks good—and more dignified—to get the endorsement of one of the group leaders.

Recently, I spoke to 60 small businesspersons on bookkeeping, IRS record-keeping requirements, business expenses, and proper tax planning. I did this as a favor to a good client who recommends about five people a year to me. Practically the entire audience turned out to be potential clients in at least one of the areas in which I practice. Before the talk my client introduced me to his group of friends, describing my business and professional credentials, and later he explained to the audience that he had been a very satisfied client of mine for three years. After my talk he made a sales pitch for me, specifically pinpointing what services I offer, what products I sell, and what a big mistake it would be not to give me a call. He came on so thick that I felt tempted to leave the room. His endorsement, however, was better than any sales pitch I could have made.

The best way to get a speaking engagement is through personal contact. Is there anyone you know who has any influence in a group that is seeking a speaker? If not, write letters to groups you may want to speak to or write to radio and TV stations, and to religious and civic groups.

Should you charge a fee? Yes and no. Yes, if the group that you speak to is not very influential; after all, you're not doing it as a matter of charity, and the likelihood of obtaining new clients may not be that great. The more established planner would be in a better position to charge a fee than the new planner. The new planner, in fact, should be satisfied just to get up in front of a group. It's great experience and can be an important part of the learning process of becoming a financial planner. I would not charge a fee if the audience was abundant in potential clients or if the engagement was for charitable purposes.

WRITING

The written word is powerful, especially when it is written in a newspaper, magazine, or book. People are highly impressed by those who get into print. There are two ways to get into print: (1) by being the author of a particular story, article, or book, and (2) by being the subject. Either way can be effective.

Just about everyone in America reads newspapers—the butcher, the baker, the candlestick maker, the nuclear physicist, airline passengers, taxi passengers, train passengers, morning commuters, evening commuters, and people who have their shoes shined. The best way to capture the public's eye is to write a Personal Finance column. Of course, the smaller the newspaper, the more chance you have to accomplish this. Obviously, the planner just starting out is not ready for the *New York Times*, but you must start somewhere. And what's wrong with writing for a town or village paper, or perhaps your local church paper? Sometimes people pay a great deal more attention to the local news than to world events. You will never know until you try. Ask local editors if they would be interested in your topic or ideas. You might be quite surprised at their enthusiasm. Financial planning is a hot topic these days. But be creative. Try some new approaches.

If you choose not to write, then perhaps you could be the subject of a story. Let me give you an example. A good friend of mine, Gailann Bruen, whom I introduced in an earlier chapter, specializes in financial planning for women, especially single, divorced, and widowed women. Gailann, as you remember, wears two hats—financial planner and therapist. Recently, Gailann was in Denver, Colorado, giving a seminar to women on financial planning. The seminar was a marvelous success, filling the hotel room to capacity. Later, when Gailann tried to analyze the reason for this tremendous turnout, she made an important discovery. She reviewed the different methods she had used to attract people. One possible reason for the large turnout was that before the seminar Gailann had distributed thousands of flyers directly to group leaders, who promised personally to hand them out. Another possibility for her success was a two-hour radio talk-show on which she had been invited to speak. Finally, a story about her and her seminar had run in the *Rocky Mountain News*. Of all the women attending Gailann's seminar, not one had read the flyer, and only one had heard the radio show. All the rest came after reading the story about her in the *Rocky Mountain News*.

The power of the press! I rest my case. Go out into the jury room, deliberate, and come back with your verdict about how the written word can enhance your public exposure.

Magazines, too, are quite important. You can write an article for a general magazine, a financial magazine, or a trade publication. No matter who you write for, you are building up your credentials and your name is getting known. Again, whether you actually write the article or become part of the article is not important. What counts is that you are getting out into the world and making things happen. No one—believe me—is going to come up to you and ask you to write an article, or to be the subject of one. It's all up to you. Make it happen.

And then there are books. Good old books. If you are willing to spend 20 or 30 hours a week—or more—writing, editing, rewriting, and re-editing, you may wish to try this approach. Many of today's successful financial planners have soared to the top of the field through the power of the pen. A case in point is Venita Van Caspel, who wrote *Money Dynamics for the Eighties* and *The Power of Money Dynamics*, published by Reston Publishing Company, Reston, VA.

The financial planner who writes a book has a big advantage over other authors of financial planning books today. The financial planner is also a *practitioner* who has a great degree of practical know-how and can help the reader by sharing useful and realistic ideas. Venita, in addition to being an author, is a skilled practitioner and a dynamic speaker. Much of her success can be attributed to the fact that she is more than just an author; she is a practicing financial planner. In fact, she has been referred to as "the First Lady of Financial Planning."

On the other hand, a great many of the financial planning books on the market today have been written by professional writers or teachers whose books are good, but only theoretical. They don't really say "how to." The planner who can put practical ideas on paper will rise above the rest.

INTERNAL NEWSLETTERS

Even if you decide that writing is not your cup of tea or that you do not seek publicity for one reason or another, you still should let your clients know that you are alive. One of the best and least expensive ways to do this is through an internal newsletter sent to clients, potential clients, business associates, former clients, the Royal Canadian Mounted Police, or anybody else that you so desire. The purpose of the internal newsletter is to inform your public what you are doing, what you are planning to do, and the ways in which you can help them. There is no one format that the newsletter must follow. It should be styled according to your type of practice and can be either service-oriented, product-oriented, or both.

A newsletter is one of the least expensive ways to capture the public's eye. I send out about 500 newsletters quarterly to all my active clients, potential clients, business associates, and anyone else whom I want to know I exist. The cost is about $60 for the newsletter and the envelopes, and another $100 for postage. I estimate that I recapture the cost at least 10 times over in terms of new clients, product and service sales, and goodwill that generates dollars at a future date. The newsletter, like advertising, becomes more effective as time goes by. It may take a while (several years) to really see the results. And if clients like your newsletters, they will show them to others who may then ask to receive your newsletter and, more often than not, become clients, too. A good-quality newsletter can cause a chain reaction of client growth.

I have been writing my newsletter for several years now, and I am still in the experimentation stage as to content and format. My newsletter is not a work of art; it's not typeset on glossy paper with photos, artwork, and logos. It is simply a two-page letter, typed in-office on an IBM Selectric, printed on colored paper, and mailed to my clients. Until very recently I was writing a four-page newsletter but I found that four pages overwhelmed the reader. My objective was for the client to read my newsletter, not to show how much I could write. Nothing fancy, nothing to rave about, but effective. I'm sure that there are hundreds of financial planners who have much better newsletters. One day I'm sure I will go to a better-quality, more sophisticated newsletter, but only after careful experimentation.

One object of each newsletter I write is to improve the style, quality, and content over the previous one. One way to determine whether you have improved or not is to get feedback from your clients regarding the current newsletter. Yes, phone them and ask them what they think. This will prove helpful to you since, first, your clients are your audience and they are the ones you are out to please; second, most will be flattered and honored to assist you; and third, that conversation could lead to further business. Frequently, a client will say to me during the course of conversation about the newsletter: "You know, Andy, I've been meaning to call you about . . ."—the perfect transition to a sale that the client has, in effect, initiated. My present newsletter covers a variety of subjects, from items of general information that can help the client (such as tax-saving ideas) to the pure marketing of my services and products. Sometimes I cover the latest results on tax shelters that my clients have invested in; sometimes I talk about tax shelters from a more general approach; sometimes I just try to motivate the client into thinking about taking some action about financial planning. In other words, I disturb. Furthermore, I try to keep the newsletter in tune with the time of year. For example, end-of-year tax-saving ideas go into the fall issue, while tax law changes will generally go into an issue after the law has taken effect. I never talk about proposed legislation because it only tends to confuse the client and may never come about. And I always write my own newsletter.

Financial planners today can generate newsletters to their clients in either of two forms. You can write your own or you can purchase a canned newsletter, printed with your name, logo, or anything else you desire. Either way is fine, and both serve the same purpose of getting your name repeatedly in front of your clients. I find a personal newsletter highly advantageous because I can completely control its content. A personalized newsletter is more my style, and besides, I like to write. But a canned newsletter is certainly better than a poorly written one or no newsletter at all. Only you can decide.

However, a financial planner, especially the small financial planner, cannot do everything. And writing a newsletter may just not be feasible for one reason or another. There is no argument that it is time consuming and takes away considerably from financial planning time. Therefore, using a professional newsletter may be the only alternative. There are several professional newsletters on the market for financial planners and most that I have seen are of high quality, on glossy paper, and come with mailing envelopes. The cost varies between 50 and 75 cents per copy. However, before you purchase a canned newsletter you should examine all the other newsletters on the market first. Examine their content over a several-month period to make sure that they are consistent with your needs. Then select the newsletter that is best suited to the type of client you represent. If you have middle-class clients and the newsletter concentrates on advanced estate planning techniques, it would be silly to send that newsletter to your clients.

Most of the newsletter services are set up to print your name, address, and logo directly on the newsletter. This is a great marketing tool, but it is a deception to your clients if they in any way believe that the newsletter was written by you or your firm. I suggest that you let your clients know that you're using a service and that you are not, in fact, the author.

How do you find a financial planning newsletter? Probably the best source is through advertisements in *The Financial Planner* magazine, published by the IAFP. The other alternative is to join the IAFP and thus get on their mailing list; all the newsletter publishers will find you.

SEMINARS

Seminars are an excellent way to get yourself in front of an audience and to get your message across. You have the option to run an educational financial planning seminar for profit based on seminar fees; you can run it as a marketing tool to attract new clients; or you can run it with other planners to accomplish whatever your specific motives may be. A successful seminar can generate a base of future clients for months or maybe years; a poorly run, unsuccessful seminar can hurt your reputation within the community in which you practice. I caution you not to run a seminar unless you are organized, well prepared, and have thought out all the contingencies and problems.

My opinion is that a seminar is not a good place to close a sale for a product or service. To begin with, a trust relationship has not yet been established. The most you can hope to accomplish at the seminar is to make people aware of their problems and of the need for financial planning. You can accomplish this by introducing them to financial planning concepts and by making them realize their shortcomings. Make them say to themselves, "Why haven't I done this before?" You must motivate them to do something now about their problems, and then sell the idea of your service.

The main objective of the financial planning seminar is to get them to come in to see you. This is really what you are trying to accomplish. The last reason in the world that people come to a seminar is to hear a sales pitch about your products. They get enough of that everywhere else. In fact, I suggest that you don't overplay your service. Save the heavy stuff for the office where you can chat one on one. You must, at your seminar, come off as *more* than a true professional. You must come off as a warm person who will be responsive to their needs. Some of the people at the seminar will be buying financial planning while the majority will be buying trust—they will be buying *you*!

10

SUCCESS IS MORE THAN A FULL-TIME VENTURE

In the sixteenth century, Spanish explorer Juan Ponce de León searched the Florida coast in the hope of finding the legendary Fountain of Youth. Needless to say, Ponce de León and the millions of explorers after him never found it. The closest anyone has ever come to discovering the eternal secret of youth was the Dannon Yogurt Company. However, their discovery was just partially successful since it only appears to work on a select group of rural Russians. Does the Fountain of Youth really exist? No one knows—and the search goes on and on and on.

With the same spirit that Ponce de León and the others had in their search for the Fountain of Youth, people throughout recorded and unrecorded history have also searched for another fountain: the Fountain of Success. Can we drink from the Fountain of Success and become successful? Unfortunately, no. Success is not so simple.

Millions of people throughout the world search daily for success, in the arts, in science, in business, in marriage, in politics, or just in survival. Some try to find success in the written word of books, others perhaps in the mountains of Nepal or the Gobi desert, and still others seek success right down the street in the local tavern. Success is truly a matter of individual taste, satisfaction, and degree. Success to one individual might be dismal failure to another. Whether rich or poor, many persons die wondering why they have never become a success.

Success generally cannot be found; it must be achieved. I view it as a function of hard work, a positive attitude, and the desire to be successful. True success cannot be inherited or purchased in the open market. It must be worked at. To be successful at anything you must spend long hours working at it without giving in to failure or obstacles along the way. Success is a matter of mind and body. You must have the overriding mental ability to drive on and the physical endurance to meet the demanding effort and hours required of your venture.

There are many things you must do to be a successful financial planner. The first thing is to realize that you cannot operate your business on a 20- or even 30-hour workweek. If you are looking for a career with nights off, and where you can play golf two or three times a week, I don't suggest having your own financial planning practice. It is certainly not unreasonable for a financial planner building up a new firm to work 60 hours a week or more. Does this frighten you? If so, perhaps you should reconsider whether you really want to work for yourself. The stories of the great achievers are filled with page after page of dull routine, working laboriously long into the night after everyone else has quit.

If you are not willing to work the long hours required of the financial planning entrepreneur, or if you feel the time and effort needed is more than you can bear, my suggestion to you is to find a business more suitable to your life-style. The chances of establishing a successful financial planning practice are remote unless you are willing to commit the time and the effort.

The small financial planner is both a planner and a marketer. As a planner you will have to spend an enormous amount of your time learning to become proficient in the products and services that you will market. The more general the financial planning practice, the more time is required to stay proficient. (Refer to Chapter 8 for the academics of financial planning.) A planner who has a general practice must stay current with investments, insurance, taxation, and estate planning, not to mention all the products there are to review. Furthermore, as a marketer, the planner must spend a great deal of time developing new clients. So do not make the mistake that I did of putting academics before marketing.

Early in my practice I made the error of subscribing to every professional publication I could get my hands on. Before long the mail carrier would deliver my morning mail in a wheelbarrow. I had four investment services, three investment magazines, *Barron's,* the *Wall Street Journal,* the *New York Times,* four financial planner periodicals, two tax services, a financial and estate planning service, four monthly life insurance magazines, a tax shelter magazine, an oil and gas magazine, a silver and gold report, a gem magazine, two coin magazines, and dozens of annual reports of various public companies. Of course, I also received, and still receive, lots of complimentary newsletters and publications from banks, mutual fund groups, diamond firms, coin dealers, tax shelter promoters, and publishing companies looking for me to subscribe to their products. And if I made a big mistake subscribing to all these publications, I made an even bigger mistake by reading most of them. Yes, I was Mr. Proficient. You couldn't ask any more of me on the academic side. However, what I was really doing was reading magazines when I should have been marketing my services and products. The more you try to better yourself, the easier it is to make this mistake.

As the checks began to thin out, I quickly realized that I would be the smartest, most up-to-date financial planner in the poorhouse. True, the quest for success does require you to put a great many hours into your business, but it also requires you to *balance* the hours intelligently between developing professional skills and developing clients. Then I realized what I had really been doing. Since I was weak at selling I was making excuses for not selling, and instead devoted my time to professional proficiency. Yes, I was working the long hours required of me but I was not being effective at all. Every time I looked at the phone and thought about calling someone, I'd turn to my large stack of unread professional material, pick up something that would kill some time, and hope that my phone would ring, so *I* wouldn't have to make a call.

In the summer of 1981 I realized that I could not survive the way I was going—no matter how many hours a week I worked. Therefore, I decided to take the Dale Carnegie Sales Course. If I was going to succeed, I knew that I had to jolt myself into marketing my services and products, and I had to do it quickly. A financial planner with a "fear of dialing" is like a pilot with a fear of flying.

It worked. My resistance to sales could not have been too great, because at the second Dale Carnegie class I was a new person. Or at least a part of me that I had never seen before came out. In fact, at the second class the other students voted me as having the best sales approach of the week, and the school rewarded me with a lead pencil. Normally, I wouldn't be too impressed by a lead pencil, but in this case it was a symbol that I had the ability to market my services and products. And this meant a lot to me.

As the weeks went by, I began to find that selling was more fun than any other part of my business. I also began to phase out all the publications and reading material that were not essential. Not only were they time consuming but they were also quite expensive. Today I read only what is absolutely necessary or of real interest to me.

The key to building a successful financial planning practice, as we have seen, is not only time in terms of lengthy hours, but also the prudent use of that time. Unproductive use of time is not only valueless, but also destructive in the sense that it wears the planner down, and exhausts, frustrates, and demoralizes. It would probably be more beneficial to go fishing for an hour than to work unproductively. The planner must face the fact that building a successful practice takes long, hard, and *fruitful* hours.

But working those long hours is only part of the story. Success also requires your full dedication and commitment to achieving your goal. You must set your sights on developing the financial planning practice that you wish to build and then let nothing along the way stop you. There will be many obstacles. There will be up days and down days. Not all the decisions you make will be right. You will no doubt make changes, for the financial planning business is a business of ongoing change. However, keep in mind that most changes you make will be beneficial to the accomplishment of your goal—building the firm that you want!

Although the financial planning business is a very special type of business—one that requires great knowledge and responsibility—the basic guidelines of succeeding with any business still apply. How many small businesses have made it because of the owner's guts and determination? How many entrepreneurs have been in the red for hundreds of thousands of dollars, on the verge of collapse, and have still gone on to cross all the valleys and reach the heights of success? Whenever a client comes in for a consultation about starting a new business, I always say that unless he or she has the burning desire to make it, don't even consider it. Motivation is at least half the battle.

There are two types of people who want to enter the small business world. There are the dreamers who do nothing about their dreams; thus their dreams never become any more than dreams, only to frustrate them in later years. These are basically unhappy people who drift through life always pushing their dreams further into the future, making excuse after excuse as to why they cannot start today. Later down the road, they concede that those dreams are too far past, and regret that they never tried to make them a reality. Then there are the dreamers who are also doers. These people never lose sight of their dreams; they have tremendous resiliency to overcome obstacles; and as each dream is turned into reality, they go on to accomplish their next dream, and so on. Successful small businesses, giant corporations, conglomerates, countries, and even empires have been built by the determined efforts and desires of dreamers.

Dreaming is wonderful. But doing is essential.

Sometimes your dreams go against what seems logical—or at least what seems logical to others. My dream began when I had a safe, secure government job as a Senior Customs Inspector at John F. Kennedy International Airport. You just don't walk away from a job like that, and historically, very few people ever have. Furthermore, I liked the job and probably was not too far from my next promotion. So what did I get in return for leaving? My own business with no certainty of a salary, piles of expenses, and bills that had to be paid even if I wasn't earning a cent, no paid vacation, no paid sick time, no pension, no benefits, lots of worries and problems, and the responsibility of feeding a family. I was on quite a few lists as being certifiable, and psychiatric care was frequently recommended. Although most of these people knew that I was a dreamer, they did not understand that I was also a *doer*. A doer is not frightened by the unknown. A doer acts, and does not only spend time dreaming. Of course, a doer does not always act without mistakes, and so must be flexible enough to change and change and change.

While writing this book, someone told me they were thinking about writing a book and asked me whether to go ahead with it. I said stop thinking about it and write it!

Looking back at my career change, I would certainly do it again. I am my own person—whether I succeed or whether I fail. Fortunately, the word "failure" is not in my vocabulary. Nor should it be in yours. To fail is to quit. And to quit is to throw a brick through those beautiful dreams.

> Dream—full time!
> Work—full time!
> Do—full time!
> Failure—Does not compute!

Charles Maher, CFP, a financial planner from Denver, Colorado, is also a doer. Charles presently has two careers, one as a television producer developing educational seminars for the Community College of Denver, and the other as a Certified Financial Planner developing a fee-only practice in his own style. I must give Charles a lot of credit for his convictions. He is absolutely convinced that pure fees is the only route to go, and that you cannot be an outstanding insurance agent, tax shelter specialist, or investment specialist and at the same time do justice to your financial planning clients.

His approach is to be a general practitioner and to surround himself with specialists who are a lot more qualified than he in their particular financial disciplines. What makes Charles' attitude so extraordinary is that he grew up hearing about the virtues of selling life insurance from his father, a life insurance agent and now a chief executive of a life insurance firm. Charles had sold life insurance for a few years but just could not buy the idea of selling it. "My objective was to do service for my clients." He now recommends that his clients purchase no-load term.

In the fee-only business it takes years to build up a solid base of clients to the point where there are enough fees to live on. But since Charles is only 30, he's not in a hurry. "I would rather do it right, work two jobs for now, than to compromise." Presently, he has 18 clients and charges an hourly fee for planning work. He estimates that the average plan takes about 16 hours of his time to complete over the course of six weeks, and costs the client about $1000. He writes complete plans only for clients who have incomes of $35,000 or more, or have a special need for a plan. For clients under $35,000 he works at a flat hourly rate.

The plans that he writes (manually) are segmented into six parts. The first part deals with establishing a good record-keeping system and gives them a grasp of where their money is going. "It seems like the more that they make, the less control they have on their money." The second part deals with the client's complete risk management program. The third part deals with investments; here he helps clients earning $35,000 and under to save 10% of their income, and clients over $35,000, 15%. The fourth part concerns taxes, and this is where he feels he works the hardest. His program sets a goal of reducing the client's marginal tax bracket by one bracket each year. The fifth part concentrates on estate planning, and the sixth part looks into investments that reduce taxes, such as shelters. Every six months he offers his clients a semi-annual review which usually runs two to four hours and costs the client between $140 and $280.

Charles Maher is a realist and has a great attitude about financial planning. He is refreshing to talk to because he views financial planning as a challenge, and knows that he will succeed. In fact, he hopes some-day to merge his broadcasting and financial planning background, producing financial planning educational productions. Naturally, he'll have to work to achieve this, and not just dream.

I'm sure he will—Charles Maher is a doer!

11

WORKING WITH OTHER PROFESSIONALS

Football, baseball, basketball, soccer, and hockey—all are team sports requiring teamwork and cooperation. But each sport also requires the effort of *individuals* to achieve the end result—winning. For instance, in football there is an offensive team, a defensive team, and a special team, each a subgroup of the main team, and each having a specific function. Then, individually, there are guards and tackles who block; defensive guards and tackles who tackle; runners; ends who catch passes; a center who hikes the ball; linebackers who tackle; safeties and defensive backs to stop passes; and finally, a quarterback to coordinate the offensive play. Each individual has a specific function, a specialty. However, without a doubt, it is the quarterback who makes things happen. He is the heart of the team. Without him all the players move in different directions, somewhat like recent Baltimore Colts teams.

Total financial planning is also a team concept. It, too, requires specialists to perform different tasks. And like football, it requires a quarterback to coordinate the client's financial program; otherwise, the result could be a disjointed effort resulting in a total fiasco. The well-balanced financial program usually requires the expertise of several skillful advisors who work with the client to fine-tune the financial program. The advisors may work together or separately. But the fact is, someone must take charge and that someone is the financial planner. As a general rule, the wealthier the client, the larger the team of advisors he or she will need. However, even persons of little affluence may require two or three advisors.

Rarely is the small financial planner able to cover all the financial functions that the client needs. I was recently approached by a potential client who could not understand why I charged a fee for my service. He said he had been to another financial planner who wouldn't charge him anything. In fact, the other planner had told him that all his program needed was deferred annuities. Then I asked him if he had a will to protect his wife and children. He said no. Did he carry an umbrella liability policy? And he said, what's that? Did he have an education fund for the children? No. I then suggested that he seriously consider paying my fee because, in the long run, it was going to be a lot cheaper this way whether he realized it or not.

Like this fellow, the public has not yet caught on to total financial planning. That is probably because there aren't too many total financial planners around. The future will be different—of that I assure you. Most financial planners still tend to limit themselves to a few products. However, as time passes and fees become more popular, this practice will change. Small independent financial planners and firms are beginning to undertake a greater variety of products and services. Yet total financial planning still requires a team consisting of various professionals. Larger firms may provide such a team in-house but the small planner must find other sources. He or she cannot do it alone.

After the financial planner has established the specific areas he or she will deal in, the next step is to make arrangements to cover all the other areas. You cannot very well tell your clients that you can provide only part of the service, and that they must go somewhere else to get the rest. That's what has happened in the past. That is the old way: the multistop service. What you must do is build a directory of other professionals to refer your clients to when you are not capable of offering a service yourself. Rather than generalize about how to work with other professionals, I have chosen to take an occupation-by-occupation approach.

THE ATTORNEY

Although all the advisors that you will work with are important, the attorney plays a critical role on the financial planning team. The one you choose should be skillful, personable, and easy for both you and your client to work with. After all, the attorney to whom you send your clients is a reflection on you.

Most lawyers, by training and experience, are skillful actors, trial lawyers especially. One of my clients is a trial lawyer with a prestigious Wall Street firm. Recently, I asked her which course in law school was most helpful to her in learning to become a trial lawyer. She said, "None." Her most important training, she emphatically stated, was acting—my client is a former actress turned trial lawyer.

Working with an attorney who can act can be to your total advantage. For instance, the attorney to whom I refer my clients goes out of his way to make me look good. He does this in three ways:

1. He is responsive to my clients and does not procrastinate when performing legal services. Some attorneys take months just to write a simple will.
2. He always makes my clients feel important and does not talk down to them.
3. In my judgment, he offers superior legal service.

Choosing an attorney to whom to refer your clients can be a most difficult task, especially since you are probably not qualified to judge his or her legal qualifications. I used several attorneys before I found one with whom I was satisfied. Selecting him, ironically, was not based solely on his skill as an attorney. Although there might be other attorneys more skillful than he, all the clients I have sent to him come back completely satisfied, thanking me for sending them to see him. What impressed me the most was that, when we first met (he was referred to me by a client), he told me which legal services he could *not* perform, rather than boasting about all the things he could do. Furthermore, he advised me right from the start to seek other counsel when cases were beyond his area of expertise. I find his frankness to be most admirable in a lawyer. A lawyer who admits there are areas of the law that he or she does not understand is a valuable asset on your financial planning team.

As a financial planner you may find yourself referring legal work to many attorneys rather than just one. Lawyers, like doctors, specialize in different areas. You might use one attorney for general work such as incorporations, partnerships, business agreements, closings, contracts, trusts, and wills; another for tax and estate planning; and perhaps another for negligence matters. It may take many years to establish satisfactory relationships with the lawyers you choose. Be patient. Ask other planners for recommendations.

The best arrangement I feel that you can have with attorneys is that of reciprocal referral. In other words, "I'll send clients to you if you send clients to me." Referrals from lawyers are important. After all, lawyers are not financial advisors, so they definitely need someone with your skills. If the attorney's client wins a big judgment and has a large sum of money to invest and plan for, you will be the first one he or she calls. Furthermore, the attorney should be responsive to *your* legal needs, both business and personal. Since you are sending the attorney business, chances are that your legal matters will be taken care of for a very reasonable charge.

And now, a very crucial point: You need an attorney to work with simply because you are not an attorney yourself. You are a financial planner. Your job, your skill, is to perform financial planning—not law. Many financial planners, unfortunately, cross over that fine line separating the two professions and perform tasks that are within a lawyer's domain. *Nothing* can be more dangerous. Here are some things financial planners do *not* do: Financial planners do not write wills, do not incorporate businesses, do not write partnership agreements, do not write buy–sell or stock redemption agreements, do not write interest-free demand notes, do not assist in divorces (only the tax consequences), do not write contracts, and do not give any legal advice, verbal or otherwise. Although you may be quite skillful in one or many areas of law, these are not your areas. This is forbidden territory, private turf—stay away. So the next time your client asks you a legal question, bite your tongue, zip the lip, simply suppress what you want to say. Tell the client that the question is legal in nature and only an attorney can answer it. If the client still demands an answer from you, after you have clearly explained the need for an attorney, see this client to the door and toss the file card into the garbage. However, if you really feel compelled to give legal advice, my suggestion is to enroll in law school and become an attorney yourself.

Dick Jones, a fellow Certified Financial Planner and attorney from Wichita, Kansas, has taken a real stand on this subject. Although he is qualified to work in both professions, he has, by choice, selected to be a financial planner. And when a client comes to Dick in need of a will or trust, he does what any skillful financial planner should do—he advises his client to see a lawyer! Here's why . . .

"It is unethical," Dick says, "for an attorney to solicit legal work through his or her financial planning practice. In most states this would be unethical under the laws of that state and the rules of the State Bar Association. The only legal work that I do is for a select group of clients whom I have represented for years. In no way do I solicit business through my financial planning practice. In fact, I actually create an awful lot of legal work for other attorneys, since I have many clients who come into my office with various legal problems. I refer these clients to different attorneys whom I consider skilled in the particular area of law in which the client has a problem."

Dick Jones, CFP, feels that his legal training and background make him a better financial planner. He sees a tremendous need for financial planning, and enjoys working with people and solving their financial problems. In fact, he recommends that attorneys coming out of law school today take a good hard look at the financial planning profession since many attorneys could have successful careers as financial planners, instead of as lawyers. "Where I come out ahead being both an attorney and a CFP is that my legal training and my 11 years of practicing law gave me a strong background enabling me to counsel and advise people better and more thoroughly in estate and financial planning matters. But my income is strictly from financial planning fees and commissions. I do not charge for legal advice."

The fine line between financial planning and law is not that easy to define. Financial planners, bankers, and real estate people cross over that boundary every day. "Financial planners must never charge for legal matters, and although they may touch on legal matters, they should make it very clear to clients that it is only their opinion. They should encourage clients to see their own attorneys."

An equally serious problem, Dick feels, occurs when attorneys cross over into the financial planner and investment advisor areas, areas where they shouldn't be. "An awful lot of attorneys do not want to admit that there are various areas of the law, as well as nonlaw areas such as financial planning, in which they are really not skilled. So rather than admit to their shortcomings by referring their clients to an expert in the field, they will give out bad or inadequate advice, or worse, they throw cold water on what someone else has suggested. This, in effect, generally means they are not familiar with the problem."

Dick suggests that you take the direct route when working with an attorney. "Tell the attorney outright that you are a financial planner and you can help his or her clients. You must make that attorney understand that you are not trying to step in and take away business. It is your goal to work as a member of the team. If you use this approach, an attorney will most likely be more receptive than if you use any other approach. You are offering to make the attorney's life easier, and there isn't a professional around who wouldn't like to figure out a way to do that. And once they are confident that you know what you're doing as a financial planner, you will have yourself some strong influential allies who will send you a lot of business as well as assist you with your mutual clients."

Being able to disclaim responsibility for legal matters is a necessity for the financial planner. I make it perfectly clear to my clients and prospective clients that I am strictly a financial planner and not a lawyer. In my SEC compliance brochure (see Chapter 4) I state the following:

"Do we provide legal services?

"No. AMR Planning Services, Inc., is a financial planner and investment advisor only, and limits itself to tax and financial matters."

Furthermore, Paragraph 15 of my financial planning contract reads as follows:

> The client is aware that AMR Planning Services, Inc., is a financial planner and investment advisor only, and does not provide legal advice or recommendations, and therefore that the client is responsible for consulting with his or her attorney before implementation of the program.

I cannot stress enough the importance of the following statement, which I have made before and I am going to make again: You are a financial planner and not an attorney. Do not in any manner practice law unless you are also a qualified attorney. Forget all the great articles you read and tapes you hear telling you about the nifty things you can do to make your clients happy and wealthy. If it involves practicing law, you can't do it. You can suggest it. You can coordinate it. You can supervise to see that it gets done. But you can't do it!

Easily understood but not easily practiced.

It is unfortunate that many aspects of financial planning, and many of the demands that clients make, touch on law. I am asked quite often to write wills. Since most financial practitioners have difficulty separating what is law from what is financial, you cannot expect the client to do so. You must not, under any circumstances, cross over the bridge into lawyerland. It is a dangerous place where the consequences of your actions may be more devastating than you can imagine.

THE ACCOUNTANT

Of all the advisors you will deal with perhaps none has more influence on a client than the accountant. This is especially true for the self-employed businessperson who employs an accountant, certified or not, to service the entire business. On the other hand, the wage earner who sees an accountant only once a year for income tax preparation does not in general rely on the accountant for other financial matters. We often hear people say, "I'll have to check with my accountant." This is because people today place tremendous stress on keeping their numbers and dollars in order. The accountant, therefore, has been put into the position of the maker or breaker of deals. And, have no doubts, one can kill a deal with the slightest nod of the head or blink of the eyes. Many times an accountant will kill a deal not because the deal is bad but because the accountant does not really understand it.

In general, accountants are conservative people. They may appear to be untrusting, but you must understand that they are getting paid by their clients to have just that kind of attitude. A person will retain an accountant not only to calculate numbers but also to evaluate choices with only the client's best interests in mind. This is especially true of the CPA. People today want a real offeree representative. And the accountant, like any other professional, is subject to the threat of mal-practice suits. Therefore, you may just have to prove your worth extra hard before you are accepted by the accountant. The accountant is not only protecting the client, but is protecting himself or herself.

Nonetheless, the accountant can be the best source of referral you will have—even better than the lawyer. You must therefore strive to establish a good relationship with one or many accountants. Of course, the chances of such a relationship developing depends on the type of practice that you have. For instance, if your firm does tax preparation or general accounting, the accountant may see you as a potential threat, as a competitor out to steal clients. Obviously, the chances of the accountant sending clients to you for financial planning may be small until you can prove that you have no interest in taking over the account-ant's clients. You must demonstrate your sincerity. On the other hand, the financial planner who does not perform in-house tax preparation or accounting is in a much better position initially to receive referrals from accountants. This is especially true if the financial planner is able to refer business back to the accountant. My firm receives a great deal of its revenue from tax accounting. I have, on occasion, referred business such as general accounting to accountants, but it is the type of business I would have no interest in anyway.

To the conceptual financial planner, the accountant is more than just a source of referral. The accountant has a unique skill that most financial planners are not trained in themselves. This is especially impor-tant for the client who owns a business. During the course of writing a financial plan an accountant may be needed to analyze an accounting practice, prepare an audit, provide information vital to a financial plan, or perform a variety of other functions. Financial planners must not only work with accountants whom they themselves select, but quite often they must work with the client's accountant—like it or not. The future of financial planning will be very interesting indeed as more and more accountants cross-train as financial planners.

THE CHARTERED LIFE UNDERWRITER

Although most life insurance situations are not too difficult to under-stand, they can at times be quite complex, even beyond the understand-ing of the financial planner. Unless, of course, the planner is also a life insurance specialist. A complex problem is most likely to arise in a business or estate planning situation. Therefore, it is recommended that the financial planner not jump into water over his or her head. Establish a relationship with a life insurance professional—or another financial planner who has a strong background or specializes in the life insurance area.

The Chartered Life Underwriter (CLU) is a person who has passed a 10-part course given by the American College in Bryn Mawr, Pennsylvania. However just because a person is a CLU does not necessarily mean that the person is capable of handling any problem that arises. A CLU, to be proficient, should have considerable practical experience. Some CLUs can out-think the keenest attorneys and accountants. There are others who are not overly swift, to say the least. Like anything else, designations and degrees do not necessarily mean that a person is competent. Some people have progressed even further than CLU and have obtained a Master of Science in Financial Services degree from the American College. The few persons I know who have graduated from this program have truly impressed me with their knowledge of life insurance.

The type of life insurance specialist you bring in will generally depend on whether you are a fee or a commission planner. The commission planner might work with an associate who is licensed by the same company and will split the commission. Or the planner might have the pull to drag in an insurance whiz from the home office to do all the hard work, while the planner retains the entire commission. Fee planners may need to develop a source of trustworthy life insurance professionals to call upon as the need arises. Since most life insurance specialists would be receiving the entire commission as well as future referrals, they should be more than happy to help you. Another alternative is to hire a life insurance professional as a consultant who would charge you or the client a service fee, present the client with the written facts, and then let you and the client decide which company and agent to deal with. As "no-load" life insurance begins to develop—and it will—the insurance consultant may become increasingly important to the fee-basis financial planner.

THE PENSION SPECIALIST OR ACTUARY

In this day and age pension planning has become a vital part of the client's financial program. The financial planner should be capable of handling most simple pensions such as an IRA, SEP, or Keogh, but going beyond those plans and into defined benefit, defined contributions, and profit-sharing plans can get quite complex. Even seemingly simple plans can get tricky at times. It is therefore best that the financial planner not try to act as a pension consultant unless the planner is, in fact, a pension expert. The repercussions of making a mistake in a client's pension can set off a chain reaction that reverberates throughout the Internal Revenue Service, the courts, the client's pocketbook, and your pocketbook as well. Pensions are a complex area that should be set up only by skillful pension consultants.

The pension consultant is an important part of the financial planning team and for that reason should be selected carefully. The planner must seek out a pension consultant who specializes in plan design, plan administration, and actuarial services. Furthermore, a truly objective pension consultant will charge a fee for his or her services, rather than relying on commissions of product sales to earn compensation. In the pension area the planner must be cautious of what *appears* free. Also, the planner should take continual service into consideration. Does the pension consultant provide administration, or will the client need to find a pension administrator once the plan has been established? Many pension consultants offer periodic seminars to clients and to planners in order to provide a high level of service.

THE INSURANCE BROKER

Homeowners insurance, automobile insurance, business insurance, liability insurance, errors and omission insurance, and so on, are all integral and necessary components of financial planning. Most financial planners, however, tend to specialize more in the tax, investment, and life insurance sectors of the planning business. Accordingly, few financial planners have adequate backgrounds in the property and casualty insurance area to do a proficient job, even though most financial planners do have some knowledge in this area. Just a little knowledge, however, can be quite dangerous.

Property and casualty insurance, an area that seems quite simple at first glance, is really a complex field. Financial planners, unless they are also insurance brokers, should develop a relationship with a professional insurance broker who is proficient in a wide range of insurance matters. My technique is to review the client's insurance, and if I see anything in the policy that appears inadequate or if I do not understand something, I check with my broker or, if need be, an insurance consultant. I then state to the client that the insurance appears inadequate for whatever reason and refer the client back to the broker or company that holds the present policy, or to a new insurance broker if the client desires one. Furthermore, since I am not an insurance broker, I *never* state in my written plans that a client's property and casualty insurance is sufficient. Even if I feel their coverage is adequate, I refer them back to their existing carrier for an update and review. A cop out, yes. But I am protecting you know who.

As with law, practicing in this area *without expertise* and *experience* can be quite dangerous, especially if, down the road, there is a liability claim against the client or the client's house burns to the ground, or so on. You, as a financial planner, should look for insurance inadequacies, and indicate to the client that there *may* be some. Then put a property and casualty insurance specialist under the spotlight. Otherwise, if you try to be what you're not, later you may be under the "hot lights."

What should you look for in a property insurance broker?

1. Make sure that the broker has been established for many years. Property casualty insurance is a field where experience is more important than schooling.
2. The broker should have a strong background in both commercial and personal lines.
3. The broker should represent companies rated A or A+ by A.M. Best. Good solid companies investigate a lot more closely the persons who are going to write business for them than do second-rate companies.
4. The broker should deal in multiple lines through several companies, since these carriers are cost competitive.
5. The broker must provide service to your client such as checking that all insureds are properly classified and that all the applicable discounts are applied to the policy. Many policies that come back to the broker from insurance companies are incorrectly discounted and classified.
6. As a general part of his business, the broker should advise on gaps in coverage and overlapping coverage.
7. In regard to claims, the broker looks out for the insured's best interest and should know how to deal with insurance companies. Brokers who produce heavy premiums will carry weight with the insurance companies.

Again, as with most other advisors, relationships with insurance brokers do not develop overnight. You may have to try many brokers over several years until you find the right one.

THE TRUST OFFICER

The trust department of a bank may offer many services of great benefit to the client. Among those are custodian accounts, acting as trustee of trusts and estates, and serving in the capacity of executor of wills, just to name a few. There are times when financial planners may be called upon to work closely with bank trust officers for the mutual benefit of the client.

Many clients prefer banks because of their conservative image and will feel more comfortable having their funds in a bank than anywhere else. The client's wishes must be respected. The trust department of a bank offers a planner the opportunity to control the client's investments, avoid a great deal of the clerical work, especially the buying and selling of securities, and to satisfy the client's desire for a conservative structure. In essence, a planner may: set up a custodial account for a client at a bank; retain the right to buy and sell securities within the account through use of a limited power of attorney; and have all paperwork performed by the bank and sent to both the client and planner. A financial planner then becomes the link between the client and the bank and should work closely with the bank's trust officer. Often, banks will handle the client's account from soup to nuts, including management of the investments and so forth. In this case, the trust officer becomes responsible for the account, and a careful selection of banks is critical for the planner and client.

OTHER ADVISORS

The type of practice a planner has and the market that the planner serves will determine what other advisors are needed. The planner may also need to work with bank loan officers, real estate brokers and appraisers, gemologists, jewelers, antique and art appraisers and specialists, and coin and stamp dealers and specialists. The list of advisors can go on endlessly, and the planner should be willing to work with almost any advisor who will benefit the client.

No matter what advisor you work with, the objective is to do what's best for your client or the advisor's client. You must always keep in mind that advising is a two-way street. At times you may need the assistance of one of the aforementioned advisors and at other times one of those advisors may need your assistance. You are a member of a team. In fact, the other professional, given confidence and trust in you, may view you as the captain. Should you be called in to advise someone else's client, you should exercise the same degree of skill and care that you would with your own client. Professional referrals are an important part of this business and may ultimately lead to a substantial portion of your income.

Remember the role of the financial planner. You are the leader of the team, the quarterback. You call the plays. You call the signals. But it is the team that scores the touchdown for the client.

12

THE OFFICE IS YOU

Earlier I mentioned that a financial planner could operate off a park bench if need be. This, of course, is an exaggeration, but it is nonetheless possible. Sounds bizarre, yet a financial planner could conceivably work from a park bench or out of a telephone booth or from a briefcase if that is the way he or she wanted to work. Furthermore, the financial planner does not initially need capitalization—just clients, the resources to live, and the desire to succeed.

Your financial planning office is an extension of yourself. It should completely reflect your style and manner of doing business. Most of the time a separate office is necessary. But not always.

The independent financial planner needs some type of working area. Some planners maintain office facilities in their homes, whereas others rent or buy space in office buildings or storefronts. The type of office a planner needs is a very personal decision. The perfect office has yet to be discovered. What is perfect for one planner may be impractical for another.

The extent of the planner's practice often dictates the type of office facility needed. If the planner conducts all meetings at the homes of clients or their places of business, simply working from an extra room of the house may suffice.

The planner who works from his or her home has a big advantage in terms of cost. The only real expenses are office equipment and telephone. Furthermore, if the room or part of the room is used exclusively for business, that portion of the house may be depreciated or that part of the rent may be expensed. However, working out of your residence has a limited application. It might not be practical if you expect to conduct a lot of business meetings or to hire several or more employees. In that case renting an office, or using a residence with an office attached and a private entrance, would be more practical.

The planner who meets frequently with clients should consider the pros and the cons of working from home:

1. An office at home might appear less businesslike to your clients than an office in a professional building, especially to new clients, professional clients, or business clients. However, once you establish your Super Trust with a client, most clients are not concerned whether you work from your home, an office building, or a tuna boat.

2. The constant parade of clients through your home may be an unfair disturbance to the rest of your family, as well as an infringement on their privacy. Your family may object to the intrusion of strangers into their homes, and the use of an attached but separate office should be considered.

3. You may have the tendency to work when you should be relaxing. Since the office is right there you might be tempted to pop up at two in the morning to do some work. Although my opinion is that the financial planner should devote a great deal of time and effort to the business, there are definite times when you must stop, rest, and be with your family. Furthermore, clients could be calling you at any hour of the day or night. Of course, these problems can be overcome through self-discipline or by simply turning off the phone. Keep in mind that an office in the home allows the planner to work when he or she feels most productive, avoiding the nine-to-five routine. One good hour's work at 11 P.M. is much more effective than three bad hours during the day.

4. You may be constantly distracted by the rest of your family. Certainly, and I'm sure you'll agree, they have every right to live a free, normal life in their own home. Your spouse or your children may need to come in to talk to you or just to get something; or your children may be making too much noise. The home office, unless both the planner and the rest of the family have the right temperament, could be a source of marital friction.

5. Your neighbors may not take too kindly to the constant coming and going of automobiles if this is the style of your practice. People who spend a lot of money to purchase a house in the suburbs are not overly thrilled at living next door or across the street from a business. And keep in mind that in some localities a home office is prohibited by local zoning codes.

Most planners, however, will use a professional office. A major objective is to locate the office where it is accessible to the majority of your clients, yet fairly close to your home. The more time you spend on the road commuting back and forth, the less time you will have for conducting your practice or for being with your family. If you must place your office a considerable distance from your home for one reason or another, you could use your commuting time effectively. Many financial planners purchase a tape recorder for the car and listen to financial planning, marketing, or educational tapes that improve them professionally.

The selection of my office location was the result of a highly scientific method. I took a child's compass and a street map of my neighborhood, placed the compass point on my house, estimated the distance between the compass point and the pencil to be about five minutes from my home, and drew a circle on the map. I then explored office buildings within that circle and found what I wanted. My office is currently about four minutes from my house.

Locating my office so close to my home has really worked well for me. I do not mean to imply that this will work for everyone. But the points I am going to bring up do deserve some consideration. Since the office is so close I am able to sleep later in the morning, rather than spending an hour or so on the highway or train, yet I still arrive at the office around 9 A.M. I generally sleep until 8:30; the average metropolitan commuter is on the road sometime between 6 and 8 A.M. Personally, since I'm a night person and tend to be quite productive in the late evening and early morning hours (11 P.M. to 4 A.M.), I like to sleep a little later in the morning. I usually do my best thinking between these hours. At times, when I work until 4 A.M. (let's not forget I'm a writer, too, and many a night I write to the tune of chirping birds), I usually sleep until 9:45 A.M. and get into the office by 10:15, refreshed and ready to deal with my clients. Commuting is not only time consuming, it also drains the body of productive energy, which is a vital necessity for the financial planner.

Having the office close to home allows me to integrate my personal life into regular business hours so that the evening hours can be used to my advantage, either personal or business. For instance, I'm able to schedule a doctor or dentist appointment during the day and, since these offices are right in the neighborhood, I'm usually back in my office within an hour. Additionally, I'm free to attend my children's school functions, a privilege that most working parents cannot enjoy. Often when I'm home late in the evening I'll find I need something from the office and, rather than dwelling on it or leaving it until the next day, I can be to the office and back within 10 minutes. Furthermore, my wife, who is an integral and vital part of my business, is able to spend considerable time in the office and still get home early for the kids or to leave if any problems arise.

Your financial planning office is truly a reflection of yourself. The building or perhaps storefront that you ultimately decide on should be attractive enough not to offend your clients. Is it wiser to take less space in a first-rate building or more space in a dingy one? If clients are going to entrust you with their money and the future of their financial lives, you cannot ask them to climb up four flights of a dimly lit, dusty, elevator-less building that is painted only once every decade and smells of mold. Renting space in a building where clients will compliment you on your taste can enhance your credibility. You certainly do not want them wondering if you are on the level, their eyes roaming for your fully packed suitcase.

One problem new financial planners have is that sometimes they tend to overassess their needs. This is especially true for office space. The small financial practitioner does not need 1000 or 2000 square feet (although your ego may tell you that you need it). Three hundred to six hundred square feet should enable you to operate effectively, depending on the location and the cost. My office is about 300 square feet and only now, after several years, am I starting to feel cramped. Do not waste your money on vast amounts of space that you don't need, hoping that one day you will. It is wise to rent a little more office space than you currently need, but not too much more. High office rental can literally kill your profit in the early years and is one of the biggest pitfalls of which the planner should beware. Also keep in mind that unless you plan on cleaning your office yourself, this expense is often additional. One thought is to hire your kids, if you have any and they are willing, to clean your office. This way they can earn some extra money and thus keep themselves fully stocked with *Star Wars* toys, Atari tapes, and Barbie dolls.

OFFICE EQUIPMENT

Once you have selected the location of your office, the next task is to plan what goes into it. Do you want modern, Early American, or Provincial? Do you want plush carpets, commercial carpet, or tile floors? Do you want brown files, gray files, or red files? And so on. What do you want your office to look like?

Furnishing and equipping an office is not as easy as it seems. There are many factors that go into the selection process. But the most important factor, I feel, is that the office must "be you." It should express, in its own decorative manner, the way you feel about things. It must also reflect your needs in relation to servicing your clients. And, of course, it must reflect your budget. The following is a list of equipment and furnishings that I consider basic to the small financial planning office:

Telephone
Typewriter
Calculator
File cabinets
Desks
Chairs
Bookcases
Refrigerator
Coffee maker
Copy machine
Answerphone
Tape recorder

Telephone

It is obvious that to survive as a financial planner you need a telephone. But there are specific phone features that you must consider. These are: (1) a second number, (2) pick-up-and-hold, (3) conference calling, and (4) long-distance calling.

You can survive with one basic instrument. But the dollars you will save in cost effectiveness may not outweigh the loss of revenue you might suffer without the additional features. First, clients do not particularly care to get a constant busy signal and may eventually get discouraged enough to seek another planner. A repetitive busy signal is just not professional. How do you feel when you keep getting a busy signal? Do you get frustrated? Do you sometimes slam down the receiver in anger? A second line is also necessary if you want conference calling, which may pay for its cost many times over. A conference call allows three or more parties to talk at one time, depending on how many lines you have. For example, suppose that you are discussing a matter with your client and a legal question arises. With the client on one line, you can call the client's attorney and the three of you can discuss the matter together. This is more effective and less time consuming than your having to call the attorney, get an answer, and then call the client back. It enables you to save time and that, of course, translates into money. Or perhaps you are discussing a shelter with your client and the client has questions for the general partner. Conference calling allows the three of you to discuss it together. The client has every right to speak to a general partner directly to ask any questions he or she wishes. There are many instances that a three-way conversation might be beneficial.

You should also consider a pick-up-and-hold feature since there may be times when you'll want to place the caller on hold so that you can think for a moment or perhaps discuss the call with someone else. A Com Key or similar type of system offers every desirable feature needed by the small planner and is expandable if your business grows.

It would also be wise to look into owning your own equipment. Prices vary, and the cost of repairs is usually extra. Although the initial purchase may be exorbitant, owning could be cheaper in the long run.

The cost of long-distance calls can get very expensive. Today, however, there are private communications companies such as MCI that offer long-distance calling at reduced rates. Some systems allow you to pay your bill through a major credit card. If you are going to be making long-distance calls, price a private system against your local phone company cost.

Also, phone numbers should be simple or easy to remember. A number like 692-7350 is probably easier to remember than, say, 692-7351.

Typewriter

Try to buy as good a typewriter as you can afford. The reason, of course, is that the quality of the typewritten word is a reflection on you and your business. A client who pays several hundred or several thousand dollars for a financial plan expects a neat, professional-looking product and not a college paper. I specifically recommend the IBM Selectric or an equivalent model of another manufacturer. If you don't wish to pay cash, most major typewriter vendors have financing plans to extend your payments over time. Depending on the style and model you select, the cost is probably between $1000 and $2000.

Calculator

A calculator to a financial planner is like a glove to a baseball player. It is absolutely essential. A ballplayer would have quite a time trying to catch a hardball with bare hands; similarly, the financial planner would have a most difficult time trying to sort out all the various numbers that come up in the course of a day. Financial planning is a numbers business. The type of client market you deal in dictates how sophisticated your calculator should be. You can choose a cheap digital; a printing calculator; a calculator with business functions, such as compounding, present value, and so on; a programmable calculator; or a VisiCalc program for your computer system. The planner who is just starting out and has not yet clearly defined his or her client market can probably start with a simple printing calculator which costs about $50 to $100 and move up from there. Personally, I prefer the printing calculators because they enable me to verify my numbers for accuracy. Remember, above all, that the numbers you give to your clients will be used to make some of the most important decisions of their lives. These decisions should not be subject to pressing a wrong calculator button. Someone's whole life may be planned around the touch of your finger. Verify!

File Cabinets

Why in the world is there any need to discuss file cabinets? Because, believe it or not, the choice of file cabinets can make quite a difference. Have you ever walked into an office where a wall of dingy gray cabinets made the room feel gloomy and boring? Would you want your clients to think they are in a government office, perhaps a subsidiary of the IRS? Buying file cabinets is not something that should take you 15 seconds to do by quickly calling up your local Sears Catalog Department. Instead, thoughtfully select the quality you need and a color that reflects the rest of your office. Good-quality file cabinets should cost about $100 to $150 apiece, but will save you a lot of aggravation over the cheap ones. You can choose a vertical, lateral, or hanging file system.

Desks

Your desk is your second home, a place where you will be spending a great deal of your time. Very often it acts as neutral territory between your client and you. If you plan on inviting clients to your office, a desk salvaged from the town dump will just not do. My desk serves as both a desk and a conference table. The side facing the client is a conference table, the legs of which are recessed so that the client can sit comfortably without knocking knees against the desk; the side facing me is a desk. Some planners, space permitting, decide not to sit with clients at a desk, but instead use a coffee table and chair (or sofa) arrangement. Still others maintain a completely separate conference room with table and chairs. Although a conference room would be appropriate for the more experienced planner, a new planner may be paying for space used very infrequently.

Chairs

Your livelihood may rest directly on the chairs that you purchase. This might sound funny, but there's truth to it. Purchase uncomfortable chairs and the client will squirm, become restless, and think about leaving your office, not about financial planning. The data-gathering interview can take two, three, or four hours or more. Consider what will happen if your client sits all that time on a skinny folding chair or a cheap vinyl chair that sticks to the skin. What are the chances of getting that client to sit cheerfully through the fact-finding, plan presentation, or implementation session? Impatient clients may very well insist that you bring the plan to their home, or that you mail it. If you work on commission and you are in the conviction stage of the sales presentation, your objective is to convince the client of your product's merit and then move toward a swift close. If your client is sitting there concentrating on a pain in the backside, and not on your presentation, the result could be the loss of that sale and possibly any future sales. And the chances are this client will never come back to your office, not because of you, but because of that back-breaking chair.

The most comfortable seats in my office are the ones meant for my clients to sit on. In fact, many of my clients have voiced displeasure at having to get up off these chairs, which are cushioned, yet firm, and covered with fabric. Generally, the more comfortable the client feels, the smoother the financial planning process will be. I definitely suggest that when purchasing chairs, place yourself in the role of the client. Think comfort, not dollars.

The client is not the only person you must consider when buying chairs for the office. You must also think of yourself and your office staff. Depending on the scope of your practice, you may spend a great deal of your working hours sitting at your desk. During the height of tax season I am generally at my desk some 10 to 16 hours a day. Therefore, in the interest of my comfort, which greatly affects my productivity, I have a chair equally as comfortable as the ones my clients use. As for employees, any physical discomfort can certainly affect work productivity. Be considerate of your workers' comfort.

Bookcases

Most financial planners, as their practices grow, begin to assemble vast collections of texts, reference books, journals, periodicals, etc. In order to conserve space, you could start with a bookcase that's about seven feet high rather than several shorter bookcases. The reason is that as your practice grows, wall space may become precious.

Refrigerator

The process of financial planning may require clients to spend lengthy hours in your office. Therefore, common courtesy and good manners oblige you to offer them a soft drink, beer, or liquor, depending on your style. It is a matter of fact—not opinion—that a glass of wine or a cold beer has done more for my practice than any Madison Avenue public relations firm ever could. *Clients respond to hospitality. Treat them like guests.* Furthermore, if you are going to serve drinks (soft or hard), be considerate of your clients' tastes. If you deal with affluent clients, don't serve "no-frills" soda, cheap beer, wine (vintage last Tuesday), and whiskey no one ever heard of. Take a lesson from the high-quality catering establishments. Serve top-shelf liquor, quality imported and domestic beer, and good wines. Nothing offends clients more than being treated below their station in life. In fact, I make it my policy to treat all my clients (affluent or not) to high-quality products. Many clients, believe it or not, do not always know whether you are doing a good job or a bad job of financial planning, but may actually base their confidence in you on how you treat them.

Unless you have a large office, a big staff, and a separate refreshment facility, you do not need a 6-foot, frost-free, ice-cube-making refrigerator. A little 2-foot box tucked away in the corner of the office is more than adequate. It should cost about $150 to $200.

Coffee Machine

Hot drinks are important, too. A drip machine that makes both coffee and hot water is a nice convenience. You can serve clients coffee, tea, herb tea, espresso (with or without anisette), hot chocolate, and soup. It is only a matter of heating up water if you use an instant product. But the point is, it is not the product that counts. It is the fact that you are offering the product. And that is important. *Hospitality* is the ice breaker. It shouldn't be overlooked.

Copy Machine

A copier is a necessity. Unless, of course, you don't mind running to the public library or drugstore several times a day to make copies, which is impractical, to say the least. However, you need not purchase a large system that sorts and collates. All the small financial planner really needs is a desktop copier. You can purchase a new machine for $1000 to $3000, or a used one for considerably less. A major consideration when purchasing a copier should be the cost of the incidentals, such as paper and toner. Some inexpensive copiers use only chemically treated paper and special toner, amounting to perhaps five cents per copy, whereas other copiers use plain bond paper and cost about a penny per copy or less. Accordingly, the number of copies you will use in a year, as well as the cost per copy, are two very important factors. Another is the price of the service contract. For example, my photocopier, unfortunately, is not cost efficient since I pay about five cents per copy. I estimate that I do about 10,000 copies per year and the service contract is $165 per year. Therefore, my total annual cost is about $665. Many copier salespersons have come to my office claiming they can reduce my cost to less than a penny per copy. "If there was a way, Mr. Rich, that I could cut your copier cost to $100 a year for paper and toner, would you buy a copier from me?" I then ask, "How much does your service contract cost?" Usually, the answer is about $800 for a dry bond copier, which is about eight cents per copy. When purchasing a copy machine, be sure to calculate the cost of the machine after depreciation and investment credit, and to figure the annual cost per copy by factoring in paper, toner, and service.

Answerphone

Do you really need an answerphone? Not necessarily. But you do need something that will serve the same function. The financial planner, like a doctor, must receive messages. Sometimes clients (like patients) have financial ailments and need to reach you quickly to get their proper financial prescription. The reception of timely messages is often critical. Whether a financial planner uses an answering service or an answerphone is really a matter of personal preference. Some clients dislike speaking to a cold-blooded machine; others dislike speaking to snippy operators who cannot assist them anyway. But the point is that some message device, human or otherwise, is absolutely essential to the planner's practice.

Tape Recorder

A tape recorder is a more valuable tool than you may realize and, believe it or not, if used correctly, could turn out to be an essential piece of financial planning equipment. First, it enables you to tape professional seminars and business meetings and to listen to financial planning, sales, and motivational tapes right in your office. It is impossible for a financial planner to read all the professional material that crosses his or her desk; if you can acquire a tape on the subject, especially regarding a current technical topic or practice management subject, listening will save you valuable time and probably enable you to retain more of the subject matter than reading will. Most convenient is a tape recorder that has a built-in cordless microphone, operates on batteries, and is small enough to carry conveniently in your pocket, handbag, or briefcase. It should cost you about $50 to $80 for the type you need.

The tape recorder becomes especially valuable to the modern financial planner during the data-gathering and fact-finding stages of the plan. Here's why. I have recently begun to experiment by taping the client during the data-gathering session. (Of course, I ask my client for permission first.) Doing this has added another dimension to the interview. When I go back over the data-gathering form, I not only read what my client said, I listen, too. It has enabled me to strengthen my understanding of the client's goals and objectives and to understand the client's feelings better—and this, I believe, is the most important part of the financial planning process. If you do not understand your client's feelings, the plan has little chance of being on target. Before I began using the recorder, I would use the data-gathering form, my written notes, and my memory to write the plan. Often, I would have to call up the client to reconfirm what was said. Sometimes it was very difficult because even the client didn't remember. Keep in mind that a skilled financial planner usually catches the client for a few precious minutes or hours when the client's guard is down—when the words flow from the heart, not merely from the mouth. The recorder hears it all and it hears it objectively.

So far my new system has increased both the sensitivity and accuracy of my written cases; it has also decreased case-writing time. I simply turn on the recorder and follow along with the data-gathering form, while listening to the recorded session. As I evaluate the accuracy of the quantitative information, I can also take a fresh look at the various nonquantitative issues by listening for the sensitivity in the client's voice. I listen carefully to the tape in order to pick up on any of the following problems:

1. Do they get highly emotional about a subject?
2. Do they tend to shy away from certain topics, skirt or avoid the question?
3. Are there conflicting answers to similar questions? Do they say one thing in the beginning of the interview and another at the end when they are starting to wear down?

4. Do they seem to be speaking of farfetched dreams rather than realistic goals and objectives?

5. Is there a real difference of opinion between spouses? Is one spouse agreeing with the other only to avoid confrontation? Does one spouse dominate?

6. Are there marital problems? If you do not catch this, the whole plan could be a waste of time.

7. Does there appear to be a question that the clients did not understand? Does their answer seem remote from the question?

8. Did they promise to get back to you with a vital piece of information?

There are many other points that you could be looking for, depending on your particular type of practice and, of course, on your clients. The idea, however, is that the proper use of a tape recorder can increase the accuracy and enhance the quality of your written financial plans manyfold—if you use it creatively, thereby adding a new dimension to the data-gathering session.

YOUR STAFF

The new financial planner, as well as the experienced one, needs responsible clerical support. This is based on the theory that the financial planner should be out generating dollars from financial planning, not sitting in the office filing or typing. This theory has strong economic merit. The financial planner—even the new financial planner—should certainly be billing at a higher rate than that paid for clerical support. Otherwise, you will not be in business very long. A financial planner, for instance, who bills at $50 or $60 an hour or more should be concentrating on financial planning and pay $6 to $10 an hour for good-quality support personnel. If you spend your time doing clerical work instead of financial planning, the cost to you will be the difference between what you could earn as a financial planner and what your clerk earns. You could even factor the cost of your clerical help into your billing rate if you desire. The point is that you must get into the habit of doing financial planning, not filing and typing. Doing your own clerical work will not help you to develop your planning practice to its full potential.

A new bakery recently opened up in my neighborhood. By the time the building structure was modified and new fixtures and equipment installed, my guess is that it cost the owner at least $150,000. Every detail was perfectly planned down to the last crumb—that is, except the hired help. After all this expense, the owner proceeded to hire two

semiconscious, bubble-gum-chewing sales clerks to represent his establishment. Even with all that elaborate preparation, do you think any
customer would keep coming back after getting wrong orders and dis-
courteous service? The point is that he failed to pay the money necessary
for experienced, courteous sales clerks with friendly smiles that say,
"Hi, glad you could come in today. Is there anything we can help you
with?", which translates to, "We value you as a customer." It is just as
important to invest in good-quality help as it is to invest in sound fixtures
and equipment. No one can see the oven in the back of the bakery. So
what if it's used and has a few scratches. But everyone can see that
"smile." The prudent businessperson must spend the money necessary
to invest in a properly placed smile. It's so important.

A financial planner, too, must invest in good-quality help and a
properly placed smile. There are no exclusions to the Human Relations
Act that exempt the financial planner, none whatsoever. The same rules
apply to you that apply to the bakery owner. If you are going to open
an office, if you are going to work 60 or 80 hours a week developing
your practice, you must have the proper backup support. This does not
mean that you need a staff of 300 employees. Just one good part-time
or full-time secretary/receptionist may suffice. Pay the money to get this
employee. But you cannot afford a secretary who answers the phone
like an employee in a muffler shop; types letters with spelling mistakes
and smothered in Ko-Rec-Type; confuses dictation; habitually puts
important documents in the wrong file; erases your original computer
diskette, backup diskette, and master program diskette in a single day;
and then growls at your clients. Pay for a smile. Pay for good-quality
help. A part-time skilled secretary is better than a full-time disaster. And
proceed with caution, please. Some secretaries can be overly efficient.
Yes, they can type 70 words per minute. Yes, they can take steno as
fast as you can dictate, and can edit your letters so that they are suitable
for the *New Yorker* magazine. And yes, they make a delicious cup of
coffee. But what good is all that if every time they answer the phone,
your callers get the third degree, and are forced to recite your Social
Security number, American Express card number, and underwear size
just to get through to you? And heaven forbid if your clients are late
paying your bill. Do you get my simple message? You can pay now for
the quality and the smile, or you can pay through the nose later. It's up
to you.

Earlier in the chapter I discussed the renting of office space. However, the subject deserves further discussion. There is no rule that you
must rent an office by yourself. Many financial planners share space
with fellow planners, while others choose to share space with other
professionals, such as lawyers or accountants. Although the sharing of

office space deprives the financial planner of a certain amount of privacy, it does have some major advantages, such as lower overhead and the integration with other professionals in terms of dual referrals. For the purpose of lowering overhead, new financial planners should consider renting office space in common with other financial planners, while pooling office staff, equipment, and research materials. Publications and professional reference books such as tax guides, estate planning reference books, and investment services can run into thousands of dollars.

Although many financial planners have strong tax backgrounds and are up-to-date on the latest tax law changes, I still feel it would be appropriate at this time to enlighten those financial planners not as well versed in the tax laws and to refresh others. Those who are very knowledgeable should move on to the next chapter.

Under Section 162 of the Internal Revenue Code, the expense for office rental is deductible against the current income. When the financial planner purchases furniture and equipment, the purchases may be depreciated over a five-year useful life under the Accelerated Cost Recovery System as follows: year 1, 15%; year 2, 22%; year 3, 21%; year 4, 21%; year 5, 21%. The Economic Recovery Act of 1981 was originally planned to increase the depreciation schedule in 1985 and again in 1986. However, the Tax Equity and Fiscal Responsibility Bill of 1982 eliminated the 1985 and 1986 increases.

Furthermore, the planner would qualify for an Investment Tax Credit of 10% of the purchase price of the furniture and equipment. Since most planners probably will lose money or break even in the first year of operation, I suggest that the new entrepreneur planner be a sole proprietor, a partner, or a stockholder of a Subchapter S Corporation. The purpose is to pass on the operating losses and the Investment Tax Credit against any other income and the before-credit tax liability. A great many new financial planners (especially fee-only) must have another source of income to survive. Otherwise, if the planner is a regular corporation, the losses and the Investment Tax Credit would be carried against the future income of the corporation. You—the financial planner—must plan your own business strategy, which should include checking with your own advisors such as your accountant and attorney.

Admittedly, many parts of this chapter may seem unnecessary and simplified. Why did I discuss things like coffee machines and photocopiers? Because they *are* important. The intent was not to add filler to the chapter but to bring to light tiny and seemingly trivial details that should not be overlooked. No matter what you decide to do, whether it's to go all the way with Persian rugs, an in-office hot tub, and a champagne cooler, to retain the services of an interior decorator to create a mood with color and style, whether to share an office with other professionals, or to work from a room of your home, your clients must feel comfortable and relaxed and ready to do business with you. In other words, the office is an integral part of your personality, an extension of yourself.

And yes—the office is you.

13

THE THEORY OF PRODUCT
DUE DILIGENCE

John D. MacDonald, in his novel *Condominium*, writes of a beautiful place in the Florida Keys, Golden Sands. This is a paradise where people live out their retirement dreams in marvelous surroundings, plush and serene in the warm Florida sun. But as the novel progresses, the reader begins to discover that Golden Sands may not be all it appears to be. Underneath that magnificent facade lies faulty workmanship and inferior-quality material, leaving the high-rise buildings vulnerable to natural disaster. Then Hurricane Ella advances toward the Keys, and Golden Sands soon crumbles like dust beneath the impact of the furious waves. The use of substandard material and workmanship has been the premise for many other disaster movies and books. In the movie *The Towering Inferno*, faulty electrical wiring was the basis of the suspense. And then, of course, there is real life. Not too long ago at the Hyatt Hotel in Kansas City, Missouri, a floor collapsed, killing scores of people and injuring many others.

Like tangible products—wiring, foundations, bridges, etc.—intangible products can be faulty, too. Although the final disaster may not be as dramatic, the result can be catastrophic nonetheless. Therefore, to avoid selecting a Golden Sands for your clients to build on or retire to, you must first thoroughly check out the material and the workmanship of the product as if you were a structural engineer.

A good financial planner must review all products carefully. The technical term that we use in the trade is "due diligence." Due diligence is analogous to a building inspection or a flight test. There is no argument that it is difficult, time consuming, and you don't get paid for doing it—but it must be done. It is an absolutely essential step that you cannot circumvent if you hope to survive.

If you don't believe there are shams in this world, ask yourself the following question: Why are there people hiding out in Costa Rica? The pages of the *Wall Street Journal* are filled with stories of fraud and mismanagement. Some of the biggest and most influential people in America today have been victims of the most useless financial product garbage and fictitious products ever invented. In some instances, financial service products may have been put together quite honestly with the promoters' most honorable intentions, but the economics or the timing or the whole concept could have been wrong. It is the job of the financial planner to place in a client's financial program the best product(s) available for that particular client's needs. If you put a product in a client's program that is inappropriate, that's as bad as choosing a poor product.

The best teacher of product due diligence, beyond a doubt, is experience. If you work with a product long enough you will begin to feel either comfortable or uncomfortable with that product. Although all the products that you use and/or recommend must be investigated (fee-only planners, although they only make recommendations, are just as responsible for due diligence, perhaps more so), the concentration of your effort must be on the products that you use most frequently and in which you place a heavy concentration of client funds.

If you lack experience in this area, the chances are you will get burned along the way. Most new financial planners lack experience. Somewhere along the way your judgment will go wrong and you are bound to make a mistake. The point is that once you do make a mistake, you must take your licks, cleanse your wounds, and vow never to make that mistake again. Mistakes are a part of life, and you must learn from them or else you are bound to make the same mistake again and again. Let's take a look at product due diligence and see how it works with some of the various products that you might select for your clients. Obviously, not all products are included. However, I have chosen what I feel the small financial planning practitioner is apt to encounter the most.

LIFE INSURANCE AND HEALTH INSURANCE

Since life insurance companies are state regulated, there is little that you have to do to check them out. To review an insurance company's financial condition, you simply obtain an analysis and rating report from A.M. Best Company, Oldwick, NJ 08858.

The A.M. Best rating is based on an analysis of the financial condition and operating performance of an insurance company. The ratings are classified in five gradations:

A+ and A   Excellent
B+   Very good
B   Good
C+   Fairly good
C   Fair

The rating reflects strengths and weaknesses in four areas: (1) competent underwriting; (2) control of expenses; (3) adequate reserves; and (4) sound investments.

The Best Report gives a synopsis of the history, management, operations, operating comments, officers, directors, and states in which the firm may write business. In order to obtain information regarding all insurance companies you can acquire the annual edition of Best's Insurance Reports.

In a great many states, the death benefit and/or cash reserves in a life insurance policy are guaranteed by a state insurance pool. You must completely understand the insurance laws in your state.

The main emphasis of product due diligence is the selection of a superior product for your client's financial program. If you represent an insurance company whose life insurance or disability income product is inferior to the majority of products on the market, your reputation as a planner could be put on the line. Since life insurance and disability income commissions may represent only a small percentage of your income, risking the loss of a client over use of an inferior product is foolish. It is highly suggested that you offer your clients a superior low-cost term product; a superior whole-life, variable-life, or universal-life product in terms of cost and cash values; and a superior disability income product. Review as many products as you can and remember that you can be flexible enough to use as many products and companies as you like. The planner's organizational relationship with life insurance companies is covered in a later chapter.

STOCKS AND BONDS

All stocks are not the same, and prices will go up and down depending on a variety of factors. Because of this, many financial planners shy away from recommending a particular stock. Today, with the array and diversity of mutual funds to choose from, it is very easy for a financial planner to be highly successful while avoiding the stock market altogether. In fact, some of the most skilled money managers operate entirely within the mutual fund world. The moral is that if you don't feel comfortable selecting individual equities for your clients—and you well may not—stay out of this market.

Financial planners who select and/or recommend stocks and bonds for their clients must base these selections on each individual client's goal and objectives. Information regarding those securities listed on the New York Stock Exchange, American Stock Exchange, or any other exchange is readily available and information regarding most over-the-counter stocks can also be obtained easily. You can obtain Standard & Poor's reports, Value Line reports, 10K's, annual reports, or interim statements. Financial planners should not be encouraging clients to buy stocks on the basis of tips, heresay, or speculation.

Bonds, which are more conservative than stocks, are easier to research., Obviously, most U.S. government securities need little research; however, other government obligations, such as certain state agencies and municipalities, may require a considerable amount of investigation. So, too, will corporations, in regard to their long-term debt and short-term paper. Most information can be easily obtained from Standard & Poor's and Moody's. Financial planners must be able to judge whether the risk involved in purchasing a second-grade obligation for a client is worth the few extra percentage points that the obligation will yield.

MUTUAL FUNDS

Mutual funds are the bread and butter of the financial planner. Again, whether you sell or whether you simply recommend, the selection process should be the same. You are seeking a product that both meets the client's objectives and, in your opinion, has demonstrated or appears to demonstrate superior performance. Information about a fund can be obtained from the fund itself via the prospectus, quarterly and annual reports issued by the fund, from Standard & Poor's (if a closed-end fund), *The Annual Weisenberger's Investment Companies, United Mutual Fund Selector, Fundscope Magazine, Johnson's Charts,* and the annual mutual fund issue of *Forbes,* to mention a few. The sources of mutual fund information are abundant.

Keep in mind that not only is product selection critical, but you must also match the investment objectives of the fund (as specified in the prospectus) with the investment objective of the client. Furthermore, the financial planner must understand how to evaluate the track record of a fund over a period of time, how and when capital gains and income dividends are distributed, and the concept of beta, which is the degree of a fund's risk relative to that of the entire market.

TAX SHELTERS

The sale and/or recommendation of tax shelters requires considerable due diligence on the part of the financial planner, especially in regard to private placements of limited partnerships. Even the public placements of venture products, such as real estate, oil and gas, equipment leasing, and so on, will require a lot more investigation on the part of the financial planner than will standard security products like stocks, bonds, and mutual funds. Just pick up the *Wall Street Journal* and read the "Who Got Indicted Today" column. Although this isn't an actual column, I'm sure that it could be, considering the volume of fraud cases. And those are just the big cases—the little ones you never hear about.

After reading through some of the articles dealing with fraud, it quickly becomes clear that the majority of fraud committed centers around tax shelters. Why? Because most people will do just about anything either to (1) get rich quick or (2) save taxes. And most tax shelters offer a combination of both.

As a smart financial planner, you should never rely on someone else to perform your due diligence. Even if you are acting in the capacity of a registered representative of a broker-dealer firm, the broker-dealer is responsible for the product due diligence. My advice is to go as far as you feel you must to check out the venture. Not only do your clients deserve this protection, but so do you. All your client knows is that you have sold and/or recommended a product to that client; your client does not want explanations as to why the general partner vacated his office in Salt Lake City without leaving a trace of himself, his staff, the proposed venture, or the partnership funds.

One of the first rules that I can give you is this: If you don't feel comfortable or confident in the area of tax shelters or with the projects in particular, stay away from them. Don't feel pressured if clients insist that you put them into tax shelter projects. Clients feel secure with a financial planner who is honest with them, and who will admit to not knowing enough about the area in general or not being familiar with the deals on the market. Take your time and learn the area correctly. It doesn't make sense to be in a hurry to put your client into a bad deal.

The first place, I feel, that a financial planner must begin the due diligence process is with the economics of the investment. The offering, whether oil or gas, real estate, leasing, breeding, and so on, must have economic merit. I tell my clients that the objective of any tax shelter venture is to make money, not to save on taxes. It does not take very much to put a losing venture together, but it takes a lot of hard work, skill, expertise, and patience to create a winner. After you have analyzed a venture that lacks economic merit, or does not meet your particular requirements, toss it into the nearest trash can.

A project without economic merit is like a movie without a plot. If the project has good economic merit, the next step is to check out the cast of characters and the stage setting. Who are the general partners? What experience do they have? What do other financial planners, attorneys, and accountants know about them? Is there a track record? Is there a criminal record? Does the reason for their taking on the project make sense? Ask them questions. Put them on the spot! After you are totally satisfied with their existence, credibility, and intent, take the numbers apart. Tax shelter projections are sometimes so incredible as to defy imagination. Establish your own parameters of what you think will happen and factor in your numbers. Today, with a microcomputer and a VisiCalc program you can analyze anything you want within seconds and change any of the variables whenever you want.

Look for the fine points. If you are analyzing an oil drilling project, for instance, and there are 10 wells in the area averaging 20 barrels of oil per day, why is the promoter projecting 30 barrels of oil per day? Does the offering speak of initial production or average production per well? This is very important because a well could have an initial production of 100 barrels of oil per day but actually drop off to 15 barrels of oil per day within a few weeks or months. Find out how the wells have done historically. What is the longevity of wells in that area? Furthermore, what is the projected price of oil? Is it projected to be increasing or declining? What is the decline curve of the wells? In real estate, is the land and/or structure being purchased at a realistic and fair price?

When you are satisfied that the numbers are realistic, the final step is to satisfy yourself as to the legitimacy of the tax consequences and the validity of the projected tax savings. Be sure to include *minimum* tax consequences. If a client is in a 50% tax bracket and has a $20,000 tax write-off, the chances are that the minimum tax will enter the picture somewhere along the line. The fact is that the client has to pay back 20% as an alternative minimum tax after exemptions under TEFRA (the Tax Equity and Fiscal Responsibility Act of 1982) for federal taxes, and perhaps a certain percentage back for state minimum tax too. *Minimum tax should not be overlooked.* A great many tax shelter promoters show their projections without regard to the minimum tax. Beware! The client's tax savings is only as good as the real tax savings and not the imagined tax savings, as calculated by many inexperienced financial planners.

Also remember that just because the deal comes in a glossy cover does not mean it's good. Public deals—the mass-marketed projects—are not necessarily better than small private placements. Nor, on the other hand, are they necessarily worse. Each partnership—public or private—should stand on its own and should be evaluated on its own merits. In fact, the NASD singles out direct participation programs (tax shelters are included) for special due diligence treatment. The NASD Due Diligence Guidelines are:

> Investigation of whether the basic economic merit of the proposed undertaking and the results of prior activities have been adequately and meaningfully disclosed
>
> Review of applicable partnership agreements for basics of legal adequacy and tax advantages
>
> Random physical inspections of properties, plant, and equipment of the sponsor and any affiliates offering services to the program
>
> Review of the financial stability, reputation within the industry, and other available information on the sponsor's background, qualifications, and experience
>
> Examination of the program for conflicts, risk factors, proposed activities, and financial status
>
> Examination of records submitted by appraisers, engineers, and financial consultants
>
> Examination of items of compensation, having an understanding of true compensation, with emphasis on disclosure of all forms of compensation
>
> Study of all tax aspects of the program to determine whether there is a reasonable basis for assuming the benefits are likely to occur
>
> Examination of experience of management and technical staff in operations and handling of funds. Likewise, examination should be made of the management projects or services offered to the program

But let's be realistic. In order for the financial planner to follow the NASD Guidelines to the letter, it would cost him or her a great deal of time and money. Sometimes this process can be shortened by using a service that analyzes tax-sheltered investments. There are several on the market which evaluate both public and private oil and gas limited partnerships. It is the private placements that are toughest, since there may be no alternative but to take a trip. And even if you do take a trip, you have to know what to look for when you get there.

The fact remains, however, that public or private, you must know with whom you are dealing.

DIAMONDS AND COLORED STONES

During 1980 and 1981 the financial planning trade magazines were filled with advertisements by diamond and colored stone firms offering gemstones with all sorts of unique and innovative programs, from guaranteed repurchase to diamonds with liquidity and diamond account books. And then what happened? Interest rates soared, forcing firms that held diamond inventories to feel the pressure, and buyers to drift to other markets seeking better investments. Also, the Australian diamond find did not help decrease supply, DeBeer's support was limited, and diamond prices nose-dived. What happened to all these firms? The majority drifted into obscurity, leaving sales reps, financial planners, and investors in the dark.

The straw that broke the camel's back was the bankruptcy of International Diamond Corporation in the spring of 1982. This bankruptcy set off a wave of liquidations in other firms, driving them into bankruptcy as well. And in some cases the firm and the principals just disappeared from the face of the earth. Many millions of dollars of clients' monies were lost because financial planners did not go far enough to investigate the backgrounds of the firm's principals, the potential for a secondary market, or the probability of an ultimate consumer.

I have learned from firsthand experience how volatile and unpredictable the diamond market can be. After using one of these liquidation firms and paying top dollar for the liquidation guarantee, I quickly reversed my position, sold out the bulk of the stones (fortunately at no loss to the client), and paid back my commissions. I then came to this conclusion, which I hold to this day: If you are going to buy stones, then purchase the stone—no frills attached—at the lowest possible price. You *must* go under the assumption that when you liquidate stones you will have to enter the market as a seller rather than rely on a guaranteed buyback by the original seller, who stands a great probability of not being around when you go to sell the stone. I suggest also that if you plan to work in this market, you take the Gemological Institute of America (GIA) Diamonds course.

A financial planner who enters the stones market must understand the mechanics of diamond color; clarity and proportion grading; the differences between the recognized gemological laboratory and foreign laboratory and domestic laboratory certificates (a diamond graded in Antwerp or Brussels may earn a much lower grade here in the United States even by the same lab); and laboratory acceptances within the diamond trade. The planner should also establish local advisory sources with which to work. My advice is to stay out of this market until you understand what you are doing—if ever.

The due diligence of the diamond market requires a great deal of care on your part. The most important thing you can do is to establish knowledgeable and reliable contacts. Closely examine the firms with which you will be doing business and concentrate your due diligence effort on these. First and foremost, examine the past history of the firm and the past history of the principals. Have the principals been in and out of the diamond business during the past several years? Ask for references. An honest person will not be afraid to open up to you. If you are considering a large purchase on behalf of your client, it might pay to drop in on the diamond vendor. And why announce that you are coming? Catch the firm in the act of doing what it really does. I once spoke to the principal of a diamond firm on the phone and was led to believe that he had a large-to-medium-size company at a posh New York East Side address. While in Manhattan one day to teach a class at New York University, I decided to stop by and see for myself. Well, the firm turned out to be the principal and his administrative assistant subletting from an accounting firm. Needless to say, the firm no longer exists. If you carefully check out some of the principals of diamond firms, you will discover long track records of deceit, and in some cases outright fraud. The effort of your due diligence should be aimed at seeking out the diamond firms with untarnished records. And don't forget to ask other financial planners for opinions and recommendations. What they say is usually very meaningful.

Once you are satisfied with the credibility of a diamond or stone firm, compare prices and stone specifications. Compare apples with apples. Avoid high-price liquidation programs. Look to see that the stones have been certified by GIA (Gemological Institute of America), EGL (European Gemological Laboratory), or IGI (International Gemological Institute). Colored stones can be certified through the GIA or the AGL (American Gemological Laboratory). Avoid any stones that are graded by foreign laboratories. Should a merchant wish to sell you a foreign-graded stone, have that stone recertified here in the United States. You will be very surprised at the difference in grading. And make sure that the stone your client receives comes sealed directly by the lab.

The financial planner should be aware of the firms with high hype; firms with massive mailings of sales literature; firms that show up at financial planner expositions, uncrate the elephants as if the circus has come to town, and wine and dine every planner to the hilt. Do you know who'll be paying for the caviar, lobster, and champagne? Your client!

In the fall of 1981 I received in the mail two tapes from a now-Chapter 11 diamond firm, demonstrating the extremes of sales hype; one tape was labeled "The Investment Diamond Market" and the other,

"The Investment Diamond Sale." In the first tape the president of the firm and three vice presidents are chatting about the great things that are happening to them: (1) they have just been joined by a company in Maryland that has 70 representatives in four states; (2) they have just opened a subsidiary corporation in Caracas, Venezuela; (3) their diamond liquity warranty is available in five languages; and (4) by the year's end the firm's president is confident that they will have sales representation in the Netherlands, Switzerland, Germany, Austria, France, and Spain. Furthermore, their business is up 46% over last year due to their program of liquidity. "Our business has been really quite good," and as a result the firm is able to raise its prices in a diamond market that is down 20 to 30%. Since July 1980, the firm's prices are up almost 48% and the current annual rate of appreciation is 26%, which is 1½ times the yield one can get in a money market fund. And one of the vice presidents, who had (just by coincidence) moved over to this firm a few weeks ago from a competitor, said he feels that the program is doing what nobody else has been able to do, which is to make their clients a profit. And all this in a declining market.

The second tape was even better.

It was a dramatization of an investment diamond sale, stressing how the company would buy back the client's diamond at 90% of the current market price; it described how the company makes its own market in diamonds, holding prices firm in declining diamond markets. The company then claimed to have "brought the sophistication of Wall Street to the diamond business, averaging four price increases per year, 6% per quarter for its customers and insulating their investors from the down moves that normally occur in the world diamond market every five or six years. In effect, the firm carries the investor along until the world diamond market returns to normal." The tape closes with the sales rep closing the sale and the investor saying that if the sales rep is wrong, "I'll eat his heart out." The sales rep comes back with, "Don't worry—they have the best program available."

On June 16, 1982, the script of the "best program available" was played under Chapter 11 of the U.S. Bankruptcy Code as the little investors watched the diamonds—for which they had paid almost double the fair market price—depreciate to about a quarter to a third of the liquidity price. Why am I singling out one firm to chastise? I'm not. That firm is typical of the high-hype, high-commission, "wine and dine" companies that have saturated the diamond market whenever the inflationary spiral begins to rise. And there will be more. Just wait! In fact, many of the same cast of characters will be back under different names, different corporations, different versions of the same scam. And there is only one way to stop them. Due diligence!

Anybody in the trade will sell you a diamond, but not everyone will buy it back. In order for a diamond firm to buy back a diamond, they must have an expectation to sell it in the near future at a higher price than they paid. Otherwise, if they have to hold the diamond for any length of time, they will buy it back only at a super attractive price. It is like any other market—the law of supply and demand dictates. Accordingly, the most any reputable firm will do is to guarantee that they will try their best to sell the diamond on a "best efforts" basis. You are almost always guaranteed a buyer, no matter how badly the market is depressed, but the price that your client receives may be a lot less than desired. Nobody can guarantee to buy back your client's stone at more than the market price unless they are in the business of taking losses. Would you pay a dollar for forty cents? I wouldn't! No reputable firm could or would either.

All the factors that apply to diamonds also apply to colored stones, except that (1) colored stones are probably harder to understand and (2) the markups in stones are a lot greater than in diamonds. In fact, I have heard from dealers that colored stones can be marked up as high as 400% and still remain competitive. Once again, it is essential that the financial planner find a trusting source when dealing in either colored stones or diamonds.

RARE COINS

Rare coins can be a very exciting investment for your clients. However, a great degree of skill and expertise is needed to select the proper investment material for the client, and also to ensure the quality of the purchase.

If anyone has earned the right to comment on numismatics it is certainly Donald H. Kagin, who holds a Bachelor of Arts Degree in Numismatics from Northwestern University and a doctorate (the first ever earned in numismatics in the United States) from the Union Graduate School in Cincinnati, Ohio. Kagin is the author of the award-winning book, *Private Gold Coins and Patterns of the United States*, published by Arco. He is also a regular columnist for *Coin World*, the largest numismatic trade paper, and he has written articles and has been quoted in numerous magazines and newspapers. He has appeared on radio and television, including ABC-TV's "Good Morning America," CBS's "700 Club," "PM Magazine," "The Joe Franklin Show," and the "NBC-TV News."

It is Don's opinion that the financial planner must go all the way in performing due diligence, especially when dealing with any hard asset, such as rare coins, stones, diamonds, and so on. About 60% of the hard-asset firms that operated in 1979, 1980, and 1981 are no longer around. The best way to really help your client is to be an informed financial planner. "Learn as much as you can to feel comfortable with the numismatics market. You will do a better job for yourself and for your client. Numismatic education is very important if you are going to deal in coins."

According to Kagin, numismatics is not for everyone, and planners must realize that coins are a long-term asset. In itself the market is very simple: Supply, demand, and conditions cause the prices of rare coins to change. In other words, the price is determined only by what a buyer is willing to pay for a coin through a dealer or a coin auction. Depending, of course, on market conditions it could take months to liquidate the investor's coins at the true market value. The key, obviously, is to match a willing buyer with the coins offered for sale.

Coins are not a short-term fad, and financial planners are cautioned that the short-term investor does not belong in this market. The difference between wholesale and retail can be 20% or more for low-ticket items, and the client will have to make up the difference through the appreciation of the coin material. The investor should hold onto the portfolio for at least three to five years. In a downward-moving coin market, the dealer's profit spread tends to be larger, since the dealer takes more of a risk of holding onto the material for a longer period of time; in an upward market, due to greater demand, the dealer's profit spread is smaller, since there is less risk of holding coin inventories during periods of greater demand. Furthermore, the rare coin market, like most other investment markets, moves in cycles. There are peaks and there are valleys, and there is always the risk that the investor will buy the right coin at the wrong time. If the client purchases a coin at the cycle peak, there is the possibility that the investor will have to wait about five years to realize satisfactory profits. Coins, historically, do not perform well during periods of prolonged recessions. It is therefore essential that the financial planner always stay informed of the conditions in the coin market.

"The most important step is due diligence," according to Kagin. "Unless the portfolio comes with a money-back grading guarantee, you cannot be certain that you are receiving properly graded coins. There is some subjectivity regarding grading, and the numismatic investment firm should be willing to either buy back the coins or put them in an auction, at the same grade that they were sold to your client." To ensure grading standards, the American Numismatic Association Certification Service in Colorado Springs has an independent coin-grading laboratory, where a coin can be graded and guaranteed that it meets or exceeds the ANA grading standards, or the client can get his or her money back.

But grading rare coins and making sure that the dealer's price is competitive are only part of the financial planner's due diligence responsibility. In my judgment a rare coin firm is no different from a diamond or colored stone firm or a tax shelter promoter. The due diligence parameters are the same. You must check to see exactly with whom you are doing business. How long has the firm been operating? What is the background of the principals in regard to professional experience? Are the principals primarily numismatists or were they in the oil business last year and the art business the year before that? If they were, the chances are good to excellent that next year they will be in the diamond business or the travel business, and your client will be left holding a bag full of misgraded coins. According to Kagin, you should ask the firm for a due diligence fact sheet stating the history, track record, and credentials of the principals as well as background and references. Next, do your homework—check out all the facts they have given you to be sure that the firm and its principals are everything they claim to be. And don't forget to check with the American Numismatic Association. A quality reputation is the most important asset that a firm can have. To ensure proper due diligence, financial planners must learn as much about the firm as possible.

"The financial planner should be very wary of freebies, very high commission rates, layer upon layer of commissions, regional directors, state directors, district directors, overrides on overrides. It is the client who ends up paying for it," Kagin says.

Every financial planner who deals or plans to deal in the coin market is advised to obtain the *ANA Grading Standards for United States Coins,* published for the American Numismatic Association, Colorado Springs, CO 80901. This handbook contains not only the grading standards for all U.S. coins but also information on investor due diligence, handling, storage and treatment of rare coins, and an appendix listing most numismatic firms.

Unless you have a deep enthusiasm for rare coins, the chances are good that you will not become a numismatist. If this is the case, you should try to develop a business relationship with a numismatist and/or dealer who is knowledgeable and is worthy of your trust and confidence.

OTHER TANGIBLES

The same rules that hold true for diamonds, colored stones, and rare coins also hold true for any other tangibles that you may sell or recommend. You certainly must know what you are doing, or at least have sources available whom you trust implicitly and who can perform your product due diligence. For the most part, diamonds, rare coins, stamps,

art, antiques, collectibles, gold, silver, and gems are inflationary investments that have shown substantial appreciation in periods of high inflation. With certain tangibles where quality plays a major part, it appears
that top-quality investments such as MS-65 coins versus AU-50 coins,
or DIF diamonds versus EVS2 diamonds, have appreciated at rates faster
than the norm for the investment. Therefore, your sources are absolutely
essential to proper due diligence. In fact, it may not be such a foolish
idea to check the tangible out with two or three sources before making
a purchase.

This chapter was written to provide the financial planner with an
overview of due diligence, not to teach due diligence—experience will
do that. Furthermore, I have spent considerably more time on diamonds,
colored stones, and coins than would appear necessary. However, I
believe that the new financial planner is more vulnerable to these markets than any other. They are unregulated glamor markets.

When you first start out in a practice, the products come fast and
furious and everything may seem overwhelming. Due diligence, accordingly, could take up a vast amount of your time. But it is not a short-term
benefit; it is a long-term necessity. And you have no choice. As a financial planner you cannot afford to recommend or sell bad products that
could destroy your reputation—your most precious asset. Proper due
diligence is essential to your longevity and survival as a financial planner. Do not take it lightly.

14

TECHNIQUES FOR SUCCESS

Many of the preceding chapters have dealt with your client's goals and objectives. Hopefully, you have understood that I have stressed this topic because of its critical importance to both your success and your client's future. Goals and objectives are so personal and important that sometimes your clients may have great difficulty expressing them to you. In fact, for a lot of people this may be harder than divulging their personal finances. A financial planner must therefore learn to become a skillful listener and a master at extracting qualitative information from the client. As the years go by and personal financial planning becomes more and more fundamental to the American way of life, financial planners will place an increasingly important role on courses in psychology, and on listening and counseling techniques.

The success or failure of a financial plan depends on whether the financial planner can ask the right questions and extract honest answers from the client. Yet the financial planner must also show sensitivity, take command of the situation in a guiding but not overbearing manner, and be a total professional from start to finish. The long-term retention of your client is often based not on the plan that you present, but on the manner in which you present it. Your clients' goals and objectives are sacrosanct to them. If you treat them lightly, your clients will treat you lightly; if you treat them with concern and respect, the chances are that your clients will view you as a very special person indeed.

Since we have already discussed the client in great detail, let me now ask you this: What are *your* goals and objectives? Are you a little surprised by this question? Well, don't be. The financial planner must have goals and objectives, too. What are your plans? How are you going to achieve them? You certainly cannot expect to solve other people's problems until you have some direction of your own.

The first goal for most financial planners—if you have not accomplished this already—is the transition from the world of working for others to the world of working for yourself. And, believe me, these are entirely different worlds. But the move obviously has to be made if you are determined to be on your own. It is unfortunate that a great many planners who read this book will never make that move. For one reason or another they will think about making the break, week after week, month after month, year after year. The excuses will multiply and they will override all the best reasons for making that break. You must face the fact that you will either do it or you won't. Don't allow yourself to drift through life in a cloud of uncertainty. Make the decision, one way or another. Only you can decide.

Although setting this goal as your top priority is certainly difficult to do, working to achieve it is even harder. And I cannot promise you will be successful, either. Simply being out on your own does not, by any means, guarantee success—but it should guarantee self-satisfaction. At least you won't be one of the millions of people who go through life regretful that they did not try to make it on their own. Before you can achieve a successful end result, you will have to bear the agony, frustration, and hard work that self-employment demands. You may decide to turn back when the sea becomes choppy, or you may continue through the storm in search of calmer waters. But at least you will be able to say that you have made an attempt to turn your goals and objectives (and dreams) into reality. As your practice begins to grow and develop you might keep the following ideas in mind. They have helped me immensely and I hope that they will help you in your development.

GET IDEAS FROM OTHERS

One of the nicest things about the financial planning business is that there is no standard way to set up your practice, as long as you stay within legal and ethical guidelines. Perhaps a few years from now your firm will even be a model for other aspiring planners. But for now, the firm you set up will not be a model from a financial planning textbook, only a product of your own imagination and creativity. From the time you begin it could take years before you are satisfied with what you have created—that is, if you are ever satisfied. And if you are like most people, your own creativity can only go so far. Quite often, you will need the help of others in one way or another.

Remember how in grade school they used to call out "Copycat!" if someone copied from another kid? Well, admit it, sometimes the other kid's ideas made a lot more sense than yours. People, by their very nature, love to copy, When I was a kid every shirt I owned had the number 7 somewhere on it, and when I ran through the grass chasing fly balls I was not Andrew Rich, but Mickey Mantle, the Yankee center-fielder. I even learned to switch hit. Whatever Mickey did, I had to do it, too. Do you ever imitate a famous singer or a movie star? Rich Little, the impressionist, has made a handsome living out of doing just that. Certainly, you have seen impressions of Tom Jones, W. C. Fields, and Mae West. Everyone, amateur or professional, does them. Do not be afraid to copy ideas from other planners. It is not sinful; it is not immoral; it simply makes good business sense, especially if the idea can help you grow or can help you financially.

Since in the financial planning business, experience is as important as textbook theory (if not more so), getting working ideas from others is crucial. Many of your most important dollar-producing ideas will surface while enjoying a cold beer or a cocktail with a professional associate. In fact, one of the most important discussions in my life occurred in May 1981 over breakfast at the Annual Conferment of the College for Financial Planning at the Sheraton DenverTech Center. It began at about a quarter to eight in the morning, a time when I have enough difficulty functioning with life, let alone partaking in heavy discussion. As I sat toying with my sausage and eggs, unsure whether to pour the cream or the orange juice into my coffee, the financial planner I was with, Nelson Kjos, CFP, asked me what I had meant the other day when I mentioned that I was hesitant about managing money. In my best morning mumble I explained that what I feared most was the tremendous responsibility and the difficulty with SEC mechanics. Then Nelson, a highly respected and successful money manager, whom I will introduce in a later chapter, began to speak, suddenly waking me as if I just plunged into the chilly Sheraton pool. He explained how he began his business, working his way from sales to fees, and how he was currently set up. Then he talked about the type of clients he handled, how he charged fees, and some of the problems that I could expect with money management clients. He also suggested that I at least give it a try. If I hated money management, I could always dump it. Since I knew I had just heard some of the most valuable advice in my life, I felt compelled to pay for breakfast. And Nelson didn't argue over that. The conversation continued again at lunch, later in the whirlpool, at the cocktail reception, the banquet, and at the bar. By 3 A.M. I had completed a graduate seminar in money management practice development. And, yes, I will admit that many of my procedures are modeled after those of Nelson Kjos. When someone has something to say, I listen, I get ideas. Especially if someone is saying, "I do it this way and it works for me." So what if I'm a copycat! In fact, don't major firms copy from others?

The beauty of the financial planning business is that other planners do not usually treat you as a competitor. It is not, by any means, a secretive profession. Most planners, in fact, are eager to talk to you about themselves, their accomplishments, the way that they write their financial plans, the products they sell, the way they get their clients, and which computer systems they use or have seen. All you have to do is ask. Planners on the whole, like to talk—especially about themselves. But that's not unusual. Dale Carnegie in his great book, *How to Win Friends and Influence People*, stresses the point that people love to talk about themselves.

Since conversation is free, it is certainly one of the best reference tools imaginable. All that you have to do is be prepared to reciprocate with conversation of your own. Besides, talking about your own practice is fun, stimulating, and ego building. And what *you* might say to another planner (seasoned or not) could help that person as much as that person has helped you. I find that the best places to stimulate practice and idea discussions are educational training sessions. There are many organizations that offer these sessions: the IAFP offers them nationally and at the local chapter level; the College for Financial Planning and the Institute of Certified Financial Planners offer excellent programs; and there are a host of other programs for people who might specialize in or wish to enhance their knowledge of a particular discipline, such as life insurance, pensions, investments, and so on. The list is endless. The objective is to broaden your horizons through both formal training and informal conversation. A formal setting is not always needed. Anywhere there are other planners really works—a bar, a restaurant, a car, a plane . . . anywhere. The point is that *you must* associate yourself with other planners as much as you can. Merge yourself into their conversations, tactfully, of course, and listen.

In our business the financial planner with "big ears" has a definite advantage. So reach into your supply of Q-Tips, swab your ears thoroughly, and start listening for profound words and novel ideas. Sometimes you can simply overhear a great idea in a discussion between other financial planners. And I suggest you carry a little notebook with you at all times. You will never know when a great idea will come along, and I certainly wouldn't trust it entirely to memory. Do not be concerned that the idea was not intended for you to hear personally. The fact is that you heard the idea, jotted it down for future use; that's all that counts. At other times, you might wish to ask someone a few questions directly. It is a nice gesture to offer to buy that person a drink, lunch, or even dinner in exchange for his or her ideas. The small investment, tax deductible, is certainly well worth it.

Another way for you to get ideas is by reading publications on all different levels. For instance, you might get an idea or two from a local newspaper that runs a feature on a financial planner or on several planners, or has a column written by a financial planner. You might even get ideas from planners who market through local advertising in newspapers, in magazines, or on radio and television. An even better way to develop ideas is to collect the advertising brochures (or Form ADV, Part II) of other planners. Most planners, if you explain that you are just starting out, will not only be glad to give you a copy, but will probably answer any questions that you have—and may even offer to help you write your ADV, Part II. There are also the professional journals and trade magazines. Each particular discipline has its own special publications. For example, if you are seeking a life insurance idea, you might try *Life Association News*, which is the official publication of NALU, the National Association of Life Underwriters, or *Life Insurance Selling*, published by Commerce Publishing, St. Louis, Missouri; these particular publications contain some interesting articles regarding insurance practice management techniques. However, at this time the best overall publication for finding ideas is *The Financial Planner* magazine, published monthly by the International Association for Financial Planning. This publication usually has several good practice management articles in each issue, and on occasion has devoted a good portion of its issue to practice management techniques. You can even pick up a general investor publication such as *Money Magazine* and get some great ideas about how other professionals manage money. The April 1981 issue featured the techniques and practices of eight of the best money managers in America, and the April 1982 issue profiled eight outstanding financial planners and their practices, including Mark McCormick of Cleveland, Ohio; Gary Pittsford of Anderson, Indiana; Alexander Armstrong of Washington, DC; Donald Wright of Philadelphia, Pennsylvania; Harold Gourges of Atlanta, Georgia; Beverly Tanner of Larkspur, California; and David Bridgforth and Eugene Duff of San Antonio, Texas. What you must keep in mind is that a great (and perhaps profitable) idea can come from just about anything you read. In fact, a great idea can even come from a note or letter that a client or potential client has sent you, suggesting that you do something you are not already doing or that you change something you are doing. Therefore, always accept criticism as a learning tool, not as an insult.

A great many financial planners will find that their automobile becomes a second home. You will need it to commute, visit clients, meet with associates and product promoters, and so on. Do not underestimate the amount of time that you will be spending on the road. However, you could put that time to productive use. Let me ask you: What do you do when you're driving in your car? Do you think? Do you curse at the traffic? Do you listen to the radio? Let me tell you what I do. When I'm not relaxing by listening to music, I listen to financial planning tapes. My suggestion is that if you do not already own one, invest in an automobile cassette player. Then, when you're not listening to Barbra Streisand or Merle Haggard, listen to what other financial planners have to say, to improve your knowledge and productivity. It makes sense. You can purchase some excellent educational and practice management technique tapes from the International Association for Financial Planning, the College for Financial Planning, the Institute of Certified Financial Planners, and Commerce Clearing House (CCH), to mention just a few sources. Certainly, most professional societies as well as a great many publishing houses market educational tapes. I also suggest motivational tapes. And soon video tapes complete with graphics and pictures will be at our disposal. I really wouldn't recommend video tapes for the car though, unless, of course, you become successful enough to hire a chauffeur. You never know!

Most of the organizations that I have mentioned above also offer seminars in practice management on the local and national level. The advantage of a seminar, of course, is that the instructor is right there to answer questions and to clarify points of information. Even some of the larger financial planning firms have set up separate corporations and divisions to offer practice management training. It is a growing concept, and the more persons that enter the financial planning profession, the bigger it will get. Most practitioners, experienced or not, are eager to learn new and better methods in which to conduct their practices. The range of seminars and imaginative topics expands manyfold each year. Unfortunately, a great many of the better seminars may not be given near your home and could be quite costly to attend, considering seminar fees, transportation costs, and meals and lodging. You must, therefore, select your seminars wisely, limiting them to those most relevant to your practice. You certainly cannot attend every seminar, nor should you want to, since attending too many would overwhelm you and take up much of your time. But keep in mind that attending professional seminars, like going to college, is an investment in your future. You might not see immediate results, but in the long run, I assure you, it will pay off.

STAY WITHIN YOUR CAPABILITY

Whether brand new or experienced, the financial planner must know where to draw the line when it comes to undertaking services and marketing products. It may be difficult to turn away business, but there are times when it may be wise to do just that. Don't practice over your head—it's too dangerous. If you make a serious error or miscalculation in a client's financial program, it could cause extreme problems later for both you and your client, especially if your client is out a lot of money and you find yourself in need of a good lawyer. Making serious errors can be as easy as pressing the wrong computer button, misinterpreting a ruling, or taking too long to process paperwork. Keep that in mind. It is easy to make errors, and hard to avoid them.

Taxation is one area where financial planners have the tendency to practice without being fully qualified. You will have to be extremely proficient in taxation if you are going to practice it. A tax error can be quite disastrous, costing the client thousands, tens of thousands, or hundreds of thousands of dollars. There are numerous provisions of the Internal Revenue Code that allow your client to make a one-time irrevocable election; there are other sections that involve statutes of limitations and penalty provisions for timely filing. There are further sections dealing with preparer penalties. Due to tax law intricacies, most CPAs, accountants, tax consultants, and tax lawyers carry plenty of malpractice insurance to hedge against the possibility of giving poor advice. Skilled as they may be, they know they are capable of making errors. They are human!

A bad experience sometimes can be the greatest teacher. When I first began to practice tax, I received a call at home from my stockbroker asking me for some very general advice regarding an IRA, apparently for his own information. He asked me the question and I came to a quick conclusion that the situation was not taxable. I even researched the CCH Federal Tax Service for him to make sure that I was right. There was obviously no question about it—there was no estate tax. All questions should be that simple. Then about six months later he called again. His voice bellowed with rage and I could hear the wire at the other end sizzle. He demanded to know what type of tax consultant I was. Stunned, I told him that I didn't have the slightest idea what he was talking about. I was mystified since he was not one of my tax clients. He then reminded me of our phone conversation six months before. "I don't see what the problem is," I said, recalling the question. "There was definitely no estate tax." "Oh, yeah? The IRS wants $9000 from her and she's going to sue me!" he responded heatedly. I demanded to know what he meant by "she" and what exactly he was talking about, and if he didn't calm down I would hang up the phone. Then the story came out.

The broker did not have the slightest idea of the difference between an income tax and estate tax. To him, a tax was a tax. Although his question six months before implied, without doubt, an *estate* tax situation, he was actually referring to an *income* tax situation. Based on my quick answer, he had advised one of his clients, a widow, to take the death proceeds of an IRA account in a lump sum rather than to roll it over into her own IRA account. As a result, the government was reaching deep down into her handbag for many thousands of dollars of income tax. And needless to say, he was blaming me. As tactfully as I could, I told him exactly what I thought of him and wished him every success before the court. Yet the fact remained that this poor woman had to pay a lot more in taxes than was necessary because of someone's bad advice. Although there was no way that I was personally responsible, I felt bad and vowed to use the experience as a learning tool. In retrospect, I realized that the stockbroker was looking for what we refer to as a free lunch to help him make a sale. But worse, he had practiced in an area that exceeded his ability—in fact, in an area where he had no ability. He should have referred this client to a CPA or tax advisor. But he didn't. The result was that he brought harm to an innocent client who relied on him for advice and he hurt himself.

Because of this incident many years ago, I learned not to give advice to anyone but paying clients and close business associates. The most I am guilty of is disturbing people and then advising them to see me professionally. I even stay out of financial and tax conversations at parties and other social events. In fact, I once told a dentist at a party who kept plugging away at me for free advice that if we went into the bathroom and he cleaned my teeth, I would then discuss tax savings techniques that he could use in his professional corporation. The financial planner, like many other service professionals, is in the advisory business and must learn that professional opinions are worth money. You cannot give your services away for nothing and expect to be viewed as a professional.

The first step you, the financial planner, should take in almost all planning cases is to obtain all the facts. Facts are your bread and butter. Once you have all the facts, you can then analyze them, judge whether you are capable of undertaking the task, and then decide what action to take. There are really only four choices: (1) decline the case; (2) refer the client to another planner; (3) do the parts you can do and refer to others whatever you cannot handle yourself; or (4) work with another knowledgeable planner who is better skilled for the case, and share the fees. Unless you are absolutely skilled in the areas of pensions, investments, taxation, and property casualty insurance, avoid them until you develop the necessary knowledge and skills.

Keep in mind that shooting from the hip will cost you somewhere down the road. It may take many years for the defect to surface. Your reputation is on the block and certainly, I'm sure, you wish to avoid the drudgery of the legal system should you be sued. Lawyers make enough; they don't need defense payments from you. Stand firmly in front of your ego and do not allow it to swell. Handle only what you are capable of handling intelligently and avoid the rest.

CREATE YOUR OWN STYLE

In the beginning of your planning career you will probably feel like the Rich Little or Frank Gorshen of the financial planning industry, imitating everyone else. But as you grow and develop, the confidence and the fire will come and you will stop pretending to be other planners. You will become yourself. When I first began, I listened to as many financial planning tapes as I could get my hands on. I set up my firm around the various tapes I heard. I even practiced in the same manner that the planners in the tapes did and charged the same fees. But then, sweet time aged my planning practice, until I saw that the time was right to break from those tapes and set up rules of my own. Generally, the self-employed are quite different from the typical wage earner in that they are strong individualists with independent ideas and great pride. It really does not matter whether they are bakery owners, candy store owners, doctors, or financial planners. Eventually, these people learn, sometimes early and sometimes later, that it is *their* business and they are going to do things their own way, in their own distinctive style— Right or wrong! Boom or bust!

The financial planner must also have style. There is no right style or wrong style, only different style—individuality. For example, no matter how successful financial planners may become, one may feel comfortable driving around in a Rolls-Royce, whereas another may feel that a Volkswagen bug is the way to go. Richard M. Silverstein, CFP, a friend of mine and a highly successful and competent financial planner from Los Angeles, California, whom I will speak about shortly, told me that he dresses each day for work in an expensive three-piece suit, silk tie, and customized shirt. That's Dick's style. Fine. My style, on the other hand, is less formal and more relaxed: Mickey Mouse T-shirts and football jerseys. Just remember that style should not be absolutely rigid, and there are times when you must step out of character. I can almost assure you that when Dick Silverstein plays tennis with a client, he does not wear a suit, nor do I wear a football jersey when I meet a client for the first time.

But style is a lot more than how you dress. It's innovation. It's creativity. In a later chapter, Eileen Sharkey, CFP, from Denver, Colorado, is quoted as saying that what excites her most about financial planning is that the rules are yours—*you* can create the type of plans that you want. And this statement hits the bull's-eye of truth dead center. Financial planning is virgin territory, like the West in the nineteenth century, just waiting for the prospectors to come along and pan for gold. Look around you. The insurance industry is in a state of cosmic change; the insurance salespeople do not know whether to sell insurance for protection or as investments; and if they sell only permanent insurance they usually wonder whether they are doing the right thing or not. At least, many of the insurance people I know wonder about this privately. But how do you say "no sale" to your livelihood. The stockbroker, on the other hand, is feeling pressure from the discount broker down the street and, in years to come, as the banking industry converges on the brokerage business, the pressure will compound. Can you see why the financial planning business is absolutely ripe for persons with fresh ideas? The creative financial planner of today will set new guidelines and rules for future planners in the years to come. So if you are determined to break away and go out on your own, you might as well go *all* the way. Be creative!

BUILD UP YOUR CREDENTIALS

Although furthering your knowledge of financial planning concepts is absolutely essential, the credentials you receive also go a long way toward building your image as a practitioner. Furthermore, credentials enhance your self-esteem, and most important, impress your clients. The rule is simple: You can impress just about anyone that you want to impress but in the end, the only people that really count are your clients. Even though it might be nice to impress other planners, they don't pay your bills. Nevertheless, you will be amazed how clients are impressed by degrees, certifications, designations, awards, publications, television and radio credits, and anything else that you can achieve. Here are some ways you can build up your credentials.

AN ADVANCED DEGREE.   An M.B.A. or M.S. in tax or financial planning is becoming increasingly important. A decade from now, as more and more colleges begin to offer advanced financial planning degrees, a master's degree in financial planning will become almost a necessity for an entry-level position. But for now, it's hot stuff! Furthermore, an advanced degree can never hurt you.

PROFESSIONAL DESIGNATION.   Although the Chartered Life Underwriter (CLU) has been around for many years, the Certified Financial Planner (CFP) and the Chartered Financial Consultant (ChFC) are fairly recent innovations. One or both of the latter two designations will prove to be very important to the financial planner. Besides prestige, they contribute to a well-rounded background.

TEACHING.   The credentials as a financial planning teacher can be quite impressive, especially on the college level. As the academic community begins to recognize the need for a financial planning curriculum, there will be a greater demand for high-quality financial planning instructors, lecturers, and professors. Clients are usually impressed by financial planners who are also college professors.

PUBLISHING.   Financial planning is a timely topic. Write articles, columns, books, and get your name into print. Then make sure that you leave your accomplishments around the office so that your clients will take notice. If I publish what I consider to be a significant article, I laminate the first page of the article and hang it on my wall. Client's are impressed and they tell other people, who are sometimes impressed enough to become new clients.

MEMBERSHIPS IN ORGANIZATIONS.   If you belong to an organization such as the IAFP, the ICFP, NALU, or a local college institute, hang those membership certificates on the office wall. In addition, many financial planners build up credentials as officers of these professional organizations. It not only helps to achieve recognition but in the process you can make a lot of good financial planning contacts who can help you in your practice.

AWARDS.   Should you receive an award that has any relevance to your financial planning practice, I would suggest that you display it proudly. Awards make you look good.

THE MEDIA.   It certainly does not hurt to be written up as part of a newspaper article or feature story or to be a guest on a radio talk-show or a television program. Should this happen to you, let your clients know about it. Of course, if you are interviewed on the "Six O'Clock News" because you've just been indicted for fraud, I wouldn't play that up; but otherwise, try to get your clients to listen to your radio broadcast or watch you on television. Today, because of the tremendous expansion of cable television, the possibility of appearing on television is not as remote as it sounds. And when your clients hear you on radio or see you on TV, they are thrilled that you handle them as clients.

Certainly, there are other credentials that you can achieve. The point is that every time that you pass another milestone—publicize it. But you must do it in a humble way. Outright boasting can have a negative effect. Do not overwhelm your clients with the fact that you are a great financial planner. It may be so, but let them discover it themselves. Clients, in fact, thrive on discovery. My technique is to leave literature in the most obvious places around my office; and relate my accomplishments to certain clients whom I know will tell a lot of other people. Your accomplishments passed from client to client will certainly have an impact. Furthermore, your credentials are a lot more important than you realize, since the background of a Registered Investment Advisor or principals of a Registered Investment Advisor firm must be stated to your clients on an annual basis. You are certainly not boasting if your background on Form ADV, Part II, is impressive—you are simply complying with the law.

LEARN TAXES

Of the disciplines of financial planning, *taxes*, I feel, are the most important. Tax theory interrelates with everything else—insurance, investments, pensions, estate planning. In fact, you cannot really have a thorough grasp of any of the other areas of financial planning without understanding taxes. Taxation is the key to effective financial planning, the nucleus from which all other planning germinates.

How much you should know about taxation is certainly not an easy question. Your degree of understanding will depend on how much you are willing to learn. At the very least, a basic knowledge is essential. To achieve this, I suggest that you take at least one course in federal income taxation and another in estate and gift taxation. Both the CFP and the ChFC programs offer these courses, or you can take them at your local college. Any school that offers an accounting program should have these courses available.

For the financial planner who wishes to pursue taxation beyond the basics—and I certainly suggest that you do—there are countless courses and programs that you can take. My philosophy, however, is that if you are going to spend the time and devote the effort to taking higher-level tax courses, you might as well pursue an advanced degree, such as an M.B.A. or an M.S. in taxation. The rationale is that an advanced degree can be another prestigious credential, another feather in your cap. Most M.B.A. or M.S. programs in taxation will offer tax courses in the following areas: individual tax; partnership tax; corporation tax; fiduciary tax; estate tax; and state tax. In addition, some schools may offer courses in estate planning, pensions, and taxation of nonprofit organizations.

For the planner who does not wish to pursue an advanced degree in taxation, I suggest continuing education and/or professional education courses. These can be taken through colleges, professional institutes, and organizations such as the AICPA (American Institute of Certified Public Accountants). Even persons with advanced degrees in taxation and CPAs, CFPs, CFCs, and CLUs, must take continuing education courses, due to the very nature of taxation and the government's policy of inconsistency. If ever I was to make an understatement, it would be to say, "Tax laws change." No sooner is a tax law passed, signed into law, and implemented than it is modified by a technical corrections act and scrapped for a new tax act. I think in my next life I would like to be reincarnated as a publisher of tax reference materials. If it were not for Prentice-Hall and Commerce Clearing House publications, even the government wouldn't know what was happening. And if you think I'm kidding, what do you think the examiners at the IRS read for information? The Code? The Regs? Publication 17? Be serious.

But understanding tax laws is one thing, and understanding tax procedure is another. Do not attempt to practice beyond your qualifications. Should you ever have a sticky problem with the IRS, there will be only so much that you can do for your client unless you are an attorney, Certified Public Accountant, or enrolled agent.

Financial planners who are not attorneys or CPAs should consider becoming enrolled agents with the IRS if they plan to work heavily in the tax area. Becoming an enrolled agent, however, is more than a mere application. The applicant must pass a rigid, four-part, two-day examination to demonstrate an in-depth working knowledge of individual, corporate, partnership, and estate gift and fiduciary taxes, as well as IRS procedures and practices. Furthermore, the applicant must pass all four parts of the exam or wait a year to retake it. For further information you can contact the district office of the Internal Revenue Service.

BELIEVE IN YOURSELF

In the 1960s Don Adams starred in a television comedy show called *Get Smart*, about a secret agent who couldn't do anything right, but was always saved by his rather good luck. In his portrayal of the bungling

Maxwell Smart, Don Adams created a character long to be remembered by many Americans. Completely entrapped by Kaos Agents and his archrival, Zigfried (Bernie Koppel), Smart would nonchalantly say something like this to Zigfried:

"Would you believe . . . that you are surrounded by the Seventh Fleet?" And when his archrival snickered, Smart would say, "Would you believe . . . the Sixth Fleet?" Then finally, when apparently no one bit: "Would you believe . . . a school of angry flounder?"

What does this have to do with financial planning?

"Would you believe that you are going to be a successful financial planner?"

"Would you believe . . . Would you believe . . . Would you believe . . . ?"

If you don't believe it, don't expect anyone else to. No one believed Maxwell Smart. Not even himself.

As a financial planner you must glow with confidence. You must be magnetic. Clients will believe in you only if you believe in yourself first. If you don't, you have a real problem and you will have to work it out. And don't assume that you'll get by with luck the way Max did. Step one, bar none, through trial and tribulation, good times and bad, up markets and down markets, through tax reduction and tax increase, you must always believe in yourself.

Should you lose this belief, even for just a moment, you must stop, reflect, take a vacation if need be, and then resume believing in yourself.

Earlier in this book you learned some of the technical, procedural, and philosophical methods that I and other planners employ. In this chapter you learned that you can and should get ideas from others, that you should work only within your ability, and you should try to create your own style. These are some of the ingredients of the success formula; however, the formula needs a special catalyst to make it really work. This catalyst is the overwhelming force that drives you on when the going gets rough. "The Force" is generated by your unquestionable belief in yourself. No one has to tell you that you can do it—you just know it.

The financial planner is certainly not unique in this belief. History, sports, business, movies, books, and television are saturated with examples of persons who believed deeply in themselves and went on to overcome all obstacles by doing what they had to do or being what they wanted to be. These people all believed in themselves, knew they could succeed, and they did. Based on the magical powers of believing in oneself, people have built empires, skyscrapers, and giant corporations and conglomerates. They have achieved fame, gold medals, and Nobel prizes. They have captured the spirit of millions of people, wined and dined with presidents, kings, and queens, and they have saved lives. Believing in yourself is the most powerful weapon. In the movie *Star Wars*, Ben Kenobi, the wise old Jedi Knight, tells young Luke Skywalker, "Believe in yourself, Luke. The Force will be with you." May the Force be with you, too.

Almost any kid can tell you about the Force. In fact, there are some adults who probably know even more than the kids. The Force is what gives the Jedi Knight power; a financial planner, too, receives power from the Force—the Force of Believing. You must believe you can do it, and you will.

Why the sermon? Because it really works, that's why. The most powerful part of your body is your mind. And you must make it work on your behalf.

The strong belief in yourself must be with you at all times. This is especially true when you first start out and the road is somewhat rocky. Once you have made it, however, believing in yourself will be a lot easier, since the tangible evidence of the fruits of your labor will be everywhere. Your name will continually be in print—on checks. In the meantime, however, you will not see much tangible evidence, only a lot of hard work, little compensation, and your dreams. Believe in your dreams and you will make them reality.

In an earlier chapter I described my career change from the U.S. Customs Service to financial planner. Now that my business is situated on solid ground, I can truly confess that there were moments when I questioned my sanity. But those moments were few and as I began to develop my business, they occurred less and less, until finally they were no more. What kept me going was the belief in my ability to create a financial planning firm in my own way—and to create one that would work. This belief in myself was the fuel that kept me going.

Now forget about me. In your realm, you are more important than I am. Have you had events in your life when you believed in yourself? That extra effort to score the winning point for your team, the test you knew you could pass, the extra push to run that last mile demanded by the nice sergeant with the potbelly and swaggerstick, or dragging yourself back to school in midlife and then graduating at the top of your class? There had to be some event in your life when you believed in yourself, and, because of that, you succeeded.

You *can* succeed in your own financial planning practice. All the conditions are right.

15

STRUCTURING YOUR ORGANIZATION SUCCESSFULLY

Building a house is a fairly standard procedure. Before a builder can install the wiring, the plumbing, the doors, the windows, or the kitchen cabinets, the frame must first be constructed. The concept of building a financial planning practice, large or small, is similar in a way to constructing a house. You should not install the products, the equipment, the furniture, or the services until you frame out what you are going to do. In other words, if you want to have a successful financial planning practice, first be an architect and design your proposed practice on a blueprint; then be an engineer and refer to your blueprint as you build, testing the structure to make sure it meets your specifications. The point is that you must first have a blueprint—a plan. Otherwise, your practice may come out lopsided, as a house without a blueprint would be. Furthermore, your blueprint need not be rigid; changes can and usually should be made, adding to, deleting from, or modifying your growing practice.

Planning what you will be doing is just as important as doing it. Therefore, I suggest that you carefully review the products and the services listed in Chapter 2 and decide which you would like to offer. But also consider what services and products you are capable of offering. Then outline your blueprint, but be sure to draw it on two different levels—the *present* and the *future*. A portion of Chapter 20 will show you how to develop a marketing plan for your business.

My original marketing plan was drawn on a large piece of oaktag and for the first six months it hung from my office wall. It was more than just an organizational chart; it served to inspire me, to remind me constantly of where I was going and what I should be doing. When I first sat down and mapped out my business, I really gave it a lot of thought. I was planning for the future and wanted to know what I would be doing in two, three, four, five years. And I was determined to set up my organization on that basis, but modifying as I went along.

The financial planner faces a lot of tough decisions along the path to the creation of a successful practice. Therefore, it is essential to associate with other financial planners to see how they have set up their organizations. There are no set rules to follow, no structured charts or tables. Planners are free to do whatever they desire as long as they comply with all the regulatory requirements of the federal and state governments. In the end, however you decide to structure your firm, it must be legally correct.

Since the vast majority of financial planners will charge fees either on a fee-only or a fee-and-commission basis, the subject of the Registered Investment Advisor becomes very important. Hopefully, it is clear to you by now that if you charge a fee, you *must* be an investment advisor. There are three practical ways to satisfy this requirement.

First, you may contract with a financial service firm or broker-dealer who is already a Registered Investment Advisor, and write cases under their investment advisor registration. I know quite a few stockbrokers who do just that. They write cases for their clients, charge a fee that is billed and collected by the firm, and then collect the fee, or most of it, from the firm. This way it is the parent firm that incurs full liability for the plan. There are some broker-dealer firms that offer this service to their reps. They act as the investment advisor and all plans must be reviewed by them—or should be. Although this arrangement seems to have a lot to offer in terms of minimum regulatory compliance, the planner loses a great deal of independence, since the financial plan must be approved by the parent advisor prior to submission to the client. Furthermore, the Registered Investment Advisor who sponsors the planner is taking an awfully big risk and must have absolute confidence in the planner.

The second method is to register with the SEC as an individual Registered Investment Advisor and to operate in that manner. A great many financial planners work just this way. You have independence, no one has to approve your plans, and it is relatively easy once the SEC has approved your registration. However, if you sell products as an individual and are also a Registered Investment Advisor, you will probably have to explain to your clients how you can be truly objective.

Another problem is that since you personally act as the investment advisor you usually have more liability exposure than the third method, the corporate Registered Investment Advisor.

The third method is to form a corporation which becomes the actual investment advisor, with you as the principal officer of the corporation. I found this to be the best method for me in terms of both growth and separation of functions. I know many other financial planners who structure their firms in this manner. Furthermore, should you someday wish to hire other planners, the corporate Registered Financial Investment Advisor is the ideal arrangement.

When I first started, my objective was to charge fees and also receive commissions. My feeling was then, and still is, that my time is of great value to me, and I do not enjoy making sales presentations knowing that I might or might not be paid. I believe that a planner should be compensated for all time devoted to a client's plan and, in this manner, the planner can be as objective as humanly possible. Knowing that you will be paid for what you are doing—without having to count on commissions—helps to ensure your integrity. If I wanted only to sell and take the risk of not being paid for my time and effort, I would actually be a pure product salesman and not a financial planner.

Frequently, I am asked by clients to review their life insurance policies. For this service I charge a fee. Why? Because I often end up recommending that the client make no change whatsoever or simply change a dividend option or just purchase a low-cost term insurance policy. If I were purely on commission, I truthfully don't know if I could afford to be quite that objective. And for this reason—to ensure my integrity and objectivity—I charge a fee. Admittedly, I hate to work for nothing, and this way I know I don't have to.

Although there are many planners who favor making product sales presentations and resign themselves to the fact that many clients will not sign on the bottom line, I personally could never get used to the idea. Furthermore, I am a poor gambler and a worse loser. To me the commission-only game is a gamble. You are betting your time and a small amount of expenses against a commission. Sometimes the commissions are small and other times they could be lottery size. But win or lose, you are risking your time, and your time should be worth money to you. So for me, fee *and* commission was the answer. No more product sales presentations—just objective advice for a price. If my clients still want to buy from me after I make it absolutely clear that they need not use the products I offer, then I write the sale. This approach places me in a no-lose situation.

On occasion, I have been criticized for costing the client more in dollars than a commission-only planner since in some cases the client has to pay my fee in addition to a commission. In that respect, the criticism is valid. However, let's examine precisely what the client has purchased. The client, in effect, has purchased two products—a tangible product and objectivity. The purchase of objectivity could turn out to be a lot cheaper for the client in the long run. Objectivity must have a price. Can a professional afford to give away services for nothing? Consider a doctor who gives you a thorough examination and then recommends that you have an operation. Whether you decide to have the operation or not, you still must *pay* for the examination. A true financial planner who gives you a "financial examination" also deserves a fee for his or her objective advice, whether or not you decide to follow the recommendations. In the case of the physician, if he or she then performs the operation, there is an additional fee for the service. The financial planner, similarly, receives additional compensation for the sale of the product. The real key to the planning process is that the initial advice must be truly objective and in the best interest of the client—not the planner.

From the very beginning my intent was to separate the services I perform from the products I sell. If I was going to wear two hats, I wanted to make sure that they were two entirely different hats. Although I was quite sensitive to the way my clients would feel, I was also concerned with the way I would feel. I needed to feel that I wore two hats. So in order to achieve this I formed AMR Planning Services, Inc., a Corporate Registered Investment Advisor firm in the fee-only business. AMR offers services only, primarily financial and tax. All clients are billed by the corporation and receive all correspondence on corporate stationery. If any selling is done, I do it as an individual operating under my securities and/or insurance licenses. The long-range plan was truly to play down my sales role, concentrate on fee-only work, and sell only as a support function of my fee services.

This chapter is about structuring your organization successfully. This refers to your financial planning organization of products and services, not the structure of your firm in terms of your employees. The following diagram is applicable to both the one-planner firm and the multiplanner firm. It is the way my organization is currently set up. Since many of the previous chapters spend a great deal of time examining financial planning, I won't say much about it now. I will only remind you not to work over your head and to experiment cautiously with new ideas. The rest of this chapter will cover ideas on how to set yourself up in the life insurance and securities business, the two most important support areas the planner should know about. The third area, tangible sales, has been thoroughly covered in the chapter on product due diligence, and I refer you back to that chapter. If you plan to market tangible products to your clients, don't be overly concerned about the structure—be more concerned about the quality of the products, fair prices, fair commissions, and the reputation of your product sources.

MY CURRENT FINANCIAL STRUCTURE

AMR PLANNING SERVICES, INC.
(Fee Only)

Financial Planning	Investment Management	Tax Preparation and Consulting	Small Business Consulting

ANDREW M. RICH, CFP
(Commissions)

Life and Health Insurance General Agent	NASD Registered Representative	Tangible Sales

LIFE INSURANCE AND HEALTH INSURANCE

Regardless of how you earn your compensation, you will certainly want to obtain the best products available for your clients. But if you sell insurance, keep in mind that your reputation and the products you use will be one and the same. To be sure you are offering competitive products, there are several ways to structure your relationship with a life insurance company or companies. There is no one best method in general. Whatever works for you, of course, is best.

The relationship you establish should be the one with which you are most comfortable from both a product and a commission standpoint. Although the commission setup is important, you should base your selection of an insurance company or companies on the products they offer rather than the compensation you will receive.

The General Agent

A general agent (GA) is a representative of a life insurance company who generally has authority to sign agreements on behalf of the company, hire agents and employees, and make suggestions and provide input regarding company management, organization, and products. For this, the general agent, in addition to the base commission, will usually receive a general agent override for subagent production, plus a healthy allowance to be used in building up the insurance agency. Sometimes the combination of the agent's commission, the general agent allowance, and the development allowance can exceed 100% of the first year's annualized premium. If the financial planner is writing insurance business, the total commissions easily can be double that of a regular agent's commission.

Although at first glance the general agent approach appears to be the way to go, it has certain drawbacks of which the planner must be aware. First, general agents are usually required to meet a minimum in annualized premium production, which can place pressure on the planner to sell insurance instead of writing financial plans. Worse, the planner might feel compelled, in order to meet a quota, to sell higher premium policies in cases where less expensive policies would be more appropriate. Most insurance companies are looking for minimums of $20,000 or $25,000 annual premiums, and some look for $50,000 to $100,000 or more. Furthermore, life insurance companies, finding that general agency structure is very costly, are becoming highly selective in their appointments of general agents. Second, a general agent is responsible for a great deal of paperwork, such as completing all agent applications, commissions, medicals, inspection reports, and policy changes. This paperwork can drain a financial planner, especially if the planner does not have adequate staff and must do a great deal of it alone. Third, to obtain a general agency you may have to sign an exclusive contract not to represent any other company or use any other products. Even if the company does let you sell other products, you may be forced to use only that company's products in order to meet a production minimum. When using only one company's products you may be fairly limited in what you can offer to your clients. Therefore, make sure that the company you represent has superior products of the type you use most. Fourth, the emphasis of the general agent may lean toward building an agency rather than on building a financial planning firm. This means that you will have to service subagents in your area, and sometimes these subagents can be a lot more trouble than the few dollars in override will be worth. There is perhaps nothing as unpredictable as promises made by certain life insurance agents.

I represent an insurance company as a general agent and am bound to use only that company's products as a general agent, but I can be a subagent for any other company that I want. I selected this arrangement because the company I represent has a variety of excellent term insurance products, and my belief (at least for the last several years) has been to use term insurance and invest the difference, which is certainly not a popular philosophy in pure life insurance circles. Recently, however, the company has introduced variable life and I am beginning to take a serious view toward permanent insurance. If your belief is whole life, that's fine, but only if you really believe in it and are not merely trying to justify high commissions. Select the company on the basis of the products you use the most.

The argument regarding term versus whole life has been going on for a long time and planners differ in their opinions. This is not a book about which one is better. My point is simply to suggest that you follow your convictions and obtain the products you really believe in, whether they be term, whole life, variable life, universal life, or any other hybrid. There is nothing as insincere as financial planners who sell whole life to their clients, but buy term for themselves. Believe in your product or don't sell it!

The Subagent

The subagent also represents a company, but reports to the general agent and does not have subproducers. This setup is quite advantageous to the financial planner. It allows more time for financial planning because after writing and submitting the application, there is nothing more to do but deliver and service the policy. It is a most convenient way for you, as a planner, to operate, since it gives you the flexibility to be licensed with as many insurance companies as you so desire. The main consideration is to select a general agent who is administratively capable—the general agent is responsible for the payment of your commissions. There are some general agents around who have to be chased for every nickel. Thus, select your general agent wisely.

The major disadvantage to this setup is that you will receive only the base commission, which is generally from 30 to 55%, depending on the product. However, if you use the time saved productively for financial planning, the loss of earnings due to the commission differential is probably well worth it. It is a matter of which method generates the most dollars and cents and how many headaches you want to avoid.

Brokering Business

This is almost the same as the subagent arrangement, except that you deal directly with the insurance company. Your commission is about the same and, depending on the company you work with, the bulk of your paperwork and the arrangements for medical examinations might be handled for you. Brokerage offers the financial planner one major advantage over using a general agent, and that is *privacy*; since you deal directly with a company, client information is kept confidential. The problem with the general agency setup is that should you decide to terminate your contract with the general agent some day down the road, your clients may get a call either from the general agent or one of the general agent's subagents suggesting that their policy be reviewed. This can happen and it has happened.

A way to prevent this is to act as a broker for the company rather than to contract with a general agent. At least, make an attempt to be a broker. Not all companies will permit you to be a broker but may insist instead that you do business through a general agent. On the other hand, certain companies will only allow you to broker business, and work directly with the company. Seek and you shall find.

In the last few years, the insurance industry has seen a major change. The consumer, plagued by a tight budget, enticed by high interest rates of alternative investments, and enlightened by modern financial education, has fled from whole life to term. The insurance companies, aware of this trend, have engaged in a term war. Today, annual renewable term (ART) costs about one dollar per thousand and even less. As a result, the profit margin on these products has been declining steadily for the insurance companies and many can no longer afford to pay 100% or better of the first-year premium to the general agent. In turn, they find it a lot more practical to deal directly with the licensed agent. It makes sense since this means eliminating another layer of commissions. There probably will be a lot more direct brokerage in the years ahead.

SECURITY PRODUCTS

Your method of doing business in the security area depends on how you structure your compensation. But regardless of how you structure compensation, the key to the success of a client's financial program is in the implementation of products into that program. If you are on a fee-only basis, then the objective is to refer the client to a trustworthy broker to implement your suggestions. A commission-only planner or a fee-and-commission planner usually does not refer security business to others. The commission-only planner instead will be relying on security sales to earn income, and would be a very unusual person to give away business. The fee-and-commission planner, on the other hand, usually operates from the two-hat approach, having products available for the clients but usually leaving the clients free to implement from whatever source they desire. In this section I will assume that most financial planners will be operating from a fee-and-commission basis.

Registered Representative

If you are going to sell security products, you must be licensed to do so. This means that you must pass an examination given by the National Association of Security Dealers. Once you pass this examination, you can be a registered representative, which means you can sell certain security products (depending on which license you hold). However, you must be licensed through a duly licensed broker-dealer firm. For the financial planner who wears two hats, this setup is the best of all alternatives. You have the opportunity to earn additional income in excess of your fees, and at the same time, you can sit back and let someone else (your broker-dealer) do all the paperwork and compliance. Accordingly, I suggest that you align yourself with a broker-dealer firm that, first and foremost, you can trust; second, that can provide you with the product or products you need; and third, that gives you a decent reallowance on the business you produce. In my opinion, the registered representative status offers the fee-and-commission financial planner a great opportunity to be a financial planner and not an administrator.

The Broker-Dealer

The alternative is for you, the financial planner, to be a broker-dealer yourself. In this capacity you will receive maximum commissions and commissions on the products that others sell; however, the cost to you in terms of depleting your financial planning time can, and probably will, be devastating. According to Donald Platz, the Operations Principal of First Eastern Equity Corporation in Armonk, New York, the firm through which I am currently licensed: "The biggest problem is that a broker-dealer spends a lot of wasted time on compliance, and this is directly computed into the loss of earning power. You can expect an NASD audit about every two years and an SEC audit about every four years, and the time that you spend with the regulatory agencies is not dollar producing time." Compliance is usually a full-time job and is not really practical in the small firm. An NASD broker-dealer will also need to hire competent clerical help to handle the paperwork, and the principals will usually need partners to produce the income. A financial planner has to choose whether to write financial plans or compliance documents. A simple choice, I believe.

However, as your financial planning practice grows, establishing your own broker-dealer firm may become more practical for a variety of reasons, such as taking internal control of the client's portfolio or designing your own product or earning override on your firm's planning practice. But in the early stages, establishing your own broker-dealer firm may not be practical for the following reasons:

1. The consumption of time is not worth the income that you lose. You are doing compliance rather than planning.
2. If you are handling customer accounts, you are going to need an extremely large outlay of capital.
3. You may have the tendency to be more of a broker-dealer to your clients than a financial planner, especially if you are marketing your own products.
4. Although the cost of setting up the firm may be small, the cost of a good SEC attorney to steer you in the right direction may be exceptionally high. Any financial planner who is also a broker-dealer will need a good SEC attorney.
5. It may take a considerable amount of time away from your planning practice to study and pass the operations principals examination, which stresses heavy accounting theory.
6. You may be ready to retire by the time the SEC and the NASD finally approve your application.
7. You will not only need to do due diligence for the products you use for your clients but you will also need to check out any products that your representatives desire to use.

All of the above may be a high price to pay for the 20 to 25% commission difference, of which a good portion could be eaten by the additional administrative expenses.

My advice to you is to talk to as many financial planners as you can; talk to those who are reps and to those who are broker-dealers. Ask them the pros and cons. It probably will not take you very long to make a decision.

16

DO YOU WANT TO MANAGE MONEY?

One of the most important decisions that you will face as a financial planner is what level of investment advisory service you will provide for your clients. This, of course, will depend on your level of expertise within the investment markets, your experience, and the degree of responsibility you are willing to undertake.

Nondiscretionary investment management simply involves giving advice to clients and then letting them make the final decision. Some financial planners will not go beyond recommending a type of investment, such as a growth mutual fund or a municipal bond, while other planners will recommend a specific mutual fund, a specific investment group, a specific stock, or a specific bond issue. For example, financial planner A tells the client to purchase an aggressive growth mutual fund and provides the client with a list of the funds and performance information. Financial planner B tells the client that 25% of the client's assets should be placed in an aggressive mutual fund, specifically recommending a fund such as Fidelity Magellan or Oppenheimer Directors. Financial planner C tells the client that 20% of the client's assets should be placed in utility stock, then specifically recommends that the client purchase 100 shares of Middle South Utilities and 100 shares of San Diego Gas and Electric. How far the financial planner goes in advising clients is a very individual matter. One thing is certain, however—a financial planner should never advise beyond his or her level of expertise. You can only hurt the client if you do.

Most financial planners today offer only nondiscretionary invest-ment advisory services in one form or another. Once the investment recommendation is made, it becomes the full responsibility of the client (and not the planner) to implement. In effect, the planner makes the suggestion and the client takes the physical action. The planner, however, can assist in productive implementation, and usually does. For instance, as part of a financial plan, the planner might recommend a specific mutual fund to the client. After reviewing the plan, the client agrees with the suggestion and asks the planner to implement the fund into the program. At that point, the planner, as a registered representa-tive, either sells the client the fund or assists in the implementation of a no-load fund. This type of financial planning is considered nondis-cretionary, since the client—and only the client—has the final say in product selection. Should the investment be switched or changed at a later date, the final authority for the switch or sale would be the client's, even though the planner had recommended the change. It is most important to understand that the concept of nondiscretionary financial advisory means that the ultimate control of the investment rests with the client, not with the planner.

Once you cross over the River of Control, you enter the Land of Discretionary Investment Management. In this land the requirement for citizenship is the taking of complete responsibility. The ultimate author-ity for the implementation of the investment is yours—the planner's. Most financial planners will not go this far and will never cross that river; however, as times change and the fee-paid business becomes more and more important to the planner, discretionary financial advisory will probably become a most significant concept.

In my practice I decided to set myself apart from the majority and to undertake discretionary money management. This involved a great deal of thought, soul searching, and discussion. It is not difficult, but it is an awesome responsibility. Before you jump into money manage-ment, you must realize that you are totally responsible for your clients' investments. You are, therefore, under a great obligation to have a full understanding of the investment markets, of the specific products avail-able, and of the future trends of investments in general. You could spend half your life reading about investments, not to mention all the required reading in the *Wall Street Journal, Barron's, Forbes, Value Line Reports, Standard & Poor's, United Mutual Fund Selector*, the *New York Times*, and company annual reports and fund prospectuses, just to men-tion a few sources. Then there are all the financial programs on both regular and cable television.

My discretionary investment advisory program revolves solely around the client's goals and objectives—not mine. This is where the discretionary financial planner differs from the portfolio manager. I do not manage in aggregate; I manage account by account. Every client's account is reviewed periodically to see if changes are needed. Although I am licensed to sell securities, I partake in *no* commissions whatsoever with discretionary accounts. I am firmly convinced that any investment advisor who has discretionary authority to manage funds should not take a cent of commissions. As a discretionary advisor you are a fiduciary to the client and are under both a strong legal and moral obligation to treat your client's account like your own.

When I purchase stocks, bonds, and other individual securities, I offer my clients the use of either a discount brokerage account or an account with a full-service broker who discounts liberally for group volume. However, it is my firm policy never to force or even try to persuade my client to use the services of any broker. The commissions paid for the purchase and/or sale of securities is strictly between the broker and the client. However, the investment advisor who represents the client should try to negotiate a better commission rate for the client. Should my client prefer that I use another broker, I will, provided that I can obtain limited power of attorney on the client's account. Recently, I have set up an arrangement with the trust department of a bank, and this appears to be going quite well. In fact, I have been using this to manage funds of institutionalized clients whereby the nursing home and medical expenses are paid directly from the account.

When mutual funds are purchased for the client's discretionary account, I use strictly no-load funds in large fund groups, so that I have the flexibility to exchange the mutual fund for another in the same group. Furthermore, I always use a fund group that has a government portfolio money market fund. In effect, I am using *market timing* techniques. However, since I am not a technical analyst and have a strong belief in a fundamental market approach (rather than a technical approach), I base my fund exchanges on longer-term trends and not the shorter-term aberrations, technical rallies, and corrections.

A big decision that a discretionary advisor must make is whether to manage funds under limited power of attorney by use of a third-party custodian, or under full power of attorney, having full custody and access to clients' funds. Taking access to client funds involves an even larger degree of responsibility, not to mention the additional SEC requirements that must be met. The most important SEC requirement is the annual certified balance sheet that must be submitted with the ADV-S.

So far I have managed to keep all my accounts in limited power of attorney where the clients retain custody of all their funds. I am able to do this by setting up mutual funds and brokerage accounts in the client's name, either addressed to my client in care of my firm or I simply receive a duplicate confirmation of the transaction. All stock certificates are either sent to the client or are held in a street name by the broker, where I am authorized to manage the account under a limited power of attorney restricted to the buying and selling of securities. There is no question that most of my clients feel better by authorizing only limited power of attorney, thereby keeping the asset in their possession. In fact, I feel better that way, too.

Even if an advisor does not take custody of the clients' funds, should a fee be charged more than six months in advance, the advisor must submit an annual certified balance sheet to the SEC. The chances are that sooner or later (probably a lot sooner than later) you could be faced with this decision.

For the planner who expects to work the athlete or entertainer market, taking full custody of funds may not be that unusual. If you are considering these markets, keep these tips in mind. First, do not commingle funds in your business account; set up separate investment accounts for each client. Second, use one account—either a bank checking or money market—as a feeder account. In other words, you are accomplishing the same thing that a bank trust department does, sweeping the uninvested balances each day in order to earn money market rates. If this procedure is infeasible or not available in your area, use a regular checking account as a feeder account, and maintain only nominal balances. If the account is large enough (over $100,000) you can always buy 7-day and 14-day commercial paper. The point is that as a fiduciary you cannot leave large sums of client money idle, accruing no interest. Certainly, you would have some explaining to do to the client and possibly to the SEC. Third, if you purchase bearer paper, either leave it in the client's account at the brokerage house or in your safety deposit box, making sure that you have the contents of the box insured. Fourth, make sure that you read and comply with the SEC bookkeeping requirements and rules. Fifth, consult with an attorney who specializes in SEC law to make sure that you are doing everything right. Sixth, abandon the thought of skipping to Costa Rica with your client's funds.

Whether you offer discretionary or nondiscretionary money management, the fact that you provide money management at all as a service is certainly a feather in your cap. A money management program may be attractive to the following group of potential clients:

Professional athletes

Entertainers

Business owners too busy to manage their own funds

Corporate executives

Retired individuals

Persons who need forced savings

Pension funds

Institutionalized persons

Small businesses

The wealthy

Presently, I have set no minimum dollar requirement on the accounts that I manage. However, I am very selective in the clients whom I will handle. The account must be conservative and the client must be easy to work with. I will not accept a short-term trading account.

The fees for my services vary accordingly, charged quarterly to the client and based on the degree of work that I am required to perform and the assets in the account. You should be aware that an investment advisor may not charge fees based on the performance of the investments but may charge on a percentage of the funds under management or some other means of compensation not involving performance.

One of the biggest problems that you will face as a money manager is internal record keeping. You must at all times know what is in each client's account. Therefore, you need a system, either manual or automated, to help you achieve this. Since I have an accounting background, creating my own internal record keeping system was not difficult to do. At present I have just moved from manual to computer using a TRS-80 Model II computer with a simple data management program (Profile Plus with a math formula upgrade). The computer will also handle various financial and tax planning projections, mailing lists, word processing, and record keeping that the business requires. Computers are discussed in more depth in Chapter 17.

Should the person just starting out in a financial planning business undertake money management? The answer, I feel, should be a qualified *no*. However, if you have experience as a portfolio manager or trust officer, it might be something to consider; in fact, it could be the focal point of your planning operation. Otherwise, discretionary money management ought to be one of the last functions you consider—if you consider it at all.

A LOOK AT A REAL PRO

A chapter about financial planners who also manage money would not be complete without including Nelson Kjos, CFP, head of Nelson Kjos & Company of Southfield, Michigan. If you ever need to speak to Nelson, he can be found in his office from 8 A.M. to 10 P.M., Monday through Thursday, and on Friday, his "short day," until 5 P.M. On the average, Nelson works about 75 hours a week, reading through his deluge of magazines and periodicals, foreign and domestic, from the *Wall Street Transcription* to the *Economist*. At last count he receives 31 magazines a month. "A good money manager is also a professional reader," he insists. "He must read in order to spot a particular trend or an action by a CEO that could indicate a reason for purchasing a security."

Working to 10 P.M. is very exciting, Nelson finds. But it is also part of his philosophy that when he works he does not let anything or anybody interfere, and when he plays he does not let anything (including work) interfere with that, either.

Nelson's day certainly is a long one. He is usually dressed by 7:15 A.M. and immediately begins his ritual of reading the *New York Times*. Then he heads for the office, 18 miles away, stopping at his post office box to pick up his *Wall Street Journal*, the second ritual of the day. Although he agrees that the 45 minutes he spends each way commuting to the office could be better used for reading, the selection of this particular location for his office was essential in order to service his clients. Southfield, Michigan, is centrally located between Detroit and Grosse Pointe, and since a major highway runs adjacent to his office, clients from almost anywhere in Michigan can reach him with little difficulty. About 90% of Nelson's appointments with clients are conducted in his office.

Nelson Kjos & Company has been registered with the Securities and Exchange Commission as an investment advisor since 1967. The firm currently manages about $28 million of assets, consisting of 150 client accounts; the largest account is about $3 million and the smallest is about $10,000. Although most clients are from Michigan, the company has clients in 17 states and several foreign countries. There are five employees, including Nelson, whose own function is that of the investment strategist. Nelson sets policy, analyzes the short-term and long-term trends in the equity market, and analyzes industries, companies, and the management of companies that his clients invest in. His other employees include a portfolio manager, an assistant portfolio manager, and two general office personnel. Although Nelson gives his "decision makers" a free hand in what securities they may select for the clients' portfolios, they are limited to a list of securities personally approved by him. The basic approach of Nelson Kjos & Company is conservatism. It is his policy not to take undue risk with client funds. Accordingly, the firm manages equity and cash only, and does not deal with fixed-income securities. The firm uses a unique concept called the Technical Tick Index, developed by Nelson, to manage client portfolios. Clients pay fees of 1% of the assets managed for accounts under $1 million and

¾% for accounts over $1 million. In addition, the firm does financial planning and manages its own asset account.

Like many other fee-only financial planners, Nelson began his career in sales. He left Wayne State University in the early sixties to become the youngest home office supervisor with Mutual Trust Life. In 1964, at 27 years of age, he became a general agent, producing $6½ million a year of paid whole-life business. But he wasn't satisfied. There had to be more challenge to life than writing whole-life policies or receiving overrides for motivating others to write business. That is when he began to think about managing other people's money. By 1967 he had nine or ten good clients and was managing $300,000. He formed Nelson Kjos & Company in 1969 and left the life insurance business altogether, devoting his entire effort to pure money management.

The bug to go back to school can be a persistent little insect that gets deep into your skin and itches. It doesn't go away until you satisfy it with knowledge. Nelson was bitten by the bug in the early seventies, but the recession, the market collapse, and the failure of Goodbody & Company, where he had most of his accounts, kept him away from the campus. In 1973 he finally enrolled at Wayne State University to finish his economics degree. Just prior to starting, however, he saw an advertisement in a financial planning magazine by the College for Financial Planning. "The people at the College spoke my language," he decided, so he opted for the College's program instead of Wayne State. In 1976 he received his CFP designation and he has been taking and teaching courses ever since. He is on the adjunct faculty staff of the College for Financial Planning and has taught all five parts of the CFP designation program. Nelson is convinced that a money manager must invest a lot in himself and spends in excess of $2000 a year just for professional courses. His favorite programs are given by the Wharton School of Finance of the University of Pennsylvania and he has completed courses in Money Management and Pension and the Financial Management of Commercial Banks.

I asked Nelson if he would recommend that a financial planner who is just starting out undertake money management. He was quick to say yes, but only if he were a money manager already or had a deep love for finance. "A financial planner—whether he manages money or not—has a mission in life to the best of his ability to increase the health, happiness and wealth through financial planning." I asked him if this referred to the client or the planner. He said, both. "The opportunity is limitless. We are currently in the 1920s of money management and financial planning. A new industry has been invented and those that get there first will fulfill their own personal gratification. Just look, there are 230 million people in America. The financial planner has the greatest opportunity to perform as a professional. The need for financial planners is geometric while the output is arithmetic."

Nelson is a disciplinarian. He has a confirmed belief in detail, organization, and advanced planning, and likes to know what he is going to be doing weeks in advance. He believes that a money manager must be programmed to handle a crisis at any time. Furthermore, a money manager or financial planner should review his or her own statement of wealth quarterly and check to see what trends are developing. This way, he feels, they will get excited seeing their own assets increase. What he finds most enjoyable about the business is the gratification of doing independent analysis of a particular industry or company, then investing into the particular security and watching the result meet his expectation. Of course, it does not always work that way, he admits, but he does it right a lot more times than he does it wrong.

As a minimum-risk investment manager, Nelson feels that his success has been based on giving more weight to the price of a stock than to its yield or its price/earnings ratio. Securities are analyzed for short-term investment (STI) and long-term investment (LTI). The STI stocks are generally held for two or three months, while the LTI stocks are held a year to a year and a half. About 40% of the assets under management are STI and 60% LTI. As in my firm, he does not take physical possession of securities, but manages entirely by use of a limited power of attorney.

I asked Nelson Kjos, CFP, if he was happy with what he has become. Nelson responded that he wouldn't want to be anything else but a money manager. At times, however, he has his moments. He feels that he tries too hard to overachieve for his clients. But he wants his clients to feel that he deserves every penny of the fees that he charges. His philosophy can be captured in a poem that he wrote in 1980 entitled, "Challenge to Victory," about maintaining momentum in one's pursuit. A financial planner, at least one who has the burning desire to be successful, should be Challenged to Victory. The poem, sent to me in May 1981, hangs on my office wall and has challenged me to write this book.

Challenge to Victory

Excitement of breathing,
And labor of living.
"How can this be?" you say.
Give me the former and
Not the latter.
For I wish the Golden Ring.

"Aha!" says another.
"I have life today,
My Journey begins.
Excitement and labor,
I fear not.
For they only challenge me
To Victory."

17

COMPUTERS FOR THE FINANCIAL PLANNER

The financial planner, like most professionals, has been swept into the age of computers. Sooner or later, the planner's very existence could depend on a system of microchips providing access to a much more sophisticated world of financial planning.

KNOW WHAT YOU WANT

Selecting a computer for your practice is not simple and could, in fact, become quite complicated, to say the least. It requires the same skill and care used in selecting products for your clients. And that means performing due diligence. Should you select the wrong product, the wrong computer system, there will only be one victim—you. And, unlike your clients, you won't have the SEC to complain to, or the bank where you send your monthly amortization payments.

Do I mean to imply that the vendors of computer systems are corrupt and delight in selling bad products to financial planners? Not in the least. The computer system vendors, for the most part, are sincere, helpful, and extremely knowledgeable—and are very conscious of tarnishing their reputations. The problem is that a great many financial planners do not understand what computers can or cannot do, or why they would even need one. Nowadays, it seems that everyone is buying a computer, so it must be the thing to do, right? Well, not so fast.

You do not need a master's degree in computer science, nor must you be able to program a computer, in order to use one. But you do need a basic understanding of computer systems to purchase one intelligently. In this chapter I will provide you with basic information on computers and, at the same time, try to remain nontechnical. Furthermore, although I refer to several specific products on the market, in no way do I either endorse or discourage their purchase. My intent is simply to point out what is available to the small financial planner, while remaining as objective as possible.

The primary reason for purchasing a computer system is to save time. Saving time means efficiency, and efficiency generally translates into dollars and cents. If a system will not increase your efficiency, you probably have no need for it. If you just want something to decorate your office and impress your clients when they walk in, which it may very well do, you don't need a complete system. Just buy a dummy keyboard and a CRT (a video display).

However, if you want a computer that you can really use, and not just window dressing, you must be practical. Don't be concerned with keeping up with the Joneses, or in this case, Merrill Lynch, Dean Witter, or Shearson. At this stage, you are no match for their technology. The point is that many a financial planner has gone out and purchased an expensive computer system when, in fact, a programmable calculator would have served the same function. The purchase of a computer system must make sense and you must justify the dollars you spend in terms of productivity.

WHAT ARE "HARDWARE" AND "SOFTWARE"?

Before you begin to look for a computer there are two terms you must be familiar with: *hardware* and *software*. The hardware is the computer itself, the physical device that you look at and touch. Usually, it consists of a video display or screen (the CRT); a keyboard for inputting; a storage unit such as a disk drive to increase the capacity of the system; a printer to produce output in the form of hardcopy; and a central processing unit (CPU), which is the nucleus of the system and is sometimes contained within one of the other components. The cost of hardware runs into thousands of dollars, or tens of thousands of dollars if you are purchasing a full turnkey system or a minicomputer. However, since microcomputers are more than sufficient for most financial planning firms (except perhaps the very large ones and multioffice firms), this chapter will stick to the microcomputer. Should you feel that your business requires a minicomputer or mainframe (it probably doesn't at this point), I suggest that you begin your search by hiring a good systems analyst.

The planner who purchases a micro, however, does not need to hire an expensive systems analyst. All the planner has to do is understand fully the need of his or her firm, comprehend the basics of computers, and then make an intelligent decision. Does this process sound familiar? Well, that's what you do every day when you write case plans and select financial service products for your clients.

Software is a set of instructions that are fed into the computer. In essence, it is what makes your computer do what you want it to do. A computer is only as good as the software that instructs it. You can, therefore, buy the most expensive, most sophisticated hardware in the world but it won't measure up if the software is inferior. Software will generally cost from a few hundred dollars for a word-processing or data management program, to several thousand dollars or more for a custom-designed package.

The most common mistake financial planners make is to look at the hardware before they look at the software. In effect, it is almost like a student who goes to a bookstore to buy a textbook, and then decides later which course to take. Financial planning systems and software people to whom I've spoken agreed unanimously on this point. Choose the software before you choose the hardware—rule number one.

DEFINE YOUR NEEDS

The second step is to *define your needs*. In other words, what do you want? What can a computer do to make you a better and more successful financial planner? Can it make the job you are doing easier and more efficient, and your business more profitable? Will it enable you to do things you are not already doing but would like to do? Will it increase your firm's productivity? Finally, is what the computer can achieve worth what it will cost?

Look at your needs for both a short-term and a long-term perspective. What specifically do you need a computer to do? Do you want it to keep internal records? Do you want it to search for client record information? Do you want the computer to perform calculations, forecast projections, analyze data? Do you want to word-process text, letters, and documents? Do you want a mailing list? Do you want it to do your accounting or your client's accounting? Do you want it to prepare tax returns or project individual, corporate, or estate taxes? In terms of financial planning, do you want to prepare a computerized plan for your client, or do you want to limit the computer output to projections for your internal use and then write the plan manually? Or do you want both capabilities? Do you want a tracking system to track the client's plan? The list is endless. It must be, since each financial planner operates in his or her own unique way, in the individual's own creative style. What one planner needs is often quite different from what another needs. Just remember: If you're not sure what your needs are, *you are not ready to purchase a computer*!

CHOOSING YOUR SOFTWARE

Once you've defined your needs, the next step is determining what software (programs) is available to handle these needs. This, in my opinion, is the most important step in buying a system and must not be taken lightly. The more time you take to complete this step, which I refer to as "the automation due diligence step," the less chance you will have of buying the wrong system. And buying the wrong system can be a very costly mistake that will frustrate you for years to come— both financially and functionally. It is like buying an expensive piece of furniture only to find that it won't go through the doorway and you have to leave it on the back porch. You must also keep in mind that, in general, no financial planning package or software will do everything you want it to do. Again, each financial planner is a unique professional and individual needs vary. Most systems and software vendors concentrate their software on what the majority of planners look for. A good system or program that you buy should be capable of accomplishing about 75 to 80% of what you desire. Of course, there is a way to meet 100% of your software needs, and that is to customize your programs. But unless you or someone in your office is able to program the system, an outside software specialist can be quite expensive, with most customized programs running into thousands of dollars.

There are a great many financial planning programs to choose from. Programs can write case financial plans; analyze capital needs; project tax shelters; analyze and project estate tax; calculate income tax; analyze investments and track portfolios; project retirement income; analyze education funds; project pensions; analyze insurance; project cash flow; maintain general ledger; and word-process verbal text. You can find a program to do just about anything. And then there is VisiCalc, a program well on its way to revolutionizing the entire software industry.

The beauty of VisiCalc is that it will run on almost any hardware. VisiCalc is like having an electronic spread sheet in front of you. Since it allows all types of calculations, you can build a whole stream of interrelated steps and view them on the spread sheet. A change in any one variable will affect all other dependent variables, according to the formulas you choose to use. It has tremendous capability in terms of forecasts and projections. In effect, the financial planner can use a computer as a huge calculator, changing formulas, design, or input at will. VisiCalc programs can be purchased in two ways. First, VisiCalc-based programs can be purchased as part of general financial planning software by certain vendors. The cost is usually several hundred dollars, but a full package including all types of financial planning software may run several thousand dollars. However, if you wish to customize the program to your own needs, most software manufacturers offer VisiCalc programs in which you set up the formulas yourself. This type of software generally costs a few hundred dollars at most.

CHOOSING YOUR HARDWARE

When you have decided what you need, and what software will do the job, it is then time to think about the hardware. First, determine what hardware is compatible with the software you desire to buy. This should eliminate a great deal of the hardware on the market. From there, select a system that you feel comfortable with, and one that will not clean out your wallet, put you into hock, or force you to go public. For example, IBM computers are probably more expensive than most personal computers on the market, but may be more sophisticated in certain ways than some other systems. You must weigh the differences in cost against the greater level of sophistication. Sometimes the differences are a lot and sometimes they are minute. However, if the software you select is compatible with one system exclusively, then obviously you have no choice. But most software should be compatible with several systems.

DO YOU WANT A TURNKEY SYSTEM?

In your search for the proper software you should investigate the financial planning systems firms who offer turnkey systems, that is, both hardware and software together. If you find a systems package to your liking, the hardware purchasing decision has been eliminated and you can usually arrange to purchase the hardware and software from one vendor. Again, you must keep in mind that, when looking at an entire system, don't be overly impressed by the hardware. Hardware is merely a tool. The software—the capability of meeting your specific needs—is what really counts. Focus your attention on what the system does and not on what it looks like. In fact, some of the full financial planning programs are so sophisticated and complete that they do everything but make the coffee.

I suggest that you review thoroughly the capabilities of the full systems on the market. Is what they have to offer compatible with your needs? Rather than mention these companies specifically, I direct you to their frequent advertisements in *The Financial Planner* magazine; most have "hands on" demonstrations at the National Convention of the IAFP and several of the local chapter forums. If you are serious about purchasing a turnkey computer system, seeing a product demonstration would be most helpful.

Purchasing a computer system out of a catalog, through a magazine, or over the telephone is out of the question. You should definitely see a demonstration of any system that you are considering. Ask the marketing representative as many detailed questions as you can think of, and collect as much information as possible. Then talk to the competitors and ask where they see weaknesses in the other company's product. I'm sure they will be more than happy to help you out. But be sure to check their opinions for validity.

Perhaps the best sources of information about a particular financial planning system are present users of that system. Chat with your fellow planners. If they are happy with their systems, ask them why. What has the system done to enhance business or to increase profits? If they are unhappy, you might not need to ask why—they will probably volunteer the information quite readily, and then some.

The next step is to analyze a full turnkey in-house system versus independent software and your own hardware. You should also keep in mind that some of the turnkey systems people also offer software to planners who have already purchased their own hardware. Take all factors into consideration—cost, capability, updating the software, maintenance. If the system goes down (breaks), how long will it take you to get it repaired? Will you be able to borrow another CPU or printer while yours is being repaired? An insurance firm in my building purchased a system and the first time it went down it took them three weeks to get it back in operation. Can you afford to have your system go down for three weeks? One of the best purchases you can make to prevent your computer from going haywire is an antistatic mat, which will discharge static electricity when the operator is on it; static electricity could cause you to lose data, or worse, blow a microchip. An antistatic mat costs somewhere between $100 and $300 and may prove to be well worth the price.

THE CENTRAL PROCESSING UNIT

When buying a computer the financial planner should know something about the internal workings of the system, since this eventually can prove to be of major importance. The real heart of the micro system or any computer system is the central processing unit (CPU). The function of the CPU is to process data according to the program's instructions and to store data in the memory. The size of the internal memory, referred to in terms of "K" (or thousand), limits the sophistication of the programs to be used with the system. The most common internal memory sizes of microcomputers adequate for the financial planner are 32K, 48K, 64K, 96K, 128K, and 256K. However, part of the memory of the system is needed for the system's internal use, and for this reason the purchaser must also know how much memory space is, in effect, available for the programs to be used. CPUs differ; this is very important, since a program that requires 50K of memory will not work on a 64K system if the 64K system needs 15K for internal use alone. Another consideration is that most microsystems have 8-bit processors, although some of the newer models come with 16. The advantage of the 16-bit processor over the 8 is that it is faster and more precise in processing information and calculating variables. It is also generally more expensive.

Even if you choose a 64K system over a more expensive 128K or 256K system, it doesn't necessarily mean that the smaller system is limited in its use. Most systems today are easily expandable to an additional several hundred thousand to several million characters, by means of a disk or expansion drive. Disk drives are relatively inexpensive, costing about $500 to $1500. Before buying any systems, check to see how expandable the system is. A multidisk drive should allow you to run several programs at one time, merging information.

SELECTING A PRINTER

However, all the computer power in the world, all the sophistication, all the most innovative projections, might not ever be seen by the client. But what is seen by the client should be terrific in terms of quality. Therefore, the output that you physically present to your client must be the same high quality that exists throughout all your work. Accordingly, you must give careful thought to the printer that you select to be certain that it meets your needs. Are you going to require a lot of hardcopy output? Is the quality of the print or the printing speed more important? Perhaps you have a great need for both speed and quality in your output.

Because of the varying needs of the consumer, many different printers are available. In my opinion, a printer is essential even if you have no intention of providing hardcopies to your clients. For one thing you will need the hardcopy for internal purposes, to provide potential financial planning solutions to problems; second, you may need hardcopy one day to justify to the SEC or a court how you arrived at your conclusions. Furthermore, having hardcopy saves you time since you will not have to turn on your system or change programs every time you need to retrieve information. For the planner who is going to provide clients with hardcopies—either support documents or verbal text—the type of printer used is very important. In fact, the type of printer that you purchase is probably one of the most important systems decisions that you will have to make. Therefore, let's review some basics about printers.

THE LETTER-QUALITY PRINTER.   If you are going to provide a word-processed case to your clients, send out good-looking letters on your stationery, or produce documents for the clients' use, the letter-quality printer is essential. The advantage, of course, is that the hardcopy output is of the same high quality as a good professional typewriter. The disadvantage is that the printer is relatively slow, usually delivering about 500 words a minute, so that it could take considerable time if you are processing multiple quantities of a document. A good letter-quality printer should cost about $1500 to $3000.

THE DOT MATRIX PRINTER.   If you need speed and are not that concerned with letter-quality copy, a dot matrix printer should serve the purpose. This, by no means, implies that the quality of the dot matrix printer is poor. In fact, some dot matrix printers produce exceptionally good-looking output. But generally, the printing is not quite equal to that of the letter-quality printer. The cost of a dot matrix printer is usually less than that of a letter-quality printer and a good one can be purchased for about $1000 to $2000. The print speed should be about three to five times as fast as that of the letter-quality printer. This printer is excellent for internal reports and for reports to clients where quality of the document is not a criterion.

A well-established financial planner may, in fact, have a need for both a letter-quality and a dot matrix printer. Space permitting, the planner can certainly own both.

PLOTTERS.   If your financial plans or output are graphic, such as line charts, pie charts, bar charts, or other types of graphs, you might wish to consider a plotter that produces graphic output. Today you can purchase plotters both in black and white and in color; the cost, including software, should be $1000 to $3000.

ALTERNATIVES TO BUYING A COMPUTER

Whether you decide to buy the hardware and software separately or to buy a complete turnkey system, the bottom line, of course, is cost. The price you pay for the system must be well worth it to you. The biggest waste of money is a computer that collects dust. Sometimes the planner will have a need for a computer, but the infrequency of its use does not warrant the cost. There are alternatives. One alternative is using a service bureau; you fill out a data input sheet and the service bureau completes the financial plan or whatever component output you have requested, using your data. This is similar to the way a tax service would prepare a tax return or a general ledger for an accountant. Usually, the cost of these plans ranges from about $50 to several hundred dollars and most, unfortunately, leave quite a bit to be desired in terms of quality and personalization. However, there are some that are exceptionally good and provide a draft to the planner prior to completing the final text. The planner may then make personalized changes, including the writing of the recommendations.

If the planner's objective is simply number crunching to be followed by the planner's own personal analysis, most of these plans are acceptable. Before experimenting with your clients, though, you should first obtain samples of these plans to see whether they meet your expectations. Many of these "canned plans" simply toss back your input in a different form, or are saturated with filler on the state of the economy, the current tax laws, or financial planning—information that the client couldn't care less about and could obtain easily from a book or newspaper. The fact is that many of these service bureau plans were designed simply to help financial product salespeople sell their products. However, as more and more planners charge fees, these plans should improve in quality, especially if the service bureaus hope to remain competitive. Recently, as financial planners have begun to take charging fees quite seriously, the plans have improved.

Another alternative to purchasing an "in-house system" is time sharing, whereby the planner buys or leases a terminal and pays for the time used to access the mainframe computer. The fees, of course, depend on the amount of time the planner will use it and could cost several hundred to several thousands of dollars plus the cost of telephoning the computer center. However, one must keep in mind that the sophistication of a mainframe computer should vastly exceed that of a micro system; also if the time-share company at the other end has done its homework, the level of your output should be sensational. However, there is the practical consideration of whether you really need the computing power of a mainframe. Again, this depends on you and the level of your clientele.

A skilled planner should review the advantages and disadvantages of time-sharing and service bureaus versus equity ownership in a system. After all, there is nothing wrong with equity ownership. It is a philosophy that we preach to our clients, isn't it? Some companies may even lease with an option to buy.

Finally, if you decide to purchase a computer, whether you decide to buy a turnkey or component system, you must keep one thing in mind. Always think to the future. Since you will not be buying a system every month, it is essential that you buy a system that not only meets today's needs but also meets tomorrow's needs. Is the system expandable? If your circumstances should change—and they probably will—will the system meet your future needs in terms of capacity and software? If you purchase a component system, will the software vendors still be manufacturing software for your computer five years from now? Will the hardware manufacturer stay up with the technology, keeping your computer compatible with the new innovative software that is sure to be introduced in the future? If you purchase a turnkey system, will your vendor continue to service your expanding needs? These are important questions, and must be answered to ensure that you are purchasing the right system today.

Financial planning is a business in which you must always think ahead. In essence, you must look to the future to solve today's client needs through tomorrow's computer technology and tomorrow's financial service products. Sometimes, it is simply good business to throw in the towel and admit that a screen, a keyboard, a magnetic disk, some wires, and those little things called microchips can do a much better job for us than we can do ourselves.

The perfect financial planning partnership is the accuracy and speed of a computer combined with the personality, integrity, and know-how of the financial planner. A computer can help you. It can make your life easier and your quality better. But it can never replace you—you will always be the planner.

18

PLANNERS ON THEIR WAY UP

One was a college teacher, one a housewife and mother, another a school teacher on a foreign exchange contract. What are they doing today? They are all financial planners building very successful practices.

The objective of writing this chapter was to demonstrate to you how a sampling of financial planners still in the early stages of professional development have made it to where they are today. The planners introduced in this chapter run their own firms and are still feeling their way around, and all are building their practices in their own way. What attracted each one to financial planning? What enticed them to go out on their own? What advice can they give to those who are two years or so behind them and ready to make the break to start their own practices?

All of these planners have their own unique style of practice, choosing the direction they feel is most suitable for them. For instance, Mimi Merrill, CFP, is a fee-only planner who had started her practice by helping primarily single and divorced women; and now, due to her rising exposure in the community, she has begun to tackle the executive and the upper-middle-income markets as well. Eileen Sharkey, CFP, was also a fee-only planner, but because she felt a loss of control in the implementation phase of the planning process she became a fee-and-commission planner. Charles Hughes, CFP, has always been a fee-and-commission planner but is probably gravitating more toward the fee area than originally expected.

The point is that they are all doing financial planning in their own way, in their own style, the way they feel financial planning should be done. I have written about them to demonstrate that there is no single way to build up a practice. There are common denominators. There are general concepts. But the financial planner cannot be a stereotype, a carbon copy of somebody else. You can start out by using similar techniques that other successful or potentially successful planners use. However, eventually the practice that you build must be designed around you.

One of the keys to becoming a successful financial planner is individualism. In fact, I have not met a successful financial planner yet who is not a very strong individualist. For you to succeed you must take a firm hold on the direction you have chosen and be guided by yourself—by your beliefs and convictions. The planners I have written about are all very strong individualists. They look, they listen, they observe, but in the end, they do what is best for themselves. And it appears that they are all on the way up because of it.

Why did I choose these particular planners? They were in the right place at the right time, I guess. There are hundreds and perhaps thousands of planners like them across the country in large cities and in small communities. However, my reason for including this chapter is that there are thousands and perhaps tens of thousands who want to be like them.

Mary ("Mimi") Merrill, CFP
Madison, Wisconsin

Back in 1976, Mimi Merrill was not thinking about being a financial planner—she was looking for one. She was also looking for something a lot deeper, something much more important than a financial planner or even her own assets—she was looking for herself. After years of being a corporate wife, married to a midlevel executive, Mimi Merrill desperately needed to find herself. Of the thousands of women who go through this midlife identity crisis, very few will ever follow their dreams and turn them into reality. Mimi, with the love of her husband and children to carry her through the long, hard hours of pursuing her dreams, set out to find the real Mimi Merrill.

When she inherited a small amount of money back in 1976, Mimi could not find a financial planner to help her. It was then that the seed for a new career in financial planning was planted. She had actually gone to see a financial planner, but the planner barely listened to anything she had to say. Instead, he offered an immediate solution to all her needs through the sale of this product and that product. "He had no sensitivity to my needs. He didn't listen to a thing we said," Mimi recently told me, even now still troubled by the way the planner had gone about his business.

So she became her own financial planner, invested her inheritance herself, and enrolled in the University of Wisconsin for a master's degree in finance as a part-time student. In 1978 she took what she then thought was a permanent career position in financial planning with a Madison, Wisconsin, firm, but soon found she was back in the pits that she had for so long sought to climb out of. After attending a training course and securing all the proper licensing requirements needed to implement products, Mimi found that she could not function as a commission-only planner. "It was the worst time of my life. I hated the thought of dialing the phone. Cold calling terrorized me. I was so unhappy that I couldn't get out of bed. I wanted in the worst way to be a financial *counselor*, not a salesperson."

It was in 1979 that Mimi read *Money Dynamics* by Venita Van Caspel and decided to enroll in the CFP program through the College for Financial Planning. This program, and her M.B.A. which she was also still pursuing, monopolized most of her hours. But in February 1981 her education and experience began to pay off as she opened Budget Counseling Service. And so that she could easily get to work and travel back and forth to school, she located the office a few blocks from the University of Wisconsin. Budget Counseling Service was designed to help the middle-income wage earner. Mimi reasoned that the rich had their advisors—the accountants, the lawyers, and investment advisors; and the less affluent had their advisors—the credit counselors. But who was helping the middle class in an objective manner? The salesman she had gone to? Obviously not. Her first clients were friends, divorced women, and referrals from psychologists. Shortly after opening her practice Mimi received her CFP designation, her M.B.A. in finance, and registered with the SEC as an investment advisor.

Mimi views success not in terms of money, but in terms of being her own person—an individualist able to do the best job she knows how for her clients. Profit is an afterthought; excellence in her profession is the prime objective. In fact, she is a firm believer that profits should be reinvested in the business and she does just that, purchasing equipment, computer hardware and software, and larger office facilities. Once she was the victim of being a corporate wife; but now she is the beneficiary, unpressured by the profit motive to support her family, allowing her husband that privilege. Mimi's advice to would-be fee-only financial planners is to have another source of income for the first few years while you are building up the business to the point where it is profitable. She feels that it takes at least two years just to develop the necessary experience and skills that you will require. For her it certainly did not come overnight, to say the least. The transition from corporate executive wife took five years of hard work, five years of devoting many hours a day to working with clients, pursuing her M.B.A. degree and CFP designation, and serving as both wife and mother.

From her two-room office on University Avenue in Madison, Wisconsin, a city of 170,000 people, she has watched her Budget Counseling Service grow. Her office is eclectically styled, upholstered chairs opposite her desk, the type of office a psychologist might have. Mimi believes in paying for high-quality professional services and not attempting to do something herself that others can do better. With that philosophy she hired a lawyer and an accountant to set up her practice properly. She has also hired a copywriter to work with her on her quarterly newsletter and a speech consultant to improve her public image. Her client base now consists of university professors, single and divorced women, middle-management executives, state and local government employees, and physicians. Her average client earns about $25,000 to $75,000 per year. Mimi rarely advertises but works mostly from referrals by clients and other professionals. To assist her in her work she has purchased an Apple II computer, a letter-quality printer, VisiCalc software for financial projections and analyses, balance sheets, and income statements, and word-processing software to write cases. She currently charges clients a fee of approximately 1% of their gross income, with a $250 minimum fee and a $750 maximum fee for a plan, or $60 an hour if the client needs specialized work rather than a complete plan. She also has an interesting policy whereby the client, in her judgment, must have the motivation and self-discipline to engage in financial planning before she will accept that person as a client.

Mimi presently holds workshops for the University of Wisconsin Extension and is on the faculty of the Financial Planning School of the Credit Union National Association, Inc., and the College for Financial Planning. She has written a financial column for a Madison-based feminist newspaper, *The Feminist Connection*, and has reviewed financial books in her column. Mimi advises fee-only financial planners to develop public-speaking skills and to write both a personal and a business financial plan for themselves. And in order to build her practice further, she is moving toward corporate seminars and the corporate executive market.

Charles Hughes, CFP
Bay Shore, New York

In 1971, Charles Hughes, CFP, made a change of careers—from college teacher to financial planning. Through the contacts of several of his former students, he first went to work for a small NASD broker-dealer firm and life general agent who specialized in newly issued securities of small companies. The transition from academia to sales was difficult itself, but was further complicated by the fact that his company provided absolutely no training in sales or products. As a result, Charles was not very comfortable making recommendations of products about which he knew very little, if anything at all. His stay with the company lasted only nine months.

Changing from job to job, however, was not what Charles wanted to do. He hooked on with Oppenheimer & Company and spent almost the next nine years there, wholesaling Oppenheimer products in the Middle Atlantic states, the Northeast, and the Southeast. Then in March 1981 he left Oppenheimer and, without any clients, tried to make it on his own.

Convinced that there was a definite need for financial planning for individuals, Charles was sure that with time people would become increasingly aware of the importance and the benefits of financial planning. Soon, he felt, the perfect marriage would take place between the public and the financial planning industry, as soon as the public became enlightened to all the benefits that financial planning could bring. "I felt I wanted to be solidly in position before both of those roads met. The decade of the eighties and beyond is going to be the period for the retail person, the person delivering directly to the clients financial products and services."

His decision to leave Oppenheimer took him a long time. It was both an emotional and a career decision. For several years he had been prepared to leave from a career standpoint, but not from an emotional one; at other times, he was ready emotionally to go out on his own but had not thought it a sound career move. Finally, in March 1981, he was ready. The move came on his thirty-eighth birthday.

In less than two years his practice has grown substantially. The firm consists of himself, his wife, who is taking the CFP designation program, and a clerical assistant; he is presently interviewing for a financial planner. He charges $60 an hour and offers three basic types of services. The Financial Focus deals with specific areas of a family's financial profile. It is a partial plan that addresses the specific needs of the client. The average Financial Focus case costs the client about $300 to $400. A comprehensive plan, on the other hand, is designed for clients earning $100,000 a year or more with a net worth in excess of $300,000, and covers all aspects of their lives. In general, the comprehensive plan will first define the client's present situation and the needs to be addressed; then it presents observations, recommendations, and an implementation schedule. Charles charges a $1000 minimum fee for this plan. The third type of service is an annual financial statement, which is a snapshot of a client's financial position and is used either as a starting point for a new client or as a review of an existing client's situation. It is a reference point for future work together and the minimum charge to the client is $150. Charles Hughes, CFP, is a licensed NASD representative, a life insurance general agent, holds a real estate sales license, and is a Registered Investment Advisor.

He believes that it is important to get involved in areas which give him exposure to the public, especially such areas as teaching and speaking. He is a regional vice president for the Institute of Certified Financial Planners and teaches courses for the College for Financial Planning, New York University, and Mount St. Vincent's College. He believes strongly in seminars and became proficient in running them while still at Oppenheimer. "Seminars are an excellent way to get out there and talk about the benefits of financial planning to as many people at one time as possible. It is both an effective and an efficient use of your time." He estimates that about 20% of the people who show up for his seminars eventually become clients.

He stresses to his clients that financial planning is a slow process. "Most clients got into their current situation over a long period of time. It's obvious that it will take some degree of time for them to put their pursuit of financial independence back on direction. I stress to them that it will take three years to see clear signs of progress, of arriving at financial independence that they did not have earlier. To see all the parts of a financial plan working together with any degree of harmony requires some time."

From his own experience Charles advises new planners making the jump to their own practice to:

1. Do more preparation while still employed at the old job, by utilizing time after working hours or on weekends. He suggests that you write a business plan, rent space, install a telephone, finalize your business name, and print stationery. Each item, no matter how trivial it seems, deserves proper time and attention.

2. Be sure that you are aware of all the regulatory implications of being a financial planner. It is not like opening up a retail store or a fast-food restaurant. The industry on any given day can be affected by any number of regulatory bodies. Therefore, secure good counsel to be

certain that you are complying with the current regulatory requirements.

3. Know what is going on in the business and do not be overcome by the desire to see your business grow. There will be times when you are faced with some very hard decisions, and at those times you will need to redefine your primary responsibility to the client. I feel that it is to provide the client with advice as objective and well informed as you are capable of giving. It also means not being distracted from that goal by any other short-term goals, however attractive those short-term goals may appear at the moment. The planner must refrain from the temptation of making a quick buck when the opportunity arises. This can become very difficult because no one is paying the bills but you.

4. Be in a position to react to the changes that occur in our business every day. Try not to marry yourself to any particular concept or any one approach because there is such a vast degree of change going on, not only with the products and services that our clients use, but also in the very structure of the financial planning profession itself. To be married to ideas at this time could prove to be detrimental in the long run.

5. Try to be as informed as possible about products and services that clients might use to implement your recommendations. Maintain a network of communications with colleagues in the business and in related fields.

The future for Charles Hughes is still unclear. But then that's not unusual because the financial planning profession, in general, is unclear as well. He is not certain whether he wants a big operation, yet he doesn't see himself continuing on his own. "I see the need of having others associated with me."

Eileen Sharkey, CFP
Denver, Colorado

In 1969, Eileen Sharkey was teaching English and European history to high school students in London, England. Today she is a dynamic young financial planner with her own practice in Denver, Colorado, destined to make her mark on the financial planning community. In the few short years that Eileen has worked in the field she has managed to build up quite a slate of credentials. She is the founder and was the first president of the Rocky Mountain Chapter of the International Association for Financial Planning and currently serves on the National Board. In addition, Eileen is the Western Regional Vice President of the Institute of Certified Financial Planners.

Eileen, who holds a Bachelor of Arts degree in History and English from the University of London, came to the United States in 1971 to teach school in Eldorado, Kansas, a suburb of Wichita. "It sounded exciting," she told me, looking back and laughing at her naiveté. "Everything is so close in England, one city is only an hour or so from the other. I thought America was somewhat like England, only bigger. I assumed Wichita was close to a suburb of New York."

It was a bit of a cultural shock to come from England to the wilds of Kansas. The first time a tornado hit, she was convinced that she would be swept away like Dorothy in *The Wizard of Oz*. When the teaching contract ran out, Eileen had the option of going back to England or staying in America. Since she had not seen Disneyland or the Grand Canyon or New Orleans or the Mardi Gras, she decided to stay and complete an American degree in history at Newman College in Wichita, Kansas. But in those days it was hard to find a job in teaching, so she made her way to Denver, found a niche in pension design and administration, and temporarily packed her chalk and rule book away.

Eileen's path to financial planning can be tracked back to *Money Magazine*, where she read a letter to the editor about the College for Financial Planning. She was fascinated by this new subject. "I always knew that there had to be more to do with your money than insurance. But I didn't know what."

Eileen completed her CFP designation in May 1978, worked for a small firm for the next few years as the in-house financial planner, and became a member of the adjunct faculty for the College in 1980; in 1981 she joined the ranks of the self-employed and opened her own practice. She now works from a professional office plaza in southeast Denver, sharing office space with an accounting firm and another financial planning firm. Because of this arrangement, she has access to computers and tax planning that she would not otherwise have. She has two employees, a secretary and a paraprofessional, and is totally wrapped up in the business 18 hours a day; this includes time she spends working for the IAFP, the College for Financial Planning, and speaking on local radio shows. "It's a fun business. It's great—a brand new area," Eileen declared. "You're on the cutting edge of a new profession. The rules are yours and you are free to create the kinds of financial plans your clients need."

Although she practices as a generalist, most of her work is in the areas of retirement planning for clients age 55 and over; single women; educators; two-income families; and small businesses. She finds older Americans fascinating to work with. They generally have a lot of knowledge and experience, but are usually very frustrated that the experience they have gathered over a lifetime does not seem to apply in dealing with the present economy. She enjoys helping these people. She has also experienced, to her advantage, reverse discrimination, where women in the business world come to her simply because she is a woman. The average income of Eileen's clients ranges from $30,000 to $80,000 per year; however, some of her clients have substantially higher incomes and above-average net worth. Only in the last year did she bring her practice from fee-only to fee-and-commission. "Many of my clients did not like going to four or five other places to implement their plan with the necessary products and services. Although I was monitoring the various transactions, my clients were more comfortable when I handled it all myself. Another reason for handling *all* of my clients' financial matters was that a few of my clients had been burned in tax shelters that were purchased through relatives. These shelters were totally inappropriate for the client, but I had no control."

Eileen presently holds a NASD license, an insurance broker and real estate license, and is registered with the SEC as an Investment Advisor. Her fee is $75 an hour; while some of her clients need only a few hours' work, others require a full case study that can run as much as $3000 or $4000 dollars. Her average financial plan usually runs $800 to $2000, with most plans averaging about $1500.

From the start, Eileen has had one goal in mind—to work as an independent practitioner. She has no desire to build a financial empire. She loves working with people, and she likes all of her clients. "The advantage of being a financial planner and/or being in business for yourself is that you can pick and choose your clients. My clients also get to pick and choose me. The first hour that we meet is at a reduced rate, and at the end of that hour there is no obligation on either of us either way. I consider it my responsibility to get them where they want to be financially." Confident that this is the business to be in, she offers the following advice to any would-be financial planner: "Practice what you preach. Write a financial plan for yourself. I know financial planners who don't even have wills. But the process of financial planning works. It matters that you start; it matters that you stick with it. Give yourself time to develop your interests. Provide services to your clients and always be honest with them."

Eileen's greatest concern today is to be able to service her clients correctly, yet she is very much afraid of overextending herself. She attributes the addition of many of her new clients to recommendations made by her existing clients, the ICFP referral service, her own visibility as a planner in her community, and new financial planners who do not yet trust their own competence in many areas. She feels that the next ten years of financial planning will prove to be extremely interesting for "whoever lives through them."

19

AND SOME WHO HAVE MADE IT

Writing a chapter about successful financial planners was indeed a pleasure. It was also an invaluable learning experience. Seeing how some "real pros" operate their practices and how they achieved their success was a rewarding experience.

The real objective of this chapter, however, is to demonstrate a key point and not to dwell on the current success of several deserving financial planners. Each of these planners worked hard to get where he is today. They are all self-made. And no one handed them a financial planning business on a silver platter. Each one went through the painful process of trial and error, building, changing, and rebuilding. Each one started from nowhere and built a successful planning practice around his own determination, ideas, goals, and hours of labor. And each practice is different from the others in its own way. These are not Supermen, nor are they Super Planners. In fact, I have never met a Super Planner, only skilled, hard-working ones. They are typical, nonetheless, of the numerous successful planners who have built practices molded from their own ideas. And there are many more like them.

Unfortunately, in a book of this size I cannot write about every successful financial planner there is. For one thing, there are too many that I know of. And for another, there are too many that I don't know of, but who, I'm sure, deserve equal credit. Not all successful financial planners maintain high visibility. There are many unsung heroes in the industry who are top-quality planners. And nobody has ever heard of them, except, of course, the people who really count—their clients. I'd have loved to write about them all, but the task would have been endless. Furthermore, each day more and more financial planners are really making it big.

My definition of a successful financial planner is one who has achieved what he or she set out to achieve. In none of these cases was it for money, although we all know that money is generally a by-product of success. A financial planner can be a monetary success and still be deeply dissatisfied with the way in which his or her practice has developed. Success means the ability to control a practice and to bring it along in the manner desired. Otherwise, there may be financial reward but there will not be true success or personal satisfaction. Success is not only measured by the opinions of the outside world but also by the inner satisfaction of the planner. To be successful, you must feel successful.

The planners that I've written about have all achieved success, and will continue to be successful, I am sure. Success is an ongoing process, a process that continues from the moment it starts.

Jim Barry, CFP, walked away from a top job with an investment company to be his own person. He started with an office, a yellow pad, and big ideas. Lawrence Krause, CFP, after building up the financial planning department of a regional brokerage firm, decided that it was time to build again, but this time he built his own firm. And the same with Dick Silverstein, CFP. He built up a successful practice from scratch while devoting a great many hours to charity and college teaching. Bob Underwood, CFP, gave up commissions forever to become "the preacher" of the fee-only practice. Their success cannot be attributed to magic or luck or being in the right place at the right time. They all had ideas and they all made those ideas work.

I have written how these four planners created successful practices, not for the sake of providing detailed biographies, but hopefully to inspire you with their successes. Remember, many of their ideas have already been proven successful. A financial planner can and should get ideas from others.

And I apologize to all the other equally successful planners who should be included in this chapter as well.

James A. Barry, CFP
Boca Raton, Florida

Jim Barry has come a long way from his meager childhood in Boston, Massachusetts. He didn't enjoy the luxury of a bathtub until he was 14. As Jim puts it, "I didn't have two nickels to rub together." Today he is president of five companies, including Asset Management Corporation of Boca Raton, Florida; he's the author of *Financial Freedom*, a book on financial planning; he lectures throughout the United States on this topic, has a television show, drives a Rolls-Royce, and is still striving for greater achievements. There aren't too many persons I know who have come so far so fast.

"I love my business. And everything I do is my business. My golf game is my business. My tennis game is my business."

Jim graduated from Burdett College in Boston, Massachusetts. He was the first on both sides of his family to attend college. Following in the footsteps of his father, who had sold life insurance for John Hancock for 33 years, Jim took a job with Hartford Life, a job that lasted nine years. The last four years there he ran an ordinary life agency of 42 agents, building it up to the number two agency in the company. "But it was a training mill. Nine or ten guys didn't last the year." When Putnam Management Company wanted to bring life insurance into the investment business, he quickly made the jump. Another nine years went by and he had worked himself up to Senior Vice President and National Sales Manager. He then decided to step up to the plate and become involved in his own business. "I knew that the name of the game was equity ownership."

What Jim had seen as he traveled throughout the United States with Putnam was a lot of very successful people who were deeply involved in their work. In fact, they were so involved that they did not have enough time for their most important asset—their families. Furthermore, they were very confused. The life insurance agent was coming at them telling them that they needed life insurance. But then the stockbroker would tell them that cash-value insurance was a lousy investment and was no hedge against inflation. So the client would buy term insurance and stocks, only to see the market go down instead of up. To add to the confusion, the CPA would come in *after* the fact, after the client had made the money, and would hand the client a tax bill, leaving the client to wonder where the CPA was the year before. "I saw people out there scattered all over God's creation not knowing what to do with their money. I saw the need to help them, the need for financial planning."

When he first started out, Jim could not quite define financial planning, but he knew that it was not simply a matter of selling life insurance, with no other products available to fill the clients' needs. But the life insurance agent claimed to be a financial planner. Jim saw that this attitude was not objective or beneficial to clients. There certainly was a need for someone who was unbiased and able to guide them, to direct them.

Although successful at Putnam, Jim was not fulfilled. He wasn't an owner—an *entrepreneur*. And that's a word Jim loved. So after 18 years of working for others, he decided to make the break. He started a company composed only of himself and his secretary, and after years as a senior executive at Putnam, learning to make his own coffee was a new experience. But it came with the territory. The first three years provided a tremendous learning experience. His first planning cases ranged from $250 to $500 in fees, a far cry from the $5000 minimum he now gets. But the development of Jim's firm was a step-by-step, crawling process. Jim credits his major breakthrough to a game plan which was developed two years into the business. The theory was that if we write financial plans for clients, we must write one for our own business. So with that in mind, he closed down shop, took his staff on a retreat, and wrote a game plan to target in on the various aspects of the business: What type of firm did they want it to be? What penetration was there to be made in the marketplace? What types of clients did they want to handle? And then they analyzed the current market situation.

Today, Asset Management Corporation is one of the top firms in the financial planning field and Jim Barry is a true leader in the profession. His firm charges a minimum fee of $5000 to write a case and has charged as much as $35,000 to $40,000. On the average, Jim earns three to four times more in commission dollars than in fees. His fees entitle clients to a written case plus six months of service. The annual renewal fee for any client is $1000. "Fees are a must. There is no such thing as a free lunch. And there is no such thing as a loss-lead item in my organization." Upon renewal, clients are then what he calls "club members"; in addition to personalized service, they are entitled to attend a quarterly financial planning seminar and workshop covering the most up-to-date techniques in tax planning, economics, the financial pyramid, and risk–reward concepts.

Jim Barry claims that his secret for success lies in his ability to be critical about himself. He advises other planners to put together a T-square of themselves, listing their pluses (strengths) on one side and their minuses (weaknesses) on the other. The only way that the process will work is by being completely honest. If you cheat, the only one you will be fooling is yourself. After you have drawn up your T-square, blank out your weaknesses, and concentrate on your strengths. "Get stronger and stronger like 'Rocky' in the movie," Jim says. But, of course, don't forget about those weaknesses. That problem, he believes, can be solved by surrounding yourself with what he refers to as "OPB" ("Other People's Brains"). He suggests that you hire the people who are competent in your weak areas, while you perfect your strong points. I thought Jim's ideas made so much sense that I included the Jim Barry T-Square on the following page. Try to evaluate yourself critically and objectively.

The Jim Barry T-Square of Yourself

Your Strengths	Your Weaknesses
Build on these	*Use other people's brains*

If this works for you, you can thank Jim Barry of Boca Raton, Florida.

Today's financial planner must not be resistant to change. Jim agrees that we are in a state of automation, but that "the best computer ever created by God is the computer that you have in your head—your brain. This is your 'hardware.' But for the brain to function it must also have a software package. Your software package consists of all your past experiences. And you must be updating your software package all the time. If you try to make today's decision using yesterday's software, you are going to do it wrong. The financial planner is traveling through unchartered waters. If you hope to be good in this business, you had better adapt to the changes that are occurring. If you don't understand the changes in financial planning, you will be like Willie Loman in *Death of a Salesman*. Dead, without knowing it. With time, you will be out of business. You have to change, to adapt to the circumstances."

One of Jim's philosophies is that he wants to be able to sleep at night. That is why *he* is the general partner of his own oil and gas and horse-breeding programs. "If I am going to be blamed for an investment going wrong, blame me directly. In the past we have made lots of monies for other companies and enjoyed the commissions. But we have not enjoyed the equity ownership. If that oil and gas program is as good as you think it is, why not own a piece of the action as well as the commissions of the program?" According to Jim, 87 to 89% of the funds raised go into each deal. He tries to structure shelters so that the client recovers the investment even before he participates. "You don't have to be dishonest to make big money. There are too many shady deals. The new financial planner should beware, because you have to live with those clients. Too many planners get wrapped up in garbage programs that come back to haunt us.

"In my practice I have stayed away from diamonds, lithographs, book deals, movie deals. I don't want funny money. I don't want multiple write-offs of 5-to-1, 6-to-1, and 7-to-1. Two years later the IRS says 'hold on, recapture, and give us some interest.' I want to know who the promoters are, who the game players are. Don't be hoodwinked by commissions, big cocktail parties and impressive meetings. Do you know who is paying for that? The end user. Of the dollars raised, what's going into the deal? I've stayed away from most private placements with the exception of my own, where I can set my own criteria that are right for the client."

Jim's definition of a financial planner relates in a way to music. "When I was much younger and living in the Boston area, my wife and kids and I used to take a blanket and go to the Charles River to listen to the Boston Pops Orchestra. If you went up to the Boston Pops Orchestra before they started, and asked the trumpet player what the most important instrument in the orchestra is, what do you think he would tell you? The trumpet, of course. Then if you went to the violin section and asked the violinist what he thought the most important instrument was, he'd say, 'It's certainly not the trumpet. That guy makes too much noise. It's the string section.' All of a sudden there was a gray-haired guy named Arthur Fiedler who said, 'I'll tell you what. We're going to start together and we're going to end together, and we're going to get all the ego problems out, and we're going to make music for that audience who came to listen to us.' That's what I do. I'm an orchestrator. I'm a quarterback of a football team. I guide, direct and call the plays. The financial planner has to be a generalist."

Furthermore, Jim insists that you must believe in your practice and you must promote that practice. "You must let people know. Tell the public what you do. Build that visibility. Let the people know who you are. You also have to be involved. You've got to be a game player. You've got to be in the arena." One of the best methods that Jim recommends for building up your practice is holding seminars. Seminars will save you a lot of prospecting, which is the advantage seminars have over taking the one-on-one route. He advises that you book a motel, put an advertisement in the paper, and then begin your performance. "When you do a seminar you are an actor, a showman; it's like Broadway." Jim's first seminars were free. Then one day he woke up to the fact that he could give these same seminars for big money. His first fee seminar was for 227 doctors who paid $100 each to attend. Needless to say, he no longer gives free seminars, except to his club members—his fee-paying clients.

Learning and sharing ideas are very important to Jim. He believes strongly in the concept of "networking," where planners exchange ideas and help each other out. He is neither threatened by other financial planners, nor does he feel that they should be threatened by him. In fact, he predicts for the future a consolidation of financial planners, a coming together for the purpose of sharing ideas, expenses, and so on. He feels that running the small one- and two-person practice is going to be tough without this consolidation. As far as learning is concerned, using tapes is the best way. And he listens to them all the time. "I'm learning every day, and the day that I think I know everything about this business, I'm dead. A financial planner never ever stops learning. And this is one business where you must give everything you've got to it."

He advises planners—young and old, experienced or inexperienced—to *listen*. It is so important. "In our business we don't listen enough and very often we don't communicate. We may think we communicate, but we don't. We're too busy selling our products. If we would listen we could empathize with others, and we'd be able to put ourselves in that other person's shoes." What upsets Jim more than anything, however, is the concept of "doom and gloom." The advice to buy gold, to buy silver, to move to the country, to buy a shotgun—he finds this advice revolting.

His career has reached the point of being more than money to Jim Barry. Money is only his way of keeping score. His philosophy is that money comes as a result of being a good game player. And if you don't have dollar signs in your eyes when you sit with your clients, if you have feelings instead, if you listen to them, if you solve their problems, you will make money. "There are three kinds of people you will meet. The first type have a way about them that makes things happen. The second type watch things happen to them. The third type scratch their heads and want to know what is going on."

It is obvious what type of person Jim Barry is.

Lawrence A. Krause, CFP
San Francisco, California

Quality. Larry Krause insists on absolute quality—without compromise. He is already producing perhaps some of the finest plans in the business. But he is still not satisfied, and is always striving to do better work. "I want to be known as a super-high-quality planner," Larry insists. And that he is.

It took him more than 10 years to make the break—from working with others to venturing out on his own. In 1968 he started out in the financial planning field as a stockbroker with a regional Midwest firm, a firm now long gone to broker-dealer heaven. The firm was big on pushing mutual funds, and in 1968 and 1969 Larry was using them conceptually, switching back and forth within the fund groups. "I guess I was doing market timing, but I didn't know what it was called." But he did well, and the mutual fund wholesalers who had money to burn in those days paid him to fly all over the country attending educational seminars in estate planning and investments, in the hope that he would use their products. This was his real education and he started to utilize the planning concepts that he had learned. "It made a lot of sense. I was doing financial planning without being aware of the term."

In 1970 he remembered someone once saying, "Go west, young man, go west," so he moved to San Francisco, taking a job first with Reynolds & Company and then moving to Sutro & Company, the oldest brokerage firm west of the Mississippi. At Sutro he proposed formalized financial planning, and was given the green light; he proceeded to create a financial planning department, which he organized and ran for five years. The idea was for the client to pay the broker, with all fees going to Larry's department. On one occasion he put together a 275-page financial plan which to this day he considers his absolute masterpiece, his "Rolls-Royce of Plans," as he calls it. "I went into absolutely everything. I even went down to the detail of what locks to put on their doors."

By 1979, however, he was becoming very frustrated working for other people's clients. His job was complicated even more by the fact that he had to make a double sale before he could write a plan. First, he had to sell the broker on the concept of financial planning, and then he had to sell the broker's client on the plan itself. Yet the five years at Sutro had been a tremendous experience, to say the least. "Sutro was a great stepping-stone. I learned to become a financial planner. And for that you need on-the-job training. In fact, I couldn't have paid them enough money for all the training that I had. I was doing financial planning for over 200 of our broker's clients, sometimes even several cases a day. That broad exposure made me a real financial planner."

However, what finally made Larry leave was the fact that he was an entrepreneur at heart. He always knew that someday he would make the break.

"From the very start I chose not to open a one-person practice, so I asked Carol Wright who had worked with me at Sutro to join me. She was a very competent planner, sensitive to people's needs. We started out with three or four clients at $90 an hour, gradually increasing our fees to $150, which is where we are now.

"We deal only with the upper-income market, and from the beginning we've been an extremely high-quality and intensely personalized financial planning firm." Currently, the firm of Lawrence A. Krause and Associates, Inc., consists of three planners, including Larry, as well as two clerical support personnel. The firm is registered with the Securities and Exchange Commission as a Registered Investment Advisor with the sole objective of providing fee-only financial planning. However, since Larry and his associates operate on both a fee and a commission basis, a separate company, K.W. Securities Corporation, was formed to act as a broker-dealer. In effect, he clearly wears two separate hats. The firm has its main office in San Francisco and a satellite in La Jolla, California.

The basic approach of Lawrence A. Krause and Associates, Inc., is personalization. "I emphasize to my clients that they are not dealing with just a firm, but with *people*. And if we are doing our job right, in both theory and practice, then our clients will be clients for life, and their kids after them.

"Financial planning is a funny business. People have some idea of what they are going to get when they go to see a lawyer or accountant, but when you go to see a financial planner you have hardly any idea. There are primarily two reasons why people walk into a financial planner's office: to lower taxes, and to get an idea of what to do about investments. Very few people walk through that door saying that they want the whole financial plan. You must educate them as to what financial planning is all about. What I tell my clients is that they are going to go through a process that I cannot really describe to them. I explain that they just have to be there to understand it. The best analogy that I can give is 'being in love'. I can write about love. I can tell them about love. But once you experience being in love yourself, it takes on a whole new dimension. The same is true of financial planning. Once you experience financial planning, it takes on a whole new dimension."

Larry believes that he does things very differently from other financial planning firms and I would certainly agree with him. His firm's clients are told point blank that if they don't feel they've received something valuable, they owe nothing! "If I didn't listen to the client, and I went off and gave them prepackaged programs rather than a plan that is personally suited to them, then I don't deserve the fee. How can I have a long-term relationship with my clients if I can't even handle their short-term goals? My reputation is more important than just trying to make money."

Ironically, 98% of the plans produced by Lawrence A. Krause and Associates, Inc., are written by hand. Although they use an Apple II computer, the output is limited to internal projections which the client never sees. "We use very few numbers and present our plan in conversation style. We use as few schedules as possible. People can't relate to all the numbers—numbers overwhelm them. In doing the plan by hand we can better relate to the client and put more of ourselves into the plan." Furthermore, at every data-gathering session there are always two or three planners present, never just one. "We want the sociological input. Some of us observe while the others write, and this way we can get that extra feeling. You can't write a financial plan by passing pieces of paper back and forth. You must be involved with the client. We are always striving to find out what is really happening."

Today the average fee for a financial plan from Lawrence A. Krause and Associates is about $7500. The clients are from all walks of life, all occupations. The practice is not limited to any one group of clients. "Clients, in general, judge you by the way you handle their investments. They look to see whether their net worth is growing. That is terribly important to them. And it is important to you. Are they staying even? We are not in the business of making money, we are in the business of preserving money."

By the same token, Larry is convinced that you have to have products available for the client. "If you are recommending a product—which is what people want us to do—you must have a certain degree of control over this product. If you simply recommend a product, and your clients run off and do what they want, you will look bad. People want that overall picture. So we have our own broker-dealer and general agency— but we treat it more like an accommodation than a sales tool."

Larry received his CFP designation in 1978 after spending two years going through the program. "The CFP program made me realize that I wasn't alone in this world and that there were other people doing real financial planning besides myself. Furthermore, it added depth and dimension to what I already knew. The strongest things that I came away with were the relationships with people from my classes. Some of these people are good friends today."

But all the education in the world, Larry insists, will not in itself make someone a financial planner, just as law school alone will not make somebody a lawyer. Only after you've been on the job do you really begin to be an attorney. "If you tried practicing law right out of

law school, you'd kill your clients. The same is true for the College for
Financial Planning or any other sophisticated financial planning program. Anybody who thinks that you just go in and come out an attorney
or a financial planner is mistaken. It is on-the-job training that one must
have. What I would like to see in the future is some type of tutorial
situation, an internship like doctors have, in order to become a financial
planner."

Lawrence A. Krause, CFP, has certain advise for the less experienced financial planner. First, he advises not to go after the lower-
income market because you will lose to Sears and American Express and
all those highly efficient companies that have the ability to use heavy
advertising; these large companies can operate much more efficiently
and at lower cost than the small financial planner. Instead, the small
planner should try to penetrate the middle- and upper-income markets,
where intense personalization will be the key factor. "The big financial
service organizations are going to be out after the mass market. What I
have done is to position myself above the mass market. I will be in the
highly personalized market that Sears or Bank of America could never
touch. It is impossible for them to compete with me. They will never
penetrate my market. However, they will do very well in the mass
market, in the sense that they will only offer limited plans and they will
leave their clients better off than they were before. The $75,000-and-up
income market is where small financial planners will have to be. Financial planners are going to have to position themselves for what people
are looking for, and that is *intensive personalization*."

Second, Larry advises keeping a low profile where computers are
concerned. This is a people business, and you can't take all your answers
from a computer—it has to come from you, the person. "A computer
can't develop that sociological side nor can it develop sensitivity."

Third, the planner should remember that he or she is not in competition with other advisors. "If we are working with other advisors and
we happen to know more than they do, we can plant the suggestion in
such a way that the advisor will come up with the idea to use in our
client's plan. We have no pride of authorship. You must keep in mind
that it becomes a losing situation for the client when you get into a
power play with that other advisor."

Larry believes that in five years at least 50% of the new financial
planners will come from an educational background rather than a sales
background. Accordingly, they will treat their clients more clinically
rather than pursuing financial planning from the sales end. More products will be suggested to do the job of solving the client's problems but
not all will be sold. He believes that much of the financial planning done
today is based on the planner providing the answer to the client even
before asking the client the question.

There are many reasons why Larry Krause has a successful practice. A major reason perhaps is that he does not believe in making a client jump hurdles. "That is what attorneys often do. People are afraid to go to attorneys because the second you talk to one, you fear he will send you a bill. We believe in keeping the door open. The client is totally free to call us at anytime—no charge.

"In fact, we beg them to call."

Dick Silverstein, CFP
Los Angeles, California

Having your office next to Beverly Hills, California, requires that it have a bit of the Hollywood touch, perhaps even resembling a movie set. With that in mind, Dick Silverstein spoke to some of his clients who were psychologists and interior decorators and commissioned them to design the ideal Hollywood office in terms of color and style. The office has been transformed into the perfect setting for the truly professional financial planner, and clients are undoubtedly impressed by the quality of the furnishings and the total appearance of the office.

"When we moved to the Westwood area of Los Angeles, a very prestigious area of high-rise buildings, our concern was how to establish what might be close to the perfect environment. We didn't want an office too modern, nor did we want an office too antique-ish. We wanted an office that expressed *us*."

It took Dick Silverstein, CFP, many years to build his firm to the high-quality organization that it is today. And, like most successful planners, he began by working for others. In the mid-sixties he went through an evolution of working for different firms. His philosophy was, and still is, to apply business and management consulting techniques to the family. With a business you would make recommendations for improving profits and making the business more successful. He applies this same approach to individuals. In effect, Dick Silverstein has been doing conceptual financial planning long before the term was ever invented: in 1969, as Executive Vice President and National Sales Manager of Bell Funding Corporation in Century City, California, he directed the operation of some 1500 salespeople, instructing his people to acquire the financial statements of their clients and examine the clients' income tax returns and insurance policies before making any recommendations.

In 1977, after receiving his CFP designation, Dick began to organize his own firm. The first step was to associate himself with an organization that was a large marketer of life insurance products. "I simply went to them and said that I wanted to create my own firm, but that I wanted to create it in a joint venture with their organization. The firm would provide individuals with financial planning services, such as life insurance, etc., and I would primarily promote it through the use of seminars." So he started out sharing joint offices with the firm. Dick had his own corporation, paid his own expenses, and provided the seminars; they handled the life insurance while he took care of asset management, tax shelters, investments, and estate planning. Two years later when he relocated the firm in Westwood, he severed the relationship with the life insurance company.

Dick has structured his organization in the following way: Silverstein & Alexander, Inc., is a broker-dealer firm and a corporate Registered Investment Advisor. The Silverstein & Alexander Financial Corporation acts as an insurance general agent and as a general partner for most syndications. There are four other professionals in the firm, including Neil Alexander, who has equity ownership, as well as three office support personnel. Almost all of their business comes from seminars and referrals from existing clients. "We try to have seminars on different topics sponsored by different organizations. As a result of my working with organized charities, I am on the Board of Directors of the American Lung Association for Los Angeles County. I have devoted quite a bit of my own time as well as my own capital to the Lung Association for personal reasons, and they have asked me to do seminars for them. They pay the entire cost and we do the seminar for nothing. Out of those seminars come business for our firm and contributions for the Lung Association." His firm also does seminars for major corporations such as Southern California Edison, a major utility in California. Silverstein & Alexander, Inc., puts on retirement planning seminars, counseling employees about retirement, about the benefits that they will receive from the company, and about how to utilize their currency and reposition their assets after retirement. They target these seminars specifically toward the members of the audience and their needs.

Dick Silverstein feels that since the United States has the largest middle class in the world, the biggest market for the financial planner can be found in the middle and upper class. Most of his clients earn from $30,000 to $100,000; however, the planning provided for each client may differ greatly and is based on variables, such as how frugal the clients have been, their age, whether they have inherited property, whether one spouse in the marriage had money to begin with. "We find that the asset base of our clients varies dramatically. In one day we can have three individuals come in all of whom are making $60,000—but one is destitute, one is doing very well, and the third has a bulk of assets to work with."

Middle-class clients are not the only people that Dick's firm services. He also has quite a few clients whose income and net worth vastly exceed the average. But these clients, he feels, you must trust with other advisors. "The beginning financial planner is frightened to death to communicate with CPAs and attorneys. Those things don't bother me. I actually prefer working with them, since they provide a base of future referrals."

The firm uses a combination of three systems for charging fees. If the individual simply desires planning and prefers to use other professionals to implement, the fees are currently $150 per hour for Dick Silverstein's time, $125 per hour for Neil Alexander's time, and $100 per hour for the time of the other planners in the firm; should the client desire implementation and monitoring, they operate on a fee-and-commission basis; and should the client simply wish to retain the firm as an agent after a preliminary work up, a commission-only arrangement is used.

Silverstein & Alexander, Inc., has recently become a broker-dealer firm for two prime reasons. First, by channeling all business through the broker-dealer firm, they deliberately forced themselves to be more highly regulated, which Dick considers a definite plus in protecting both their clients' and their own interest. And second, they began to market their own products and to structure carefully very conservative real estate partnerships for their clients. However, Dick warns, "The small individual should not become a broker-dealer until he or she has had many, many years with a broker-dealer firm, has obtained a principal's license, and thoroughly understands what it is to manage a brokerage office for a broker-dealer firm. Otherwise the mounds of paperwork could cause real problems."

In August 1981, Dick Silverstein appeared in *Time* magazine in an article that discussed, " 'Money U', The College for Financial Planning" and cited him as one of the most successful Certified Financial Planners in the United States. He has been interviewed and quoted in numerous publications, including the *Los Angeles Times, Herald Examiner, Venture Magazine,* and *The Registered Representative;* he has also appeared on both television and radio in the Los Angeles area. Success to Dick Silverstein, however, is more than a matter of money. He spends a great deal of his time teaching college, at great financial loss to himself. For the past six years he has acted as a coordinator for all the teaching activities of the College for Financial Planning in the greater Los Angeles area; he has also been most influential in extending the College's course of study to the major universities through the Affiliated College Program. He currently teaches the CFP program at the University of Southern California. "I am a great believer that, without our own continuing education, we are going to fail in this business. It is vital for financial planners to spend a great deal of their time in their own continuing education, even more so than the accountant and the attorney." In addition to teaching the CFP program at USC, he teaches basic investments at a California community college. "Teaching is so time consuming, but I really enjoy it. It is tremendously ego-satisfying. But I'm also a great believer in the idea that you have to do something for the community, to give what you can to the community that supports you. I take a lot from the community, and this is one of the reasons why I believe in doing a lot of work for organized charities and education."

As with any business there are good times, there are bad times, and there are problems. Dick's main problem was finding clients to whom to sell his services and products, and also finding good products to sell. The difficulty was with the evaluation of products. Due diligence is always a problem since it is so time consuming.

Dick has chosen to do seminars because he feels that this way he can approach more people simultaneously than in a one-on-one situation. He offers the following advice to new planners.

"For many, many years to come, financial planning will continue to be a very profitable profession that can absorb a large number of people into it. There really isn't any competition among financial planners right now. And I think that if the individual starting out has patience, then that is the key. It's almost as if we could tell new planners to lean a ladder against the wall and if they climb that ladder one rung at a time they will get to the top; but if they are looking for instant gratification and want to become successful overnight, they are going to miss all the little nuances and details on how to become successful and stay successful. At the first meeting I tell my clients that we are not just going to be analyzing what you are doing and discussing your wishes, dreams, goals and ambitions with you, but we will also be judging each other. You judge me and see whether you can be comfortable working with me, and have confidence and trust in me. And quite frankly, I will judge you to see if I can work with you. There are just some personalities that I cannot work with."

Dick Silverstein advises the new financial planner to be a good time manager, although he will quickly admit to some major shortcomings in that area. "I am probably the most organized disorganized person that exists. I look at piles of paper on my desk which get sorted and moved from one pile to another. It is a terrible problem, especially in the latter part of the year when people are interested in tax-advantaged investments. Time is a major problem when doing due diligence and looking into situations; this may involve traveling to determine what is a good investment and what is not a good investment for our clients, or traveling to acquire property for our clients outside California. And then I need time for my own continuing education, time for my own personal needs like teaching, donating time to charity, and meeting with clients. It becomes an overwhelming and difficult situation. My administrative assistant is my right-hand person; she schedules my time and keeps my calendar for me. I tell her what days I want to spend in the office and when I need to be out of the office. And she builds around that."

It has been said that the true mark of a real professional is admitting your weakness.

Dick Silverstein is a true, true professional in every sense of the word.

Robert J. Underwood, CFP
Birmingham, Alabama

Bob's philosophy is simple: "The difference between the commission-only planner, the fee-and-commission planner, and the fee-only planner is *objectivity*. The commission system works against the person you're serving. The client has to pay more than his or her own fair share to cover the cost of trying to sell to others who don't buy." Bob speaks from experience, since he has worked from all three angles.

From 1963 to 1968 Bob worked in the commission-only business, and then in 1969 he became a fee-and-commission planner. However, in 1974 he burned the last of his security and insurance licenses and became a fee-only financial planner. He likes to refer to this period of his life as, "When I went legit!"

Bob feels there are several things wrong with the commission-only arrangement. First, the planner is psychologically influenced by the need to earn commissions, thereby making it difficult to be purely objective. As a fee-basis planner you can be a buyer for your client rather than a seller to your client. In effect, the fees are the same whether the client does everything you've advised the client to do or nothing, and the only way to hold on to that client is through positive results. The second problem is that the planner who only sells will look to the broker-dealer or life general agent for information, while the fee-basis financial planner is out digging under rocks trying to help clients. Bob's point is that the fee-only financial planner uses more tools than products. "I have no limits in solving their problems. The guy who is going to sell something does have a limit, which is the products he has available to sell. I can go anywhere I want to."

In a seminar that Bob gives on the fee-paid financial planning practice, for both the College for Financial Planning and the IAFP, he talks about the "lullabies, legends and lies" regarding the fee-only practice. The first myth is that fee-only planners don't implement, and that's just not true, he says. "Fee-basis financial planners are heavy into implementation because clients will judge you on what you did for them. It is crucial that the fee-only planner implement because if you don't implement, your clients will not recommend additional people to you and the professionals you work with, the CPA and the attorney, will not be satisfied. Seventy-five percent of my business comes from CPAs and attorneys." The only exception Bob knows of is a major Big Eight accounting firm, but the small individual fee-only financial planner must implement to stay in business.

The second myth is that it costs the client double because of the fee. But this isn't so, either. The fee-only planner, for the most part, uses no-load products and is able to squeeze the front-end loads out of a program. Besides, the client is better off paying fees since the fees are tax deductible; commissions are never deductible until the investment is sold at the other end and offset against the gain or added to the loss. A fee-only financial planner, however, should not be charging the clients $1000 if only saving the client $900.

The third myth in financial planning is that you cannot make any money in the fee-basis business. The fact is that the commission planner spends a great deal of time and money in order to get in front of clients and must also spend a great deal of time in activities not connected to financial planning. A fee-only planner, realistically, should build up enough to live on in a year. It's no different from any other business.

The best way for you, as a new financial planner, to get into the fee-only business is to sit down and make a list of all the things you can do to save your clients money. Then—at your expense—take a CPA to lunch (CPAs will never resist going to lunch when you are paying). At lunch explain to the CPA what you can do for the client and for that CPA. If you do your job right, "and provide a real honest-to-goodness service, the CPA's billings should increase, your billings will increase, and the client will be 400% better off than before." Bob advises that you go to the CPA firms and attorneys and simply tell them you are starting a fee-basis financial planning practice. Then tell them how you can benefit both them and their clients. You might be surprised at the response you'll get from another professional who has been constantly badgered through the years by promoters with phony investment deals for putting clients into. "Most CPAs will not recommend that their clients do something. They will recommend that their clients *not* do something. Now the client will get something done that has been put off for five or ten or perhaps fifteen years."

In 1974 when Bob entered the fee-paid business, his minimum fee was $3500 a year. About the eighth or ninth client who came to him was a junk dealer who did not bat an eye when Bob told him the fee would be $3500. The man said it was like telling him it was free, because the fee was tax deductible. And in those days the 70% tax bracket (the junk dealer's bracket) was the top bracket. That's when Bob realized he'd have no problem in getting his fees. Today, since his clients are mainly businesspersons, he uses this system: He charges his client a monthly fee equal to the monthly salary of the client's lowest-paid employee; however, the first month's fee is three times the normal monthly fee in order to cover his startup costs. It is not until after the data-gathering interview that Bob quotes the number of months that the plan will take and at that time the client can decide whether or not to go ahead with the plan. The shortest time span has been six months, with the average monthly fee (after the startup) about $650 to $700. However, Bob insists that between the concept interview and data-gathering interview, the client must check his references, or else he will not proceed to the data-gathering interview. "I want the client to know at that point that I can do the job." After the plan has been completed, Bob is put on a quarterly retainer by each client. If at any time his clients feel that they are not getting their money's worth, they do not have to send in the fee. His quarterly retainer fee is $1000.

It was four years ago that Bob made the decision to work with only people who were "fun." As a result, he is convinced that he ended up with a much better group of clients. His staff consists of two other financial planners and an office manager. And no employee of his firm may hold any product license whatsoever.

Is the fee-paid movement strong? Bob Underwood, CFP, is certainly convinced that it is. He is presently in the process of putting together a network of fee-basis financial planners to share information with one another. "The biggest problem for the new planner is knowing where to find good products." Bob's theory is that by being part of a group the planner can usually find someone within that group who specializes in a particular area. Together they can help develop a better deal for the client, so that 95% of the dollars goes into the investment, not just 70%. "In many of the tax shelters, even those of the big firms, as much as 40% of the dollars raised goes to the general partner, the general partner affiliates, and the broker for commission. That investment then has to be successful for years just to get back to the break-even point. There is really no need for that since there are plenty of people who are excellent managers of real estate, for instance, who want to manage and are willing to take their share of the profits on the other end. And they should be paid for their expertise when they negotiate for property at below the fair market value. The *Wall Street Journal* had an article about financial planning, the CFP and the IAFP, and wrote two sentences about a group of fee-paid financial planners. We have had over 2000 requests for fee-only financial planners in various areas of the country."

Bob's idea is that a network of fee-only financial planners will cut down considerably on the normal production time of the planner, such as time spent on product research, since fee-paid planners can easily check with the network for information. "It is as much our responsibility to keep people out of bad deals as to get them into good ones. What we need are polyunsaturated investments—all the fat squeezed out—and to really have our clients make more money. The number one problem for a fee-basis financial planner is how to screen the deals. It is impossible in this business to be an expert in every field. They haven't yet made the planner who is. In essence, out on your own you will be taken to the cleaners; but together, people with expertise in each different field will help screen the deal for type, structure and so on."

If there is one thing that you can say about Bob Underwood, CFP, it is that he is a "people" person. This, he feels, is the key to his success. "Financial planning is very much a people business. It is understanding your clients' needs and wants and goals and being able to look at their problems through their eyes, and then taking your expertise and superimposing it over their needs to come up with a solution to their problems. It is very important to understand your clients and their needs in order to solve any of their problems. It is 100% a people business.

"There are times when a client will talk to you about a problem that you know nothing about. And in the process of just talking to you, the client will come up with the answer. Is it even worth it to the client to pay me that fee?

"Most people in America have learned to make money by getting a good education. They get a good job and they make more money. But no one ever told them what to do with the money once they have made it. And what we as financial planners should be able to do is show them how to make their money go a little further. But first you need to know their problems and be aware of their comfort level. I am sure that I can design the world's greatest financial plan. There isn't any doubt in my mind that I can look at your problems and come out with the absolutely best thing for you to do in every circumstance. But if you can't sleep at night with it, if you are going to lie there and toss and turn, we are better off with the second-best plan, the third-best plan or the fourth-best plan, which at least you can sleep with. The plan must fit you—you should not have to fit the plan. And that's why it is such a people business and will always be. The computers can crunch the numbers for us, but they can never eliminate that 'how do you feel about this and about that?' The big companies have a problem because this is such a people business. They, in fact, look for people whom they can fit into their program rather than programs that will fit people. Financial planning is complex. You need to know how the client views the problem. You need that 'one-on-one'."

A financial planner, according to Bob, is someone who gathers the data first before coming up with any solutions. The planner must first find out what the client's problems are. Then he or she reviews the problems, taking into consideration the client's temperament, and comes back to the client with a way to get the most mileage out of the client's money and other assets. The written financial plan tells the client what to do, when to do it, and also how to do it. Furthermore, after the plan has been put into place, the planner checks back with the client periodically to see if the plan is still on target.

To say that Bob Underwood is a very unselfish person is an understatement. He devotes much of his time to strengthening the foundation of the financial planning profession, building organizations, and speaking to new financial planners about his convictions and his beliefs. It has been said that one of the true marks of a real professional is putting something besides money back into the industry. "If someone doesn't pay the dues, the industry isn't going to get any better. I firmly believe that you cannot give more than you get back. If you keep giving it will eventually come back. It is the law of cause and effect. If I had had someone to steer me on, I wouldn't have made nearly the mistakes that I made.

"If some financial planners can head other financial planners in the right direction, then those others will do a good job for their clients, and the financial planning industry is going to get a better name. If more people understood what financial planning was all about, our jobs would be a lot easier."

Bob's fee-only planning organization is called "SIFA," the Society for Independent Financial Advisors, discussed in an earlier chapter. He devotes much of his time to developing the organization.

Whether you agree with Bob's approach or whether you are totally convinced that the commission route is the avenue for you, just listening to Bob Underwood give one of his seminars is an enlightening experience. You cannot really call yourself objective until you have heard him.

20

YOU—THE PLANNER

Since the business, the livelihood, of the financial planner is to develop goal-oriented financial plans for other people, it makes a great deal of sense for planners to develop one or several plans for themselves. Planners, by virtue of their occupation, are not exempt from their own planning. In other words, practice what you preach.

There are two types of plans that financial planners would be wise to create for themselves. The first is a business marketing and strategy plan designed to help you along so that you can reach your business goals and objectives on target; the second is a personal financial plan no different from any you would write for a client. Both plans should be independent of each other and are designed to achieve different goals. Both plans are equally important. A financial plan and a marketing plan are like maps—they provide direction. And the planner, like everyone else, needs direction, too. In fact, since the financial planning business thrives on the concept of change, keeping close track of your own direction and development is a wise idea.

The business strategy and marketing plan that you write for your business is vital to your continuous uninterrupted growth. The format you use is insignificant. The ideas are what count. Furthermore, the writing of the plan will force you to look under many rocks, evaluate both old and new concepts, change direction, and bring you closer to the real world in terms of what's happening. Your business strategy and marketing plan also requires periodic updating. It explores many areas of your practice, and with each update the areas that you cover should become more and more complete.

The plan might begin with a summary or listing of what services you'd like to offer your clients now, and then explore what services you might wish to offer them in the near future. Take this same approach with products. And because the financial planning environment changes so rapidly, I feel you should concentrate on the present and near-future. Trying to determine what you'll be providing 10 years from now could prove a bit unrealistic, since financial planning and financial service products may be very much altered by changes in the economy, legislation, and even the weather, as projected by Iben Browning at the 1982 Convention of the IAFP. There is only one certainty in financial planning and that is *change*. It will happen. Just what changes will occur is another question, one that very few can answer with much accuracy. If you try to devise a strategy that is too long range, events might not quite happen the way you projected them. Keep your planning short term to intermediate term. I cannot see developing a strategy for longer than a five-year period.

The next step of the plan is to target your market as described in Chapter 2. Then review your compensation arrangements. Are you a fee planner? Are you a commission planner? Are you a fee-and-commission planner? Are you happier charging fees or earning commissions? If you charge fees, how much do you charge for a plan? Do you feel that your fees are adequate? Do you want to write more plans at a lower rate per plan, or fewer plans at a higher rate per plan? How many plans do you reasonably expect to write in the coming year? Try to be realistic. In fact, I suggest that you set up a low estimate and a high estimate, and average the two. Then project your revenue. Will you be receiving fees from any other sources? If you are receiving commissions, how much do you expect to receive? Projecting commission income, of course, is a lot more difficult than projecting fees. It is very hard to foresee the big sale that will make the whole year worthwhile—or the several-month dry spell that you were not expecting. Try to compare expenses with revenue. Are you currently buying items that are unnecessary? Are there things you know you will have to buy? Will you need more office space? Admittedly, these things are very difficult to project. But the sheer task of just attempting to do this will give you greater insight into your own business and where you are heading. To assist you in preparing financial projections, I suggest that you refer to the chart that I have provided later in this chapter.

Although all of your expenses are important, some are more heavily weighted than others. Perhaps one of the most important expenses that you must consider in a marketing plan is advertising and promotion. And there is more to it than just dollars. It is a question of philosophy. Are you going to keep a low profile, or are you going to go all out and saturate the media? What has been the result of your promotional activity in the past? Are you keeping tabs? You should be. Analyze why clients come to you. Is there a way of increasing your publicity? And do you want to? For instance, if you rely on client or other professional referrals and have been doing quite well this way, you might not want to spend the time answering an abundance of queries from persons curious about financial planning. Remember that the small financial planning firm is not a large company that can afford to send out pounds of advertising literature just to get an ounce of results. If you do advertise, will you target on a select market?

Perhaps the most difficult part of the marketing plan is the evaluation of your strengths and your weaknesses in relation to the firm, and to the firm's principal—you! It is not easy to evaluate yourself objectively. There is a strong tendency to be either overcritical or undercritical. Nevertheless, you must try. The process whereby you list your strengths and weaknesses should not be attempted in 5 or 10 minutes, writing down the first things that come to mind. Take as long as you need, a week, two weeks, a month, more. But you must get it down on paper. Then analyze ways either to build or sustain your strengths and to improve or eliminate your weaknesses. Finally, once you have developed your plan, you must implement your own suggestions. For instance, if one of your weaknesses is that you are shy and have difficulty selling yourself to new clients, what are you going to do about it? Mope about it, or take a human relations or sales training course? Take a good look at that firm of yours, or that firm you are going to start once you leave your present job. And do not forget to write down in your plan the date you intend to leave that job.

The last part of your plan is the most important. It is the Action Program. These are the things you will do, the steps that you will take to achieve your business objectives, and the approximate dates that you plan to accomplish these things. It might be the purchase of an asset, like a computer, or the raising of plan fees, or a rewrite of the annual or semiannual review process. Or it might be achieving a personal product license such as NASD, or the completion of an academic degree or professional designation program. In other words, it can be anything that you are going to do.

The following action ideas were taken from the marketing plan of Mimi Merrill of Madison, Wisconsin, of whom I spoke in Chapter 18.

A. *Product Development*

1. Purchase printer/word processor to go with Apple II computer; update software and applications.

2. Streamline business systems and rewrite business plan.

3. Update and add to consumer information file.

4. Attend continuing education seminars and national conventions to keep timely on financial and economic trends and delivery of financial services.

5. Retain professional membership in IACP and ICFP.

6. Subscribe to and study professional journals such as *WSJ, Forbes, Business Week, Personal Finance, The Financial Planner,* and *Money Magazine.* Subscribe to personal advisory newsletters such as *Personal Finance.* Read all the current new books on financial theory and trends.

7. Complete examinations to become registered with the SEC and the state as a Registered Investment Advisor.

8. Complete M.B.A. in Finance in August 1982.

B. *Communication*

1. *Personal Selling:*

    a. *Seminars.* Conduct seminars free for service organizations in the community. Send flyer to all organization presidents and follow up with telephone calls.

    b. *Initial consultation.* Offer free initial consultation. Get prospect to open up about their financial problems and offer to help provide them with some alternatives to deal with these problems. Negotiate a price and get them to sign a contract.

    c. *"Networking."* Personal meetings with other community professionals to share with them the goals and objectives of the firm and offer to work with them with their clients. Objective: Professional referrals.

    d. *Social contacts.* Maintain membership in community professional civic and social organizations.

2. *Public Relations:*

    a. *Newspaper column.* Continue to provide a free newspaper column on economic issues for women for a feminist newspaper. Column is headlined with picture and logo.

    b. *Newletters.* Send to prospects, clients, and opinion leaders.

    c. *Radio and TV appearances.* Talk about budgeting or special issues.

    d. *Publicity.* Put together a publicity package and talk to business editors—suburban papers.

3. *Direct Mail:*
   a. Select *mailing list* of community opinion leaders and send brochure and newsletter.
   b. *Letters* to lawyers, realtors, ministers, and counselors, describing services and including a brochure.
   c. A series of *letters* to prospects who ask for information.
   d. Follow-up *mailings* to clients, getting market research, and hopefully referrals, and follow-up visits.
   e. *Thank-you note* to anyone who refers a prospect to the business.
4. *Advertising:*
   a. Awareness ads in *This Is Madison, Wisconsin,* and the *Civic Center Program* (for symphony) in September and January.
   b. Small budgeting ad in *Feminist Connection* and *Isthmus* once a quarter.
   c. Further research with marketing consultant regarding other advertising program.

C. **Image and Packaging**
   1. Work with marketing consultant to develop new name, logo, graphics, and brochure (e.g., Mary Merrill Associates, Ltd.).
   2. Change organization from sole proprietorship to Subchapter S Corporation (family corporation).
   3. Develop a theme to be used to tie together image and communication.
   4. Consider relocating office in August 1982 to more prestigious location, such as the Piare Square Building.
   5. Continue to put emphasis on office appearance, personal appearance, and wardrobe.

You should always keep in mind that your plan is not carved in stone. Circumstances change. You must be flexible and willing to reevaluate your plan whenever necessary and to change your direction should a change be in order. There is a very good chance that your progress will be either a lot faster or a lot slower than you anticipate. However, once you are more established, you should be better able to judge your pace, and your marketing plan will be more in synch with your expectations.

Once you have finished your marketing plan there is yet another plan to write. And that is your own personal financial plan. It is extremely important. From experience, I can tell you that financial planners, like many other professionals and businesspersons, can get so involved in their work that they forget to take care of their own personal needs. It is like the lawyer who does not have a will, the accountant who does not file a tax return, or the doctor who smokes six packs of cigarettes a day. Well, the financial planner is no different from these professionals. If you feel that other people have a need for financial plans, why would you have any less of a need? You need one as much as anyone else.

If you think that your own financial plan will be easier to write than a plan for someone else, you are very much mistaken. Your plan will probably be a lot more difficult. The problem is that you are too close to the source. It is like asking a devoted grandfather at his grandchild's Little League game to tell you which kid is the best on the team. Once again, just as you acknowledged your strengths and weaknesses in the marketing plan, true objectivity is put to the test. When you hold a data-gathering session with a client, you sometimes must pull information from the client through skilled questioning techniques. But with your own plan no one else is there to ask the questions. You must force yourself to be completely honest. Once you can put your personal goals and objectives down on paper, you'll be well on your way to writing a good plan for yourself.

And when you finish writing that plan—implement!

DEALING WITH YOUR OWN INCOME AND EXPENSES

There are many problems facing the new business owner today—inexperience, volatile interest rates, undefined markets, unproductive employees. But the biggest problem, I feel, is undercapitalization—not having adequate liquidity and reserves to deal with the trials and tribulations of the early years, when expenses are high and income dribbles in. It is not unusual by any means for the new business owner to write many more checks than the income will cover. Therefore, the ability to weather the storm, to maintain cash flow, becomes vitally important. The lack of adequate capital, whether equity or debt, is the biggest cause of a new business to go down the tubes.

Is financial planning different from any other new business? Yes and no. Yes, in the sense that adequate working capital and reserves are needed to build up a planning firm to any degree of sophistication. No, in the sense that you need very little capital if you are content to remain very small. Fortunately, the financial planning firm, like many other personal service businesses, does not need nearly as much startup capital as the average retail firm. The only major capital outlay required is for fixtures and equipment, and the amount spent on these depends directly on the planner's taste, the scope and level of the practice, and the caliber of potential clients. Furthermore, the new financial planner, like any new business owner just starting out, has a definite need for personal cash reserves in order to adequately cover living expenses until the business grows enough to draw profit—or salary, if corporate. There is no specific length of time during which the new planner will need this cash backup; it all depends on how long it takes to develop an adequate clientele so that the revenues can exceed the expenses (including capital investment needed for growth). Then, and only then, can profit be withdrawn, provided that the cash flow of the business is not impeded.

Usually, there is a time lag involved between providing a service or selling a product, and receiving compensation. It may be a matter of several days, weeks, months, or perhaps even a year or more. Yes it could even be longer than one year before you actually receive the money that you have earned today. And keep in mind that tomorrow's income will neither pay this month's mortgage nor put dinner on your table tonight. It is, therefore, a matter of necessity that the financial planner have a sufficient source of liquid funds on which to live and with which to carry on the normal operations of the business.

Let me give you a few specific examples of the need for reserve funds. A financial planner sells the client a life insurance policy. The policy may take a month or more for the underwriting to be completed and for the policy to be issued by the insurance company. The planner will then collect the first quarterly premium from the client and submit it to the home office. In all probability, the first commission check (based on only a fractional amount of the first quarterly premium) will not arrive for another month or two—if you are lucky. Already, two to four months have elapsed from the time of application to the time the first commission check finally arrives. And the second, third, and fourth quarterly commissions will not arrive for another three, six, and nine months. This "fee lag" may also occur when the planner sells limited partnerships and takes a subscription from the client for the sale of an oil and gas shelter. It could take several months for the limited partnership to close, and several more months for the general partner to distribute the commission check to the broker-dealer, and for the broker-dealer to then pay the planner. Another case of "fee lag" may involve a new financial planner who writes a fee-paid plan for a client without charging an up-front fee because he or she lacks the confidence to demand a fee in advance. An established planner, on the other hand, will generally dictate payment terms, asking for 25 to 50% or even the full case fee in advance. Should the client not wish to meet these terms, the planner simply does not write the plan. Most established financial planners do not negotiate fees, and are not fearful of losing a client's business, as they already have established clients and other business coming in. But the new financial planner is hungry—hungry to write cases, hungry to obtain new clients, hungry to make a mark on the financial planning world, and hungry for dinner! The new planner is afraid that asking for too large a fee in advance will scare the client away, and therefore may offer a very liberal fee payment schedule to the client, asking for a nominal amount in advance (if anything), and so much per month after the plan has already been written. In this case the planner will receive payment spread over a period of many months.

I have experimented with all types of fee payment schedules but have not found any one method that is totally satisfactory. In the past, I have geared my fee schedule to the client's financial situation. If I was dealing with an established tax client or someone who was recommended by a responsible client or associate, I usually charged a nominal fee in advance. Upon completion of the plan, about a month later, I billed the client for the balance. In some cases I allowed my clients to extend their payments over a longer period; at times I even made the suggestion myself if I felt that my fees placed a strain on the client's emergency funds. Only now, after several years of practice, am I beginning to set policy. The new policy stems from the frustration of chasing clients to collect fees and my belief that any "serious" financial planning client should be willing to pay an up-front fee. Accordingly, I now collect half at the data-gathering session and the balance when the plan is presented to the client. From experience, I have found that "unserious" financial planning clients, those who never had any intention of ever paying for a written financial plan in the first place, will attempt to engage in a financial plan with no up-front fee. That way they will have nothing to lose. Only people very serious about financial planning will put up half the plan fee in advance. At this stage, I am interested only in serious long-term clients.

Can a new planner be this choosy? No way. The new planner will generally be quite receptive to generous fee terms just to get the business.

However, to be honest, my policy is not cast of iron or unbendable. There are still many times that I get very little in advance, very little when I'm finished, and very little for a long, long time. But I must be absolutely certain of the client, the client's integrity, and the client's willingness to pay my fee when he or she can afford to do so. An experienced financial planner should be able to sense which clients they can plan for in good faith.

The slow, sometimes tedious collection of accounts receivable is admittedly not a sound business practice. The probability of bad debt increases significantly for each day that an account receivable is overdue. The accounting term for this is known as "aging of accounts," which simply means placing more risk on longer-due accounts.

Why then would I continue to use this often ill-advised business practice? Because I actually consider it a good business practice for the financial planner—who, don't forget, is in a "people" business. In fact, it is the most "people" business that I know. The medical profession deals with organs, the legal profession deals with precedent, the accounting profession deals with numbers and systems. In the financial planning business we deal with people—their feelings, their emotions, their goals and objectives, which are far more important than their dollars and their shares of stock. In financial planning, qualitative is as important, if not more so, than quantitative. Do not forget that these clients are the very people who pay for your house, your car, your food, your children's education. It is not only *what* you do for them financially, but *how* you do it, that builds the lasting bond between you and your client. You must remember that your client could generate for you thousands or maybe tens of thousands of dollars in fees and/or commissions over the course of your career. For you to lose this because the client perceives that you do not care enough would be foolish. Above anything else the client must know that you really care.

If I sense a real problem with a client, I simply do not take on the case. No exceptions. This includes any suspicion that the client might not pay the fee. Experience is the best teacher; after you get burned a few times, you learn. Before I take on a new case I give the client a thorough interview. Now and then I encounter someone for whom I would not be comfortable writing a plan or managing funds. There is only one way, I feel, to handle this situation and that is to tell the person, tactfully, of course, goodbye. I generally explain to the person that I do not have the expertise to write the type of plan they desire. By doing this I have placed 100% of the inadequacy upon myself and there is nothing they can really say. They usually thank me for my honesty.

Since the flow of income may be sporadic at first, the financial planner should strive to keep expenses down. The fixed costs, not the variable costs, are the most dangerous. Fixed costs are those that do not change with the volume of business; these costs (rent, salaries, professional publications, etc.) can be adjusted only by a drastic change in circumstance, such as breaking a lease or firing an employee. But these are not everyday occurrences. Your fixed costs should not be significantly increased unless a higher level of business warrants the additional expenditures. Furthermore, you must give careful thought to the long-term ramifications of any new fixed costs. Here are six major points to consider:

1. Avoid renting an office that is too expensive. It is better to

negotiate a shorter-term lease with moderate rent. You can always work your way up to a larger and more luxurious office when and if you need one. By following this suggestion you will avoid putting undue pressure on yourself to write that many more cases a month or to close so many more sales just to pay the rent. Also, you might consider sharing office space with another professional, such as a lawyer or accountant. There are many successful planners who prefer this arrangement. Another alternative is to work from your home; however, I would not advise this setup unless the business facility is completely set off from the rest of your living quarters.

2. Before you purchase a computer or word processor, know exactly what you want it to do and how much you wish to spend. Just because computers are the "in thing" does not mean that you have to run out immediately and spend thousands of dollars on one. A computer should only be purchased when the planner can no longer function without one. Certainly, you will not have to be told when that time has arrived. I can guarantee, though, that this will not happen until you have built a fairly large client base.

3. Do not purchase every publication on the market. Buy only what you need. I am referring primarily to the professional services that can cost several hundred to several thousand dollars a year, although even the cost of $5 and $10 magazines can really mount up if you buy enough. Besides, if you spend your entire day reading magazines and professional publications, you will have no time to write financial plans.

4. Increase your staff size only as the need arises. I suggest that you hire a secretary who can also function as a receptionist and administrative assistant. Start with a part-time secretary and increase the hours to full time when necessary. Hiring a secretary is very important to the financial planner; it keeps the planner from getting into the habit of doing clerical work instead of doing financial planning. The theory is that if you bill at the rate of $60 an hour, and a secretary would have cost $8 an hour, you have lost $52 for the hour that you did secretarial work instead of financial planning.

5. Don't go berserk buying fancy, expensive sales and promotional literature and logos. The chances are that you will change your business 82 times before you get it the way you want it. For you to go out and buy an abundance of expensive promotional material will, in all likelihood, result in a large supply of wastepaper.

6. Don't go insane with telephones. Your telephone company is rich enough and does not need your charitable support. I survived with one number and two phones for a year and then worked my way up to a Com Key system with two numbers. Start out with the basic service, and modify your system any time you feel that it is warranted.

Keep your costs as low as possible. It is so important that I must emphasize it again and again. Low cost is a key factor in your growth. Keeping your costs down will enable you to operate free of pressure, thereby allowing you to structure your business the way you desire. If your costs are high, you may tend to structure your business in a manner alien to you simply because you are under a great deal of pressure to meet your monthly expenses. Later, as you start getting into the swing of the business, you can take on a greater degree of expenses. And more risk.

Another reason for keeping your costs low is that many of your early purchases will eventually result in waste, as your business evolves and begins to take shape. For example, brochures, stationery, and business cards might become obsolete if, soon after you have them printed, you come up with new and better ideas. It is important to buy smaller quantities of supplies more frequently rather than larger quantities of discounted supplies that will just decorate the trash can. Paying more per unit and using it all is usually less expensive than paying less per unit and wasting half.

No matter how much you try to keep your costs down, you cannot avoid expenses altogether. One way for the planner to meet fixed costs, such as rent, phone, insurance, and professional publications, is to develop an income tax business. Fees for income tax preparation are steady and can really help pay for some of your initial fixed costs—not to mention that this is an excellent way to develop financial planning clients.

A major problem that financial planners usually face, especially those who rely on commissions, is an uneven stream of income. You may not see a check for several weeks, and then all of a sudden thousands of dollars will roll in when you least expect it. As a new planner, your first challenge is surviving during this period of dollar inactivity, and being able to pay the bills. Because your personal financial reputation is so important, you cannot afford to become a credit risk or to mar your personal reputation in any way. Don't forget, you are a model. People look up to you. They respect your opinion and your suggestions. How confident would they feel if they knew that you had three pages of negative information on a TRW report? This is why your *own* financial planning is so vital.

THE PLANNER'S FINANCIAL PROJECTION

The following list should help you to see where you will stand financially.

Revenue

Fees:
      Financial plans (number × price)   _____
      Hourly consulting   _____
      Investment management   _____
      Tax planning   _____
      Tax preparation   _____
      Accounting/bookkeeping   _____
      Other   _____
          Total fees   _____
Commissions:
      Mutual funds   _____
      Life insurance   _____
      Health insurance   _____
      Group insurance   _____
      Annuities   _____
      Property/casualty insurance   _____
      Tax shelters   _____
      Royalties   _____
      Tangibles   _____
      Other   _____
          Total commissions   _____
          Other income   _____
            Total revenue   _____

Expenses

      Accounting and legal fees   _____
      Advertising   _____
      Bank charges   _____
      Computer software   _____
      Depreciation   _____
      Entertainment   _____
      Insurance   _____
      Interest   _____
      Meals and lodging   _____
      Medical reimbursement plan   _____
      Office repairs and cleaning   _____
      Office supplies   _____

Postage and delivery   _____
Printing   _____
Professional association dues   _____
Professional courses and
    seminars   _____
Professional publications and
    tapes   _____
Regulatory and license   _____
Rent   _____
Salary   _____
Taxes   _____
Telephone   _____
Travel and transportation   _____
Miscellaneous   _____
Other   _____
        Total expenses   _____

Total projected revenue   _____
Total projected expenses   _____
Total net profit   _____

YOUR HEALTH AND YOUR FAMILY

"There is nothing more important than your business!"

It's an interesting thought. It certainly is a positive statement. But it is simply not true!

There are things more important than your financial planning practice—you, your health, and your family, to name a few.

The way to develop a successful financial planning practice is through a positive and healthy mental attitude. You must feel good about yourself. If you lack confidence in yourself, how do you expect your clients to take you seriously when you offer a suggestion? You may lack confidence in only a particular area of financial planning. In fact, you should. There is no one who knows everything about financial planning, and I seriously doubt that there ever will be. But you must have overall confidence in your ability as a planner and you must spill over this confidence to your clients. The planner is somewhat like the sun; he or she must radiate light—the light of inspiration to guide the client.

A healthy mental attitude generates from within. It is an internal function of the body, the mind. On the other hand, insincerity or acting is an external function. It is a way of role playing and lasts only until the final curtain falls. The financial planner must not be caught playing a role. The spirit behind the planner's task must come from within.

Feeling good about yourself is more than just mental; it is physical, too. Financial planners must keep in mind that they are in the service business and like most other service businesses, the major asset is you—the planner. Should you break down, should you malfunction, should you run out of gas, much of your business—if not all of it—will stand idle. Granted, disability income insurance will replace some of the loss of your income, but it will never begin to replace the loss of your potential.

So there is a conflict. On the one hand, you must work hard to make your business successful and, on the other hand, you must rest. Both are vital to your well-being. You cannot work yourself to the point of physical exhaustion or mental depression (or both), nor can you build a successful planning practice between vacations or from the golf course or tennis court. You must reach a point of equilibrium between work and play—otherwise, the law of diminishing returns will certainly hold true. And only you can pinpoint your particular point of equilibrium. For some this might mean a very long workweek; for others the work-week may be considerably shorter. But there is one thing that I feel should always be true. Work should be fun!

I love financial planning. And so does every successful planner that I have ever come across. You must love financial planning or you should not be in this profession. This profession—especially owning your own firm—cannot be a compromise with another job or another profession that you would prefer to be in. If you have chosen to be a financial planner, you should have no desire to be anything else. Then, given your love for the profession and your ability to control your own destiny, work should indeed be fun.

Individuals have a great deal of control over their mental health. It is possible for the planner, by making work fun, to reach the highest plateau of gratification during the ups and still weather the downs without tumbling into the valley of despair. Our physical health is a little more difficult. Many times a sickness or injury occurs that is beyond our control; however, it is certainly foolish to invite it. Since you are the major asset of your business, it is no more than common sense to realize that you must take care of yourself. Be careful to watch your diet and your intake of liquor. The financial planner may spend a great deal of time socializing while working: for example, going to lunch or dinner with clients or business associates, or attending educational seminars, conventions, and professional meetings where the dinner table or the cocktail lounge is a major forum for meaningful discussion. You should pay as much attention to the calories as to the topic you are discussing. In fact, the biggest problem I have attending these meetings is that I eat because the food is there and not because I am hungry. It is truly amazing that I have the ability to say no to thousands of commission dollars staring me in the face if I feel that an investment is not suitable for my client, but I have practically no will power to turn down a chocolate mousse or a candy apple or a dish of ice cream topped with hot fudge.

My intent is not to preach about what to eat and what to drink. I should be the last person in this world to offer that advice. On many occasions I have had a candy apple for breakfast, sushi (raw fish) for lunch, and an ice cream sundae for dinner. At times, I have the tendency to feel sorry for myself for working so many long hours, so I treat myself to these delicious little rewards of life. But experience tells me that we can only do that for so long. You—the financial planning machine— require a high grade of fuel to run on. And you must pay attention to your diet or you'll be going in for repairs a lot sooner than expected. And, of course, it goes without saying that everyone needs some form of daily exercise—a long day of financial planning often means a lot of sitting.

The financial planner who lives alone with no family ties is primarily concerned with his or her own well-being. But if you are married and/or have children, much more is demanded of you. There may be a wife or husband, or tykes or teenagers, around the house to consider. These people require as much of your time—or more—as your clients. This is, indeed, a difficult problem! There is no question that you need a great many hours of the day to develop your practice effectively. But you must put things in their proper perspective, and always remind yourself what is really most important to you. Regretfully, there are no easy answers I can offer. I can only tell you that you must force yourself to make time for your loved ones. There is nothing worse than missing your children grow up, and not really knowing who they are. The years can never be replaced. And there won't be anyone to blame but yourself if this happens. I can think of no better way to clarify this advice than to suggest that you listen to a song by the late songwriter and musician Harry Chapin, entitled, "The Cat's in the Cradle." It's a song that describes the apologies made by a busy father to his growing son, and his regrets in later years.

TOMORROW

Hopefully, by now you have determined that the journey into your own financial planning practice will not be an easy one. And if you have already started your own practice, this should be evident by now. But planners are not alone. In many other professions, success does not come easily. Doctors go through eight years of school and several years of internship before they are qualified to call themselves doctors. A lawyer goes through seven years of school, practices for a few years, and then may be faced with the critical decision of whether to continue in the legal profession or to enter another one more suitable. The financial planner cannot expect to be a financial planner overnight. It just doesn't happen. There is too much information to pursue, both theoretical and practical. A doctor never knows it all; a lawyer never learns it all; nor will a financial planner.

It should be obvious by now that financial planning is a building process. The work that you do for your clients is a process. And building your firm is a process, too. Both require patience. Financial planning is not an impatient science. You must experiment like any other science to make a discovery. You must work at it. You must learn. Every little nook and cranny of your business can be a learning experience. The best text you will ever read is your own book, entitled *Mistakes I Have Made*. In the beginning it will be a multivolume text, and as your practice develops it should thin out to soft cover. But it will never end. You will never stop making mistakes. You are human. And human beings always make mistakes. That is one of the great things about being human. Could you live in a perfect world? I know I couldn't. In fact, in the perfect world your business wouldn't survive because your clients wouldn't need you. They'd be perfect, too!

Enough about perfection. Let's discuss imperfection. Since you will most assuredly be imperfect, you must compensate by adjusting your level of integrity. Ethically, you must be nearly perfect. Telling a client that a product is not needed, and thereby costing yourself a big commission, is tough. But there is really no other option. And once you can pass that hurdle you are well on the road to making it as a financial planner. If you never cross that hurdle, you may make it *financially*, but you will never make it as a financial planner. Making a lot of money and being a financial planner are not always one and the same. I hope this is understood by now.

The financial planner of tomorrow faces tremendous challenges down the road. If the challenges can be met, the opportunity is abundant. As I stated in Chapter 1, "the streets are paved with gold." And I really meant that. There is a great opportunity for the small independent financial planner. Those willing to pay their dues through hard work, patience, and ethics in today's world will become the very successful financial planners of tomorrow.

The small financial planning practice, however, is not for everyone. Perhaps you agree with what I have said in this book. And perhaps it sounds appealing. But maybe it's just not for you. The one thing that you cannot do is force yourself to be self-employed when you really don't have it in your heart. So what can you do?

Consider becoming a financial planner who works for someone else. The road for you will be paved with silver, the next best thing to gold. Obtain your financial planning credentials, your degrees, your designations, your training. Shortly, the demand for a person with your skills will vastly exceed the supply. You will be one step ahead.

Fred Tillman, CFP, has a master's degree in finance from the Wharton School of the University of Pennsylvania and a law degree from the University of Oklahoma. Currently, he heads what is perhaps the most advanced financial planning education program in the world: Georgia State University in Atlanta, Georgia, now offers a Doctorate in Financial Planning.

According to Fred Tillman, "The need for financial planners in years ahead will be staggering. I am excited by the opportunities that I see." He predicts the need for four types of people, especially as the multiproduct companies, the conglomerates, make their presence felt in the marketplace. First, there will be a need for the *specialist, the estate planner*, the person who can develop new and innovative products for service and product firms. There will be a greater need for the specialist because more people will be demanding products as we get more and more sophisticated on the consumer end, which is happening already. Second, he sees the need for the *comprehensive financial planner*, the person who can truly write a comprehensive objective plan. This person could either operate as an individual practitioner or as an employee of a multiproduct firm. Third, the large companies will need a *manager of financial services* within the organization. This manager will work all the way from the policy level to the strategic level and all the way down through operations, coordinating the delivery of the financial services and products. And finally, he sees the need for *teachers*. Once the educational institutions catch on to what's happening, they will need good financial planning teachers.

So if the small practice is not for you, it is by no means the end of the world, or the end of financial planning. You can still be a financial planner. No matter who you will work for—yourself, a conglomerate, a medium-size firm—the basic rules still apply. The source of a person's paycheck is not what makes a person a financial planner. It is what you do and the way you treat your clients that make you a financial planner.

You can think all you want about what you'll be doing tomorrow. But you must start today.

What are you waiting for?

Appendix A

Form ADV and Instructions

FORM ADV

INSTRUCTION SHEET

OMB Approval
OMB #3235-0049
Expires August 30, 1984

APPLICATION FOR REGISTRATION AS AN INVESTMENT ADVISER OR TO AMEND SUCH AN APPLICATION UNDER THE INVESTMENT ADVISERS ACT OF 1940

General Instructions for Preparing and Filing Form ADV

1. This Form and any Schedules and continuation sheets required in connection with it shall be completed and filed in triplicate with the Securities and Exchange Commission, Washington, D.C. 20549. Retain one additional copy for your records. All information required by Form ADV and any Schedule thereunder must be submitted on the officially prescribed forms (or mechanical reproductions thereof). Additional copies are available at any office of the Commission.

2. Form ADV consists of two parts, Part I and Part II. Both parts shall be completed and filed with the Commission.

3. At the time of the filing of an application for registration under the Act, the applicant shall pay to the Commission a fee of $150, no part of which shall be refunded. There is no fee for the filing of any amendments to Form ADV.

4. Each copy of the execution page must contain an original manual signature of the appropriate duly authorized individual. *Mechanical reproductions of signatures are not acceptable.* All other pages containing correct information may be mechanically reproduced by any method producing clear, legible copies of identical type size. Copies must be on 8½ x 11 inch paper.

5. If Form ADV is filed by a sole proprietor, it shall be signed by the proprietor; if it is filed by a partnership, it shall be signed in the name of the partnership by a general partner; if it is filed by an unincorporated organization or association which is not a partnership, it shall be signed in the name of such organization or association by the managing agent--i.e., a duly authorized person who directs or manages or who participates in directing or managing its affairs; if it is filed by a corporation, it shall be signed in the name of the corporation by a principal officer duly authorized.

6. If the space provided for any answer on the Form is insufficient, the complete answer shall be prepared on Schedule E with respect to Part I of the Form and on Schedule F with respect to Part II of the Form, which shall be attached to the Form. If the space provided for any answer on the Schedules is insufficient, the answer shall be completed on additional copies of the applicable Schedule which shall also be attached to the Form.

7. Individuals' names, except for executing signatures, shall be given in full wherever required (last name, first name, middle name). The full middle name is required. Initials are not acceptable unless the individual legally has only an initial. If this is the case, so indicate by "NMN" after the initial.

8. Definitions: Unless the context otherwise requires:

   a. All terms used in the Form have the same meaning as in the Investment Advisers Act of 1940 and the rules and regulations thereunder.

   b. "Jurisdiction" means a state, a territory, the District of Columbia, the Commonwealth of Puerto Rico, or any subdivision or regulatory body thereof.

   c. "Applicant" means the investment adviser or person which will be the investment adviser and not the individual completing the form unless they are identical. "Applicant" includes a "Registrant."

   d. "Self-Regulatory Organization" means any national securities exchange, national securities association, or clearing agency, registered under the Securities Exchange Act of 1934.

   e. "Client" means an investment advisory client.

9. **Under Sections 203(c), 204, 206, and 211(a) of the Investment Advisers Act of 1940 and the rules and regulations thereunder, the Commission is authorized to solicit the information required by this Form from applicants for registration as investment advisers. The information specified by this Form** *(other than social security numbers)* **must be provided prior to the processing of any application. Disclosure of social security numbers is voluntary. The information will be used for the purpose of determining whether the Commission should grant or deny registration to an applicant and other regulatory purposes. Social security numbers will assist the Commission in identifying applicants and, therefore, in promptly processing applications. Information supplied on this Form will be included in the public files of the Commission and will be available for inspection by any interested person. A Form which is not prepared and executed in compliance with applicable requirements may be returned as not acceptable for filing. Acceptance of this Form, however, shall not constitute any finding that it has been filed as required or that the information submitted is true, current, or complete. Intentional misstatements or omissions of fact constitute Federal criminal violations.** *(See 18 U.S.C. 1001 and 15 U.S.C. 80b-17.)*

Special Instructions for Filing Form ADV as an Application

10. If Form ADV is being filed as an application for registration, all applicable items must be answered in full. If any "item" is not applicable, indicate by "none" or "N/A" as appropriate. Items requiring information relating to the business activities of applicant should be answered to disclose what such activities will be when registration becomes effective.

11. If any non-resident of the United States is named in the Form, consult Rule 0-2 to determine whether he is required to file a consent to service of process and a power of attorney. Non-residents of the United States should also consult Rule 204-2(j) under the Act concerning the notice or undertaking relating to books and records which non-resident investment advisers are required to file with Form ADV.

Special Instructions for Amending Form ADV

12. Rule 204-1(b)(1) requires that if the information contained in response to questions 2, 4, 6, 10, 12(a), 12(b), and 14 of Part I of any application for registration as an investment adviser, or in any amendment thereto, becomes inaccurate for any reason, or if the information contained in response to questions 5, 7, 8, 9, and 11 of Part I or any question in Part II (except question 13) of any application for registration as an investment adviser becomes inaccurate in a material manner, the investment adviser shall promptly file an amendment on Form ADV correcting such information. In addition, if the information contained in response to questions 5, 7, 8, 9, and 11 of Part I or any question in Part II (except question 13) of any application for registration as an investment adviser, or in any amendment thereto, becomes inaccurate, but not in a material manner, or the information contained in response to questions 12(c), 13, 15, and 16 of Part I of any application for registration becomes inaccurate for any reason, the investment adviser shall file an amendment on Form ADV correcting such information no later than 90 days after the end of applicant's fiscal year. In addition, a balance sheet, as required by question 17 of Part I or question 13 of Part II shall be filed no later than 90 days after the end of applicant's fiscal year.

If the information contained in response to question 3 of Part I becomes inaccurate, the investment adviser shall file an amendment on Form ADV correcting such information no later than 90 days after the end of applicant's fiscal year. However, if the investment adviser's license has been withdrawn or involuntarily terminated, the investment adviser shall promptly file an amendment.

13. When an amendment is necessary, only the pages being amended, the execution page and page 1 of Part I need be filed, although these must be completed in full. Three copies of each of such pages should be filed.

CAUTION: When any item on a page is amended, it is necessary to answer all items on the page being amended. Pages which contain obsolete information are retired to the Commission's inactive files.

Special Instructions as to Specific Items on Form ADV

14. Item 2(a) - Include a street address; post office box numbers alone are not acceptable.

15. Item 3(a) - Key to State Abbreviations

AL - Alabama	KY - Kentucky	ND - North Dakota
AK - Alaska	LA - Louisiana	OH - Ohio
AZ - Arizona	ME - Maine	OK - Oklahoma
AR - Arkansas	MD - Maryland	OR - Oregon
CA - California	MA - Massachusetts	PA - Pennsylvania
CO - Colorado	MI - Michigan	RI - Rhode Island
CT - Connecticut	MN - Minnesota	SC - South Carolina
DE - Delaware	MS - Mississippi	SD - South Dakota
DC - District of Columbia	MO - Missouri	TN - Tennessee
FL - Florida	MT - Montana	TX - Texas
GA - Georgia	NE - Nebraska	UT - Utah
HI - Hawaii	NV - Nevada	VT - Vermont
ID - Idaho	NH - New Hampshire	VA - Virginia
IL - Illionis	NJ - New Jersey	WA - Washington
IN - Indiana	NM - New Mexico	WV - West Virginia
IA - Iowa	NY - New York	WI - Wisconsin
KS - Kansas	NC - North Carolina	WY - Wyoming
		PR - Puerto Rico

16. Item 8(b) - If a registered partnership is dissolved and a new one is created to continue the business of the old one, the new partnership must file a new or successor application as an investment adviser.

17. Item 10 - Check answers to Items 2(a), 8, and 9 of Part I and the related Schedules for the names of all persons who are covered by any of the subsections of Item 10 of Part I. Similarly, any persons who directly or indirectly control or are controlled by the applicant, including any employee, are covered by Item 10 of Part I. For each affirmative answer, list each person involved on a separate Schedule D and explain these incidents, including, for example, the parties involved, time and place, subject matter, and the outcome of the proceedings.

Special Instructions relating to Schedules

18. Schedule A - Schedule A is for corporations.

    (If applicant is owned directly, or indirectly through one or more intermediaries, by a corporation, then such corporation's shareholders should be considered in determining who must be listed on Schedule A.)

19. Schedule B - Schedule B is for partnerships.

20. Schedule C - Schedule C is to be completed only by organizations or associations which are not sole proprietorships, partnerships, or corporations.

21. Schedule D - Schedule D is to be filed for the following classes of persons:

    (a) Each natural person named in Items 2(a), 8, or 9 or any Schedule thereunder, except that Schedule D need not be furnished for any person who meets both the following conditions: (1) he owns less than 10% of any class of equity security of the applicant; and (2) he is not an officer, director or person with similar status or functions.

    (b) Each person subject to any action reported under Item 10; and

    (c) (1) Each member of applicant's investment committee or similar group, if any, which determines or approves what investment advice shall generally be rendered by applicant to any client, or to which clients such investment advice shall be rendered.

       (2) In the absence of an investment committee or similar group, each person associated with applicant who determines or approves what investment advice shall be rendered by applicant to any client, or to which clients such investment advice shall be rendered (if more than five such persons, it is necessary to complete a separate Schedule D only for those persons having supervisory responsibility over those persons described in this paragraph)

22. Schedule E - Schedule E may be used (1) where the space provided for any answer in Part I of the Form is insufficient, or (2) in response to each item in Part I of the Form which requires the submission of Schedule E. Schedule E should not be used when the space on any other Schedule is insufficient. In that case use additional copies of the applicable Schedule.

23. Schedule F - Schedule F may be used (1) where the space provided for any answer in Part II of the Form is insufficient, or (2) in response to each item in Part II of the Form which requires the submission of Schedule F. Schedule F should not be used when the space on any other Schedule is insufficient. In that case use additional copies of the applicable Schedule.

24. Schedule G - Schedule G is for the balance sheet required by Item 17 of Part I and Item 13 of Part II.

25. Execution - The execution must include an original manual signature. *(Mechanical reproductions of signatures are not acceptable.)*

FORM ADV
Part I
(revised 7-31-79)
Page 1

APPLICATION FOR REGISTRATION AS AN INVESTMENT ADVISER OR TO AMEND SUCH AN APPLICATION UNDER THE INVESTMENT ADVISERS ACT OF 1940

Securities and Exchange Commission, Washington, D.C. 20549

OFFICIAL USE

GENERAL: Read all instructions before preparing the Form. Please print or type all responses. If this Form is filed as an amendment, a completed and signed execution page, Page 1 of Part I (this page) and those pages containing items which are being amended or which have changed since the previous filing must be filed. Such pages should be completed in full. Submit check for $150 if this is an application for registration. Return in triplicate.

☐ *Check here if change of address*

1. (a) if this is an APPLICATION for registration, check here ☐ and complete all items in full.

   (b) If this is an AMENDMENT to an application, check here ☐ and specify below all items which are amended.

      Item(s) _____ of Part I of Form ADV   Schedule A ☐   Schedule B ☐

      Item(s) _____ of Part II of Form ADV   Schedule C ☐   Schedule D ☐

                                                           Schedule E ☐   Schedule F ☐

                                                             Schedule G ☐

2. (a) Exact name, principal business address, mailing address, if different, and telephone number of applicant:

   Full name of applicant *(If sole proprietor, state last, first, and middle name):*   IRS Empl. Ident. No.:

_____

   Name under which business is conducted, if different:

_____

   If name of business is hereby amended, state previous name:

_____

   Address of principal place of business: *(Do not use P.O. Box Number)*

_____

   (NUMBER AND STREET)   (CITY)   (STATE)   (ZIP CODE)

   Mailing Address, if different:

_____

   (NUMBER AND STREET)   (CITY)   (STATE)   (ZIP CODE)

   Telephone Number:

_____

   (AREA CODE)   (TELEPHONE NUMBER)

   Address of each location of the books and records applicant is required to maintain, pursuant to Section 204 of the Investment Advisers Act of 1940 and the rules thereunder, if different from address of principal place of business:

_____

   (NUMBER AND STREET)   (CITY)   (STATE)   (ZIP CODE)

ALL OF THE ITEMS ON THIS PAGE MUST BE ANSWERED AND COMPLETED IN FULL

2. (b) Persons to contact for further information concerning this Form:

_____   _____
(NAME)   (TITLE)

_____   _____
(MAILING ADDRESS)   (TELEPHONE NO.)

2. (c) Applicant consents that notice of any proceeding before the Commission in connection with its application for or registration as an investment adviser may be given by sending notice by registered or certified mail or confirmed telegram to the person named at the address given.

_____   _____   _____
(LAST NAME)   (FIRST NAME)   (MIDDLE NAME)

_____   _____   _____   _____
(NUMBER AND STREET)   (CITY)   (STATE)   (ZIP CODE)

2. (d) Does applicant have offices other than that mentioned in Item 2(a)?   YES ☐   NO ☐
(If "yes," state their addresses and telephone numbers on Schedule E.)

2. (e) Applicant's fiscal year ends: ☐ (MONTH)   ☐ (DAY)

3. (a) Applicant is filing or has filed its application for registration or license as an investment adviser with the following: *(Place a code after each applicable jurisdiction in accordance with the following: If application is pending, insert number "1"; if presently or previously registered or licensed, insert number "2".)*

AL __ AK __ AZ __ AR __ CA __ CO __ CT __ DE __ DC __ FL __ GA __ HI __ ID __ IL __ IN __ IA __

KS __ KY __ LA __ ME __ MD __ MA __ MI __ MN __ MS __ MO __ MT __ NE __ NV __ NH __ NJ __ NM __

NY __ NC __ ND __ OH __ OK __ OR __ PA __ RI __ SC __ SD __ TN __ TX __ UT __ VT __ VA __ WA __

WV __ WI __ WY __ PR __ Other _____
(SPECIFY)

3. (b) If any license or registration listed above is of a restricted nature or has been suspended or involuntarily terminated, or withdrawn or voluntarily terminated, explain on Schedule E.

4. Applicant is a:

☐ Corporation   ☐ Partnership   ☐ Sole Proprietorship

☐ Other _____
(SPECIFY)

If any item on this page is amended, you must answer in full all other items on this page and file with a completed and signed execution page and Page 1 of Part I. No Schedule required by any item on this page need be filed with an amended item unless the Schedule itself is amended.

WARNING: Failure to keep this form current and failure to keep accurate books and records as required by the Federal securities laws would violate such Federal securities laws and may result in disciplinary, administrative, injunctive or criminal action. INTENTIONAL MISSTATEMENTS OR OMISSIONS OF FACTS MAY CONSTITUTE CRIMINAL VIOLATIONS.

5. If applicant is a corporation:

   (a) Date and place of incorporation:

      Date _____ State: _____
      (MONTH · DAY · YEAR)

   (b) List below each class of equity security:

CLASS	VOTING	NON-VOTING
_____	☐	☐
_____	☐	☐
_____	☐	☐

6. If applicant is a sole proprietor, state current legal residence address and social security number.

      Social Security No.: _____

   _____
   (NUMBER AND STREET)   (CITY)   (STATE)   (ZIP CODE)

7. (a) Is applicant filing this application as a successor who is taking over all or substantially all of the assets and liabilities and continuing the business of a registered investment adviser? If "yes," state: . . . .   YES ☐   NO ☐

   (1) Date of Succession: _____

   (2) Full name, IRS Empl. Ident. No. and SEC File No. of predecessor:

      Name: _____

      IRS Empl. Ident. No.: _____

      SEC File Number: _____

   (b) Has applicant, during the previous ten years, merged with or acquired another registered investment adviser? *(If "yes," explain on Schedule E.)* . . . .   YES ☐   NO ☐

8. (a) If applicant is a corporation, complete Schedule A.

   (b) If applicant is a partnership, complete Schedule B.

   (c) If applicant is other than a sole proprietorship, partnership, or corporation, complete Schedule C.

If any item on this page is amended, you must answer in full all other items on this page and file with a completed and signed execution page and Page 1 of Part I. No Schedule required by any item on this page need be filed with an amended item unless the Schedule itself is amended.

FORM ADV PART I Page 4

9. (a) Does any person not named in Items 2(a) and 8, or any Schedule thereunder, directly or indirectly through agreement or otherwise, exercise or have the power to exercise a controlling influence over the management or policies of applicant?. . . . . YES ☐ NO ☐
(If "yes," state on Schedule E the exact name of each person (if individual, state last, first, and middle names) and describe the agreement or other basis through which such person exercises or has the power to exercise a controlling influence.)

(b) Is the business of applicant wholly or partially financed, directly or indirectly, by any person not named in Items 2(a) and 8, or any Schedule thereunder, in any manner other than by: (1) a public offering of securities made pursuant to the Securities Act of 1933; (2) credit extended in the ordinary course of business by suppliers, banks and others; or (3) a satisfactory subordination agreement, as defined in Rule 15c3-1 under the Securities Exchange Act of 1934 (17 CFR 240.15c3-1)?. . . . . YES ☐ NO ☐
(If "yes," state on Schedule E the exact name (last, first, middle) of each person and describe the agreement or arrangement through which such financing is made available, including the amount thereof.)

10. State whether the applicant, any person named in Items 2(a), 8 or 9, or any Schedule thereunder, or any other person directly or indirectly controlling, or controlled by applicant, including any clerical or ministerial employee of applicant:

(a) Has been found by the Securities and Exchange Commission or any jurisdiction to have willfully made or caused to be made in any application for registration or report required to be filed with the Commission under the Investment Advisers Act of 1940 or in any proceeding before the Commission with respect to registration, any statement which was at the time and in the light of the circumstances under which it was made false or misleading with respect to any material fact, or to have omitted to state in any such application or report any material fact which is required to be stated therein . . . . YES ☐ NO ☐

(b) Has been convicted of or has pleaded nolo contendere to, within 10 years preceding the filing of any application for registration or at any time thereafter, any felony or misdemeanor:

(i) involving the purchase or sale of any security, the taking of a false oath, the making of a false report, bribery, perjury, burglary, or conspiracy to commit any such offense;. YES ☐ NO ☐

(ii) arising out of the conduct of the business of a broker, dealer, municipal securities dealer, investment adviser, bank, insurance company, or fiduciary;. . . . . YES ☐ NO ☐

(iii) involving the larceny, theft, robbery, extortion, forgery, counterfeiting, fraudulent concealment, embezzlement, fraudulent conversion, or misappropriation of funds or securities; or. . . . . YES ☐ NO ☐

(iv) involving the violation of Section 152, 1341, 1342 or 1343 or Chapter 25 or 47 of Title 18, United States Code (concealment of assets, false oaths and claims, or bribery, in any bankruptcy proceeding; mail fraud, fraud by wire, including telephone, telegraph, radio or television; counterfeiting, forgery, fraud, false statements) . . . . . . YES ☐ NO ☐

If any item on this page is amended, you must answer in full all other items on this page and file with a completed and signed execution page and Page 1 of Part I. No Schedule required by any item on this page need be filed with an amended item unless the Schedule itself is amended.

10. (c) Is permanently or temporarily enjoined by order, judgment, or decree of any court of competent jurisdiction from acting as an investment adviser, underwriter, broker, dealer, or municipal securities dealer, or as an affiliated person or employee of any investment company, bank, or insurance company, or from engaging in or continuing any conduct or practice in connection with any such activity, or in connection with the purchase or sale of any security or arising out of any securities or investment advisory activity......

YES ☐ NO ☐

(d) Has been found by the Securities and Exchange Commission or any other jurisdiction to have willfully violated or willfully aided, abetted, counseled, commanded, induced, or procured the violation by any other person of any provision of the Securities Act of 1933, the Securities Exchange Act of 1934, the Investment Company Act of 1940, the Investment Advisers Act of 1940, the rules or regulations under any of such statutes, or the rules of the Municipal Securities Rulemaking Board, or to have failed reasonably to supervise, with a view to preventing violations of the provisions of such statutes, rules, and regulations, another person who commits such a violation, if such other person is subject to his supervision, or to have been unable to comply with any of the foregoing provisions ....

YES ☐ NO ☐

(e) Is subject to an order of the Securities and Exchange Commission entered pursuant to Section 203(f) of the Investment Advisers Act of 1940 barring or suspending the right of such person to be associated with an investment adviser which order is in effect with respect to such person ....

YES ☐ NO ☐

(f) Has been denied membership or registration with, or participation in, or has been suspended, revoked or expelled from membership, participation in or registration with any self-regulatory organization registered under the Securities Exchange Act of 1934......

YES ☐ NO ☐

(g) Has been denied registration (license) with, or suspended, revoked or expelled from registration (license) with the Securities and Exchange Commission or any jurisdiction (or any agency thereof) as a broker, dealer, investment adviser, securities salesman, or municipal securities dealer, or has been barred from being associated with a person engaged in such business ....

YES ☐ NO ☐

(h) Has been found to have been a cause of (1) the denial, suspension, or revocation of any person's (a) registration with the Securities and Exchange Commission or any jurisdiction (or any agency thereof), or (b) membership or participation in any self-regulatory organization registered under the Securities Exchange Act of 1934; or (2) any person's expulsion from such self-regulatory organization.................................

YES ☐ NO ☐

(i) Has been, within the past 10 years, the subject of any cease and desist, desist, and refrain, prohibition, or similar order which was issued by the United States or any jurisdiction arising out of the conduct of the business of a broker, dealer, municipal securities dealer or investment adviser ....

YES ☐ NO ☐

If any item on this page is amended, you must answer in full all other items on this page and file with a completed and signed execution page and Page 1 of Part I. No Schedule required by any item on this page need be filed with an amended item unless the Schedule itself is amended.

OFFICIAL USE

(j)   Has been the subject of any order, judgment, decree or other sanction of a foreign court, foreign exchange, or foreign governmental or regulatory agency arising out of any securities or investment advisory activities . . . .

YES ☐   NO ☐

(k)   State whether applicant, any person named in Items 2(a), 8 or 9, or any Schedule thereunder, or any other person directly or indirectly controlling or controlled by applicant, including any employee, is presently the subject of any public proceedings in which an adverse decision would result in any of the foregoing questions being answered "yes." . . .

YES ☐   NO ☐

11.   Complete a separate Schedule D for each appropriate person in accordance with the instructions thereon and instruction 21 to this Form.

12.   Does applicant, or any person associated with applicant, have custody or possession of, or have authority to obtain custody or possession of:

(a)   Securities of any client?   . . . .

YES ☐   NO ☐

(b)   Funds of any client? . . . .

YES ☐   NO ☐

Reminder: Rule 206(4)-2 contains special provisions relating to investment advisers who have custody or possession of securities or funds of their advisory clients.

(c)   If the answer to any of the foregoing questions of Item 12 is "yes," provide the approximate value of the clients' funds and securities in applicant's custody or possession as of the end of the last fiscal year . . . .   _____

13.   (a)   State the number of persons employed by applicant, other than clerical or ministerial employees . . . .   _____

(b)   Does a substantial part of applicant's investment advisory business consist of rendering "investment supervisory services" as defined in Section 202 (a)(13) of the Act? . . . .

YES ☐   NO ☐

14.   Is applicant a defendant in any material civil litigation relating to its business as an investment adviser? . . . .
(If "yes," explain on Schedule E.)

YES ☐   NO ☐

If any item on this page is amended, you must answer in full all other items on this page and file with a completed and signed execution page and Page 1 of Part I. No Schedule required by any item on this page need be filed with an amended item unless the Schedule itself is amended.

FORM ADV PART I Page 7

15. (i) Opposite each of the following types of clients for which the applicant generally provides discretionary account management place a numeral indicating its rank (largest = 1) according to the approximate dollar amount under management in each category as of the end of applicant's last fiscal year. Omit any category where the dollar amount under management is less than (a) 10% of the amount stated in response to Item 15(ii) (b) or (b) $50,000, whichever is lesser.

a) Individuals . . . . _____

b) Registered investment companies . . . . _____

c) Pension and profit-sharing plans . . . . _____

d) Banks . . . . _____

e) Charitable institutions . . . . _____

f) Educational institutions . . . . _____

g) Trust accounts . . . . _____

h) Corporations . . . . _____

i) Insurance companies . . . . _____

j) Other (explain on Schedule E) . . . . _____

(If the applicant imposes any limitations on the types of clients it will accept, explain on Schedule E.)

(ii) (a) Total number of accounts under discretionary management as of the end of the last fiscal year . . . . _____

(b) Approximate aggregate market value of such accounts as of the end of the last fiscal year. *(Round off to nearest hundred)* . . . . _____

(iii) Approximate number of accounts under discretionary management in the following size categories as of the end of the last fiscal year:

a) Less than $10,000 . . . . _____

b) $10,000 — less than $50,000 . . . . _____

c) $50,000 — less than $200,000 . . . . _____

d) $200,000 — less than $500,000 . . . . _____

e) $500,000 — less than $1,000,000 . . . . _____

f) $1,000,000 or more . . . . _____

If any item on this page is amended, you must answer in full all other items on this page and file with a completed and signed execution page and Page 1 of Part I. No Schedule required by any item on this page need be filed with an amended item unless the Schedule itself is amended.

16. (i) Opposite each of the following types of clients for which the applicant generally provides account management or supervision on other than a discretionary basis place a numeral indicating its rank (largest = 1) according to the approximate dollar amount under management in each category as of the end of the applicant's last fiscal year. Omit any category where the dollar amount under management is less than (a) 10% of the amount stated in response to Item 16(ii) (b) or (b) $50,000, whichever is lesser.

a) Individuals . . . . _____

b) Registered investment companies . . . . _____

c) Pension and profit-sharing plans . . . . _____

d) Banks . . . . _____

e) Charitable institutions . . . . _____

f) Educational institutions . . . . _____

g) Trust accounts . . . . _____

h) Corporations . . . . _____

i) Insurance companies . . . . _____

j) Other (explain on Schedule E) . . . . _____

(If the applicant imposes any limitations on the types of clients it will accept, explain on Schedule E.)

(ii) (a) Total number of accounts under management or supervision on other than a discretionary basis as of the end of the last fiscal year . . . . _____

(b) Approximate market value of such accounts as of the end of the last fiscal year. *(Round off to nearest hundred)* . . . . _____

(iii) Approximate number of such accounts in the following size categories as of the end of the last fiscal year:

a) Less than $10,000 . . . . _____

b) $10,000 — less than $50,000 . . . . _____

c) $50,000 — less than $200,000 . . . . _____

d) $200,000 — less than $500,000 . . . . _____

e) $500,000 — less than $1,000,000 . . . . _____

f) $1,000,000 or more . . . . _____

If any item on this page is amended, you must answer in full all other items on this page and file with a completed and signed execution page and Page 1 of Part I. No Schedule required by any item on this page need be filed with an amended item unless the Schedule itself is amended.

17. Every applicant not subject to the requirement of Part II - Item 13 shall provide on Schedule G a balance sheet as of the end of applicant's most recent fiscal year. The balance sheet need not be audited by an independent public accountant. The balance sheet shall be prepared in accordance with generally accepted accounting principles and shall show assets and liabilities related to the advisory business separately from other business and personal assets and liabilities. The statement shall be accompanied by a note stating the accounting principles and practices followed in its preparation, the basis at which securities are included and other notes as may be necessary for an understanding of the statement. If securities are included at cost, their market or fair value shall be shown parenthetically.

Has applicant provided a balance sheet on Schedule G pursuant to this Item? . . . .

YES ☐   NO ☐

If any item on this page is amended, you must answer in full all other items on this page and file with a completed and signed execution page and Page 1 of Part I. No Schedule required by any item on this page need be filed with an amended item unless the Schedule itself is amended.

272

FORM ADV   PART II   Page 1

Name of Investment Adviser:

_____

Address:

_____
        (NUMBER AND STREET)   (CITY)   (STATE)   (ZIP CODE)

Telephone Number:

_____ _____
(AREA CODE)   (NUMBER)

     Part II of Form ADV, the application for registration as an investment adviser under the Investment Advisers Act of 1940, contains information relating to the investment adviser and the nature of his business. Items 1 through 4 relate to general information about the adviser's basic operations including the types of services offered and the fees charged, the types of clients advised, the types of investments generally recommended, the methods of analysis, the types of investment strategies employed, and the sources of information used by the adviser in formulating recommendations. Items 5 and 6 provide information concerning any educational and business standards applicable to persons associated with the adviser and the actual educational and business backgrounds of certain persons associated with the adviser. Items 7 through 9 contain information about other business activities of the adviser, other activities or affiliations of the adviser in the securities industry, and his participation in connection with securities transactions of clients. Items 10 through 12 provide additional information for clients whose accounts are managed by the adviser including conditions for managing investment advisory accounts, the nature of the adviser's discretionary authority, if any, with respect to clients' accounts, and the process of reviewing investment advisory accounts. Item 11 also contains information about brokerage placement practices of the adviser. Item 13 contains, for certain advisers, a certified balance sheet.

    The information regarding the investment adviser contained in Part II of Form ADV has not been passed upon or approved by the Securities and Exchange Commission nor has the Commission passed upon or approved the qualifications or business practices of the investment adviser described in Part II.

FORM ADV PART II Page 2

1. **Advisory Services and Fees.** Does applicant:

a) Furnish "investment supervisory services," defined as the giving of continuous advice to clients as to the investment of funds on the basis of individual needs of each client, e.g., the nature and amount of other assets, investments and insurance, and the nature and extent of the personal and family obligations of each client (distinguished from continuous advice of any nature which is not based on consideration of such relevant individual factors)? . . . . YES ☐ NO ☐

b) Manage investment advisory accounts under circumstances not involving investment supervisory services? . . . . YES ☐ NO ☐

c) Furnish investment advice through consultations (not as part of (a) or (b) above)?. . . . . . YES ☐ NO ☐

d) Issue periodic publications relating to securities on a subscription basis? . . . . YES ☐ NO ☐

e) Prepare or issue special reports or analyses relating to securities, not included in any service described above? . . . . YES ☐ NO ☐

f) Prepare or issue, not as part of any service described above, any charts, graphs, formulas, or other devices which clients may use to evaluate securities?. . . . . YES ☐ NO ☐

g) Furnish advice to clients on any matters not involving securities on other than an incidental basis?. . . . . YES ☐ NO ☐

h) Furnish investment advice in any manner not described above? . . . . YES ☐ NO ☐

(In each case in which the answer to the preceding paragraphs is "yes," the applicant shall describe such services and the fees for such services on Schedule F, including the basis or bases of compensation, e.g., a percentage of the assets under management, hourly charges, a fixed fee or an annual subscription fee in the case of a periodic publication for the services which the investment adviser provides, and the amounts charged, e.g., 1% per annum, applicant's basic fee schedule and an indication that its fees are negotiable, if such is the case, and when such compensation is payable. If such compensation is payable prior to the rendering of the services relating thereto, the applicant should expain to what extent and under what conditions such compensation is refundable.

In addition, those applicants who answered "yes" to questions (d) and (e) above should include the name of each publication or analysis issued on a regular basis and a general description of any special reports or analyses to be issued on an irregular basis.

The applicant should set forth the procedures and conditions, if any, pursuant to which the applicant or any client may terminate an investment advisory contract prior to the termination date set forth in the contract.)

If any item on this page is amended, you must answer in full all other items on this page and file with a completed and signed execution page and Page 1 of Part I. No Schedule required by any item on this page need be filed with an amended item unless the Schedule itself is amended.

2. **Types of Clients.** List the type or types of clients for which the investment adviser generally provides investment advice, including but not limited to, individuals or specified classes of individuals, banks, investment companies and pension and profit-sharing plans.

3. **Types of Securities.** Check the types of securities concerning which the applicant generally provides investment advice:

a)   Equity securities

			YES	NO
	1) exchange listed securities		☐	☐
	2) securities traded over-the-counter		☐	☐
b)	Corporate debt securities		☐	☐
c)	Warrants		☐	☐
d)	Commercial paper		☐	☐
e)	Bank certificates of deposit		☐	☐
f)	Municipal securities		☐	☐

g)   Investment company securities

			YES	NO
	1) variable life insurance		☐	☐
	2) variable annuities		☐	☐
	3) mutual fund shares		☐	☐
h)	United States government securities		☐	☐

i)   Options contracts on

			YES	NO
	1) securities		☐	☐
	2) commodities		☐	☐

j)   Interests in partnerships investing in

			YES	NO
	1) real estate		☐	☐
	2) oil and gas interests		☐	☐
	3) other *(explain on Schedule F)*		☐	☐
k)	Other *(explain on Schedule F)*		☐	☐

If any item on this page is amended, you must answer in full all other items on this page and file with a completed and signed execution page and Page 1 of Part I. No Schedule required by any item on this page need be filed with an amended item unless the Schedule itself is amended.

FORM ADV PART II Page 4

4. Methods of Analysis, Sources of Information, and Investment Strategies.

a) Relate in a narrative fashion the applicant's method or methods of security analysis, e.g., fundamental analysis, technical analysis, cyclical analysis or charting.

b) Relate in a narrative fashion the principal sources of information applicant uses, e.g., financial newspapers and magazines, company prepared information (i.e., annual reports, prospectuses, filings with the Commission, press releases), inspections of corporate activities, research materials prepared by others, or corporate rating services.

c) Relate in a narrative fashion the types of investment strategies generally recommended or used to implement any investment advice rendered to clients, e.g., long term purchases (securities will be held at least one year except in unusual circumstances), short term purchases (securities will generally be sold within one year after purchase), trading (securities will generally be sold within 30 days after purchase), short sales, margin transactions, or option writing, including covered options, uncovered options, and spreading strategies.

If any item on this page is amended, you must answer in full all other items on this page and file with a completed and signed execution page and Page 1 of Part I. No Schedule required by any item on this page need be filed with an amended item unless the Schedule itself is amended.

5. **Education and Business Standards.** Are there any general standards of education and business background which applicant requires of persons associated with applicant (other than persons whose functions are solely clerical or ministerial whose functions or duties relate to providing investment advice to clients?. . . . .

YES ☐ NO ☐

(If "yes," describe such standards briefly on Schedule F).

6. **Education and Business Background.**

   a) Applicant shall set forth the name, age, formal education after high school, and, for the preceding five years, the business background of each member of the investment adviser's investment committee or similar group, if any, which determines or approves what investment advice shall generally be rendered by the investment adviser to any client or to which client such investment advice shall be rendered.

   b) If applicant does not have an investment committee or similar committee, applicant shall set forth the name, age, formal education after high school, and, for the preceding five years, the business background of each person associated with the investment adviser who determines or approves what investment advice shall be rendered by the investment adviser *(if more than five such persons, it shall be sufficient to limit this information to persons having supervisory responsibility over those persons described in this paragraph).*

If any item on this page is amended, you must answer in full all other items on this page and file with a completed and signed execution page and Page 1 of Part I. No Schedule required by any item on this page need be filed with an amended item unless the Schedule itself is amended.

FORM ADV PART II Page 6

7. Other Business Activities.

a) Is applicant engaged in any business or profession other than acting as an investment adviser? . . . . YES ☐ NO ☐

b) Does applicant offer or sell any type of product, other than investment advice concerning securities, to clients? . . . . YES ☐ NO ☐

(If the answer to item (a) or (b) is "yes," describe briefly on Schedule F such other activities.)

c) Is the principal business of applicant that of an investment adviser? . . . . YES ☐ NO ☐

8. Other Securities Industry Activities or Affiliations.

a) Is applicant registered (or does applicant have an application for registration pending) as broker or dealer? . . . . YES ☐ NO ☐

b) Is applicant affiliated with any broker, dealer, investment company or another investment adviser? . . . . YES ☐ NO ☐

(If "yes," state the nature of such affiliation and the business relationship, if any, between such entity and applicant on Schedule F.)

NOTE: *Pursuant to Section 202 (a)(12) of the Act [15 U.S.C. 80b-2(a)(12)], the term "affiliated person" has the same meaning as in Section 2(a)(3) of the Investment Company Act of 1940 [15 U.S.C. 80a-2(a)(3)], which, as relevant, means*

"(A) any person directly or indirectly owning, controlling, or holding with power to vote, 5 per centum or more of the outstanding voting securities of such other person; (B) any person 5 per centum or more whose outstanding voting securities are directly or indirectly owned, controlled, or held with power to vote, by such other person; (C) any person directly or indirectly controlling, controlled by, or under common control with, such other person; (D) any officer, director, partner, co-partner, or employee of such other person . . . ."

If any item on this page is amended, you must answer in full all other items on this page and file with a completed and signed execution page and Page 1 of Part I. No Schedule required by any item on this page need be filed with an amended item unless the Schedule itself is amended.

9. **Participation or Interest in Securities Transactions.** Does applicant:

(a) As principal, sell securities to or buy securities from any (investment advisory) client?.......... ....
YES ☐   NO ☐

(b) Effect securities transactions for compensation as broker or agent for any (investment advisory) client?...................................
YES ☐   NO ☐

(c) As broker or agent for any person other than a (investment advisory) client, sell securities to or buy securities from clients? ....
YES ☐   NO ☐

(d) Recommend to (investment advisory) clients or prospective clients, the purchase or sale of securities in which the applicant, directly or indirectly, has a position or interest?...
YES ☐   NO ☐

(If the answer to any of the foregoing questions of Item 9 is "yes," describe on Schedule F the circumstances in which the investment adviser engages in such transactions and any internal procedures the investment adviser has concerning conflicts of interest in such transactions.)

(e) Impose any restrictions upon itself or any person associated with it in connection with the purchase or sale, directly or indirectly, for its or their account of securities recommended to clients? *(If the answer to this paragraph is "yes," describe such restrictions on Schedule F.)* ....
YES ☐   NO ☐

(If applicant provides investment supervisory services (as defined in Section 202(a) (13) of the Act [15 U.S.C. 80b-2(a)(13)] or manages investment advisory accounts for clients under circumstances not involving investment supervisory services, answer Items 10 through 12. If applicant does not provide any of the foregoing services, Item 11 must, nevertheless, be answered if applicant determines or suggests the broker or dealer through which or the commission rates at which securities transactions for client accounts are effected.)

10. **Conditions for Managing Accounts.** Does applicant generally require a minimum dollar amount of assets for or generally impose any other conditions on the establishment or maintenance of an investment advisory account? ....
YES ☐   NO ☐

(If "yes," describe such minimum and/or other conditions on Schedule F.)

If any item on this page is amended, you must answer in full all other items on this page and file with a completed and signed execution page and Page 1 of Part I. No Schedule required by any item on this page need be filed with an amended item unless the Schedule itself is amended.

FORM ADV PART II Page 8

11. **Investment or Brokerage Discretion.** Does applicant or any person associated with applicant have discretionary authority to make any of the following determinations without obtaining the consent of the investment advisory client before the transactions are effected:

		YES	NO
---	---	:-::	:-:
(a)	Which securities are to be bought or sold?	☐	☐
(b)	The total amount of the securities to be bought or sold?.....................	☐	☐
(c)	Through which broker or dealer securities are to be bought or sold?	☐	☐
(d)	The commission rates at which securities transactions for client accounts are effected?...	☐	☐

(If the answer to any question of Item 11 is "yes" and there are limitations on such authority, describe such limitations on Schedule F.

If applicant or any person associated with applicant determines or suggests the broker or brokers through whom, or the commission rates at which, securities transactions for client accounts are executed, describe on Schedule F how brokers will be selected to effect securities transactions and how evaluations will be made of the overall reasonableness of brokerage commissions paid, including factors considered in these determinations. If the receipt of products or services other than brokerage or research services is such a factor, this description should specify them. If the receipt of research services is such a factor in selecting brokers, this description should identify the nature of such research services.

State on Schedule F if applicant may pay a broker a brokerage commission in excess of that which another broker might have charged for effecting the same transactions, in recognition of the value of (a) brokerage or (b) research services provided by the broker.

If applicable, explain that research services furnished by brokers through whom applicant effects securities transactions may be used in servicing all of applicant's accounts and that not all such services may be used by applicant in connection with the accounts which paid commissions to the broker providing such services; or, if other policies or practices are applicable with respect to the allocation of research services provided by brokers, explain on Schedule F such policies and practices.

If, during the last fiscal year, applicant, pursuant to an agreement or understanding with a broker or otherwise through an internal allocation procedure, directed brokerage transactions to a broker or brokers because of research services provided, identify and briefly describe on Schedule F such arrangements.)

If any item on this page is amended, you must answer in full all other items on this page and file with a completed and signed execution page and Page 1 of Part I. No Schedule required by any item on this page need be filed with an amended item unless the Schedule itself is amended.

12. **Review of Accounts.**

(a) Describe briefly below the process pursuant to which the applicant reviews investment advisory accounts, including, but not limited to, the category of personnel performing the review, the frequency of review, the number of accounts assigned to account managers, factors which trigger reviews, the sequence in which accounts are reviewed and the matters reviewed.

(b) State below the general frequency and nature of any reports regularly furnished to clients concerning their investment advisory accounts.

13. **Balance Sheet.** Every applicant who has custody or possession of clients' funds or securities, or requires prepayment of advisory fees six months or more in advance and in excess of $500 per client, shall provide on Schedule G a balance sheet as of the end of applicant's most recent fiscal year. The balance sheet shall be audited by an independent public accountant. The balance sheet shall be prepared in accordance with generally accepted accounting principles and shall show assets and liabilities related to the advisory business separately from other business and personal assets and liabilities. The statement shall be accompanied by a note stating the accounting principles and practices followed in its preparation, the basis at which securities are included and other notes as may be necessary for an understanding of the statement. If securities are included at cost, their market or fair value shall be shown parenthetically.

YES   NO

Has applicant provided a balance sheet on Schedule G pursuant to this Item? . . . .   ☐   ☐

If any item on this page is amended, you must answer in full all other items on this page and file with a completed and signed execution page and Page 1 of Part I. No Schedule required by any item on this page need be filed with an amended item unless the Schedule itself is amended.

Schedule A of

FORM ADV ☐

FORM BD ☐

FOR CORPORATIONS

(Answers in response to Item 8(a) of Part I of FORM ADV or Item 8(a) of FORM BD.)

Date as stated on the execution page of FORM ADV or FORM BD accompanying this Schedule:

WARNING: Failure to keep this form current and failure to keep accurate books and records as required by the Federal securities laws would violate such Federal securities laws and may result in disciplinary, administrative, injunctive or criminal action. INTENTIONAL MISSTATEMENTS OR OMISSIONS OF FACTS MAY CONSTITUTE CRIMINAL VIOLATIONS.

I. Full name of applicant exactly as stated in Item 2(a) of Part I of FORM ADV or Item 2(a) of FORM BD:

IRS Empl. Ident. No.:

OFFICIAL USE

II. Name under which business is conducted if different:

III. Complete and mark appropriate columns for (a) each officer, director, and person with similar status or functions, and (b) each other person who is, directly or indirectly, the beneficial owner of 1% or more of the outstanding shares of any class of equity security of applicant unless applicant is the issuer of a security registered pursuant to Section 12 of the Securities Exchange Act of 1934 (or the issuer of a security which is exempted pursuant to Subsections (g)(2)(B) or (g)(2)(G) thereof) in which case each other person who is, directly or indirectly, the beneficial owner of 5% or more of the outstanding shares of any such registered class of equity security of applicant. Thus, if applicant is owned directly, or indirectly through one or more intermediaries, by a corporation, then such corporation's shareholders should be considered in determining who must be listed on Schedule A. Place an asterisk (*) after the names of the persons for whom a change in title, status, or stock ownership is being reported. Place a double asterisk (**) after the names of the persons which are ADDED to those furnished in the most recent previous filing. Designate percentage of ownership as follows: If none, enter "none," above 0% to less than 1%, enter "A," 1% to less than 5%, enter "B," 5% to less than 10%, enter "C," 10% to less than 25%, enter "D," 25% to less than 50%, enter "E," 50% to less than 75%, enter "F," 75% to 100% enter "G."

FULL NAME			RELATIONSHIP			Official Use Only	Ownership Code	Class of Equity Security	Social Security Number
			Beginning Date		Title or Status				
Last	First	Middle	Mo.	Yr.					
						01			
						02			
						03			
						04			
						05			
						06			
						07			
						08			
						09			
						10			
						11			
						12			

IV. List below names reported in the most recent previous filing pursuant to this Item which are DELETED hereby:

FULL NAME			Ending Date		Social Security Number	OFFICIAL USE
Last	First	Middle	Mo.	Yr.		

If any item on this page is amended, you must answer in full all other items on this page and file with a completed and signed execution page of Form BD or with a completed and signed execution page and Page 1 of Part I of Form ADV.

Schedule B of

FORM ADV ☐
FORM BD ☐

OFFICIAL USE

FOR PARTNERSHIPS
(Answers in response to Item 8(b) of Part I of FORM ADV or Item 8(b) of FORM BD.)

Date as stated on the execution page of FORM ADV or FORM BD accompanying this Schedule:

I. Full name of applicant exactly as stated in Item 2(a) of Part I of FORM ADV or Item 2(a) of FORM BD:	IRS Empl. Ident. No.: / OFFICIAL USE

II. Name under which business is conducted if different:

III. List all general, limited, and special partners. For each partner, complete and mark appropriate columns below. Place an asterisk (*) after the names of persons for whom a change in title, status, or partnership interest is being reported. Place a double asterisk (**) after the names of persons which are ADDED to those furnished in the most recent previous filing. Designate percentage of capital contribution as follows: If none enter "none," above 0% to less than 1%, enter "A," 1% to less than 5%, enter "B," 5% to less than 10%, enter "C," 10% to less than 25%, enter "D," 25% to less than 50%, enter "E," 50% to less than 75%, enter "F," 75% to 100%, enter "G."

FULL NAME			Beginning Date		Type of Partner	Official Use Only	Capital Contribution Code	Social Security Number
Last	First	Middle	Mo.	Yr.				
						01		
						02		
						03		
						04		
						05		
						06		
						07		
						08		
						09		
						10		
						11		
						12		

IV. List below names reported in the most recent previous filing pursuant to this Item which are DELETED hereby:

FULL NAME			Ending Date		Social Security Number	OFFICIAL USE
Last	First	Middle	Mo.	Yr.		

If any item on this page is amended, you must answer in full all other items on this page and file with a completed and signed execution page of Form BD or with a completed and signed execution page and Page 1 of Part I of Form ADV.

Schedule C of

FORM ADV ☐
FORM BD ☐

FOR APPLICANTS OTHER THAN SOLE PROPRIETORS, PARTNERSHIPS AND CORPORATIONS

(Answers in response to Item 8(c) of Part I of FORM ADV or Item 8(c) of FORM BD.)

Date as stated on the execution page of FORM ADV or FORM BD accompanying this Schedule:

WARNING: Failure to keep this form current and failure to keep accurate books and records as required by the Federal securities laws would violate such Federal securities laws and may result in disciplinary, administrative, injunctive or criminal action. INTENTIONAL MISSTATEMENTS OR OMISSIONS OF FACTS MAY CONSTITUTE CRIMINAL VIOLATIONS.

I. Full name of applicant exactly as stated in Item 2(a) of Part I of FORM ADV or Item 2(a) of FORM BD:

IRS Empl. Ident. No.:

II. Name under which business is conducted if different:

III. List below any person, including a trustee, who directs, manages, or participates in directing or managing the affairs of applicant. As to each person listed below, state his title or status and describe the nature of his authority and his beneficial interest in applicant. Place an asterisk (*) after the names of persons for whom a change in title, status, or interest is being reported. Place a double asterisk (**) after the names of persons which are ADDED to those furnished in the most recent previous filing.

FULL NAME			Relationship			Social Security Number	Description of Authority and Beneficial Interest
			Beginning Date		Title or Status		
Last	First	Middle	Mo.	Yr.			

IV. List below names reported in the most recent previous filing pursuant to this Item which are DELETED hereby:

FULL NAME			Ending Date		Social Security Number	OFFICIAL USE
Last	First	Middle	Mo.	Yr.		

If any item on this page is amended, you must answer in full all other items on this page and file with a completed and signed execution page of Form BD or with a completed and signed execution page and Page 1 of Part I of Form ADV.

Schedule D of

FORM ADV ☐
FORM BD ☐

OFFICIAL USE

(Answers in response to Item 11 of Part I of FORM ADV or Item 12 of FORM BD.)

Date as stated on the execution page of FORM ADV or FORM BD accompanying this Schedule:

NOTE: (a) Complete a separate Schedule D for each natural person named in Items 2(a), 8 or 9 of Part I of Form ADV or Items 2(a), 8 or 9 of Form BD or any Schedule thereunder, except that Schedule D need not be furnished for any person who meets both of the following conditions: (1) he owns less than 10% of any class of equity security of applicant; and (2) he is not an officer, director, or person with similar status or function.

(b) Complete a separate Schedule D for each person subject to any action reported under Item 10 of Part I of Form ADV or Item 10 of Form BD.

(c) State all names in the order of last name, first name, full middle name. If any person legally has only an initial, so indicate after the initial.

(d) Applicants who are completing Schedule D in response to Item 11 of Part I of Form ADV should also complete a separate Schedule D for: (1) each member of applicant's investment committee or similar group, if any, which determines or approves what investment advice shall generally be rendered by applicant to any client, or to which clients such investment advice shall be rendered; or (2) in the absence of an investment committee or similar group, each person associated with applicant who determines or approves what investment advice shall be rendered by applicant to any client, or to which clients such investment advice shall be rendered (if more than five such persons, it is necessary to complete a separate Schedule D only for those persons having supervisory responsibility over those persons described in this paragraph).

I. Full name of applicant exactly as stated in Item 2(a) of Part I of FORM ADV or Item 2(a) of FORM BD:

IRS Empl. Ident. No.:

II. Full name of person for whom this Schedule is being completed:

IRS Empl. Ident. No. or Soc. Sec. No.:

III. (a) Residence address of person:

(NUMBER AND STREET)　　(CITY)　　(STATE)　　(ZIP CODE)

(b) Date of Birth:　　(c) City of Birth:　　(d) State or Province:　　(e) Country:

IV. NAMES USED: Furnish below a list of all names other than the name stated in Item II of this Schedule the individual is or has been known by or uses or has used, including maiden name if applicable. If applicant is not or has not been known by any other name or does not or has not used any other name, state "None."

(LAST)　　(FIRST)　　(MIDDLE)

If any item on this page is amended, you must answer in full all other items on this page and file with a completed and signed execution page of Form BD or with a completed and signed execution page and Page 1 of Part I of Form ADV.

Schedule D of FORM ADV ☐
FORM BD ☐   Page 2

I. Full name of applicant exactly as stated in Item 2(a) of Part I of FORM ADV or Item 2(a) of FORM BD:

IRS Empl. Ident. No.:

V. EDUCATION: Furnish below a description of the education of the person named in Item II of this Schedule (include name and location of last high school attended, name and location of any college or university attended, degree received and year it was received).

VI. BUSINESS BACKGROUND: Furnish below a complete consecutive statement of all business experience and employment for the past ten years. List the most recent position first. If none, state "None."

Name of Firm and Address	Kind of Business	Exact Nature of Connection or Employment	Beginning Date		Ending Date	
			Mo.	Yr.	Mo.	Yr.

VII. PROCEEDINGS: If any answer to any paragraph of Item 10 is "Yes" with respect to the person for whom this Schedule is being completed, furnish the following details:

Applicable Part and Question of Item 10	Title or Description of Action	Name and Location of Court, Agency, Jurisdiction or Self-Regulatory Organization	Nature and Date of and Disposition of Proceeding

If any item on this page is amended, you must answer in full all other items on this page and file with a completed and signed execution page of Form BD or with a completed and signed execution page and Page 1 of Part I of Form ADV.

Schedule E of FORM ADV

(CONTINUATION SHEET FOR PART I OF FORM ADV)

(Do not use this Schedule as a continuation sheet for
Part II of FORM ADV or Schedules A, B, C, and D.)

Date as stated on the execution page of FORM
ADV accompanying this Schedule:

I. Full name of applicant exactly as stated in Item 2(a)
of Part I of Form ADV:

IRS Empl. Ident. No.:

Item of Form (identify)	ANSWER

If any item on this page is amended, you must answer in full all other items on this page and file with a completed and signed execution page and Page 1 of Part I.

WARNING: Failure to keep this form current and failure to keep accurate books and records as required by the Federal securities laws would violate such Federal securities laws and may result in disciplinary, administrative, injunctive or criminal action.

INTENTIONAL MISSTATEMENTS OR OMISSIONS OF FACTS MAY CONSTITUTE CRIMINAL VIOLATIONS.

Schedule F of FORM ADV

(CONTINUATION SHEET FOR PART II OF FORM ADV)

(Do not use this Schedule as a continuation sheet for
Part I of FORM ADV or Schedules A, B, C, and D.)

Date as stated on the execution page of FORM
ADV accompanying this Schedule:

I. Full name of applicant exactly as stated in Item 2(a)
of Part I of FORM ADV:

IRS Empl. Ident. No.:

Item of Form (identify)	ANSWER

If any item on this page is amended, you must answer in full all other items on this page and file with a completed and signed execution page and Page 1 of Part I.

288

Schedule G of FORM ADV

(Answer in Response to Item 17 of Part I or
Item 13 of Part II of FORM ADV or Item 4 of FORM ADV—S

Date as given on the execution page of
FORM ADV accompanying this Schedule:

I. Full name of applicant exactly as stated in Item 2(a)
of Part I of FORM ADV:

IRS Emp. Ident. No.:

WARNING: Failure to keep this form current and failure to keep accurate books and records as required by the Federal securities laws would violate such Federal securities laws and may result in disciplinary, administrative, injunctive or criminal action.

INTENTIONAL MISSTATEMENTS OR OMISSIONS OF FACTS MAY CONSTITUTE CRIMINAL VIOLATIONS.

*If any item on this page is amended, you must answer in full all other items on this page and file
with a completed and signed execution page and Page 1 of Part I.*

FORM ADV Execution Page

EXECUTION: The applicant submitting this Form and its attachments and the person by whom it is executed represent hereby that all information contained therein is true, current and complete. It is understood that all required Items and Schedules are considered integral parts of this Form and that the submission of any amendment represents that all unamended Items and Schedules remain true, current and complete as required.

Dated the _____ day of _____ 19 ___

_____
(Name of Corporation, Partnership or other organization)

_____
(Manual Signature of Sole Proprietor, General Partner,
Managing Agent or Principal Officer)

_____
(Title)

ALL OF THE ITEMS ON THIS PAGE MUST BE ANSWERED AND COMPLETED IN FULL

Appendix B

Important Questions You Should Ask About AMR Planning Services, Inc.

AMR PLANNING SERVICES, INC.
8243 Jericho Turnpike
Woodbury, New York   11797

Registered Investment Advisor   Telephone: (516) 692-7350

In order to provide you with background information regarding AMR Planning Services, Inc., here are some questions that you might have.

This brochure is in lieu of Form ADV Part II, required by the Securities and Exchange Commission, to be given to all potential clients by investment advisors prior to any contractual agreement.

1. *What is AMR Planning Services, Inc.?*
   AMR Planning Services, Inc., is a financial planning advisory firm registered with the Securities and Exchange Commission as a Corporate Registered Investment Advisor. Our Securities and Exchange Commission file number is 801-15442. We also maintain a current investment advisory registration with the New York State Department of Law.

2. *What is a Registered Investment Advisor?*
   An Investment Advisor is a fiduciary who has a duty of undivided loyalty to his investment advisory clients and must deal fairly and honestly with them. Any person or entity that holds itself out as a financial planner must be registered with the Security and Exchange Commission as an Investment Advisor. A Registered Investment Advisor is a representative of the client.

3. *What does AMR Planning Services, Inc., sell?*
Sound financial planning advice regarding taxes, investments, insurance, pensions, retirement, and general financial matters. We also offer an ongoing service through our investment tracking program and selectively manage client accounts.

4. *Whom do we serve?*
Individuals and businesses.

5. *Who can benefit most by our services?*
Anyone who has a financial, tax or investment problem, or who wishes to plan prudently for his or her financial future. Furthermore, persons who desire a higher, more sophisticated level of financial planning services may find our programs appealing.

6. *How much money do you need to start a financial program?*
There is no minimum or maximum dollar requirement. We recognize that persons with little or no assets have financial problems, too.

7. *What is a financial plan?*
An in-depth review of your financial situation, taking into account your goals and objectives, and focusing on income tax planning, asset management, estate planning, risk management, educational planning and retirement. The plan analyzes and recommends ways that you can achieve your financial objectives.

8. *How much do we charge for planning services?*
Our current rate is $75 per hour for financial planning consulting. However, in most cases, we will quote a flat fee for our service.

9. *What is AMR TRACKING?*
An innovative program whereby we track a client's investments, keep track of the current market value and advise periodic changes. We meet frequently with our clients and review accounts for changes in investments and for ongoing tax planning. The system is computerized and clients periodically receive a detailed report of their AMR TRACKING account. Clients are billed a flat quarterly fee for this service.

10. *Do we offer money management?*
Yes. But we reserve the right to select accounts. All assets are managed under limited power of attorney whereby the client retains custody of all funds. This service may appeal to persons too busy to manage their own accounts, athletes and entertainers, and persons confined to institutions.

11. *Are the fees tax deductible?*
Always. Section 212 of the Internal Revenue Code permits an itemized deduction for tax and/or investment advice.

12. *Do we sell financial planning products, such as investments, insurance, tax shelters?*
No. AMR Planning Services, Inc., sells only financial planning advice on a fee-paid basis. Certain financial service product, however, can be purchased from Andrew M. Rich, CFP, or from any other source.

13. *If you use AMR Planning Services, Inc., to develop a financial planning program, are you obligated to purchase the recommended products?*
Absolutely not. In fact, you are encouraged to shop around for the best available products.

14. *Does AMR Planning Services, Inc., only provide complete programs?*
No. Although a complete program is most likely beneficial, we can limit our advisory services to your specific needs.

15. *Does AMR Planning Services, Inc., offer a tax service?*
Most definitely. We believe income taxes are the central focal point of most financial programs. Therefore, we offer an income tax preparation service. Unless you are a business client who has a business accountant to prepare your taxes, it is recommended that you use us to prepare your taxes. The charges for this service are in addition to financial planning, tracking or money management.

16. *Do we provide legal services?*
No. AMR Planning Services, Inc., is a financial planner and investment advisor only, and limits itself to financial and tax matters.

17. *What types of securities do we provide advice for?*
Equities, corporate bonds, commercial paper, bank deposits, municipal securities, mutual funds, variable annuities, limited partnerships (tax shelters), and diamonds and other precious stones. We do not provide advice for options and/or commodity futures.

18. *What method of analysis do we use to analyze investments?*
We do not use technical analysis or charting. We do use a fundamental approach, such as economic conditions, earnings, industry outlook, politics (as it relates to the investment), historical data, price-earnings ratios, dividends, general level of interest rates, company management and tax benefits.

19. *Do we guarantee investment performance?*
No.

20. *Will client information be kept confidential?*
Yes. It is the law.

21. *Once a program is completed, does our relationship end?*
Absolutely not. Financial planning is a process and not a one-shot deal.

We offer ongoing service, periodic review, and day-to-day consultation if necessary.

22. *How do you get started?*
Contact us at the above phone number, tell us your problem, and find out if we can be of assistance to you.

ANDREW MICHAEL RICH, CFP
BUSINESS AND EDUCATIONAL BACKGROUND

Andrew Michael Rich, President of AMR Planning Services, Inc., is thirty-seven years of age. He earned a Bachelor of Arts degree in Economics from Queens College of the City University of New York in 1969. In 1979, he received a Master of Science degree in Taxation from the School of Professional Accountancy, Long Island University, C.W. Post Center.

Mr. Rich holds a Certified Financial Planner designation from the College for Financial Planning, Denver, Colorado, and is a member of that school's adjunct faculty.

Currently, Mr. Rich is a Lecturer of Financial Planning and Coordinator for the Financial Planning Program at New York University, School of Continuing Education.

Organization memberships include The Institute of Certified Financial Planners, The International Association for Financial Planning, and the Tax Institute of C.W. Post College.

In addition to acting as President of AMR Planning Services, Inc., he is an NASD Registered Representative licensed through First Eastern Equity Corporation, Armonk, New York, and USLICO Securities Corporation, Washington, DC. He is also a General Agent for Bankers Security Life Insurance Society, Washington, DC.

Mr. Rich is the author of *How to Survive and Succeed in the Small Financial Planning Practice*, published by Reston Publishing Co., Inc., in 1984. He appeared in the May 1982 issue of *Money Magazine*.

Information regarding the investment advisor contained in the aforementioned has neither been passed upon nor approved by the Securities and Exchange Commission, nor has the Commission passed upon or approved the qualifications or business practices of the investment advisor.

Appendix C

Release IA-770 from the Securities and Exchange Commission

SECURITIES AND EXCHANGE COMMISSION
17 CFR Part 276

(Release No. IA-770)
Applicability of the Investment Advisers Act to Financial Planners, Pension Consultants, and Other Persons Who Provide Investment Advisory Services as an Integral Component of Other Financially Related Services

AGENCY. Securities and Exchange Commission.

ACTION. Statement of staff interpretive position.

SUMMARY. The Commission is publishing the views of the staff of the Division of Investment Advisers Act of 1940 to financial planners, pension consultants, and other persons who, as an integral component of other financially related services, provide investment advisory services to others for compensation. The purpose of this release is to call to the attention of persons providing such services, as well as members of the general public who may utilize such services, the circumstances under which persons providing these services would be investment advisers under the Advisers Act and subject to the Act's registration, antifraud and other provisions. The guidance provided in this release should assist providers of financial advisory services in complying with the Advisers Act and reduce the number of requests for staff interpretive or no-action advice with respect to the applicability of the Advisers Act to such persons where the requests do not present any novel, factual or interpretive issues. With one exception the interpretive views set forth in the release are based on positions consistently taken by the staff in the past. In the case of the one exception, the position articulated in the release may have the effect of excepting from the definition of investment adviser certain persons the staff would not regard as being in the business of providing investment advice.

For further information contact:

Mary S. Champagne, Esq.
Investment Advisers Study Group
Division of Investment Management
Securities and Exchange Commission
500 North Capitol Street
Washington, DC 20549
(202) 272-2041

Supplementary Information

The staff of the Commission has received numerous requests for staff interpretive or no-action advice concerning the applicability of the Investment Advisers Act of 1940 (15 U.S.C. 80b-1 *et seq.*) ("Advisers Act") to persons, such as financial planners, pension consultants, sports and entertainment representatives and others, who provide investment advisory services as an integral component of, or bundled with, other financially related services. In addition, it appears that many of these persons may not be aware of the provisions of the federal securities laws which may be applicable to their activities, particularly the fiduciary standards and registration requirements of the Advisers Act. It is the view of the staff that, for the reasons set forth below, many of the persons providing such services to the public are investment advisers under the definition of investment adviser contained in Section 202(a)(11) of the Advisers Act (15 U.S.C. 80b-2(a)(11)) and are not entitled to rely on any of the exceptions from that definition provided in clauses (A) to (F) of Section 202(a)(11). An investment adviser who uses the mails or any means or instrumentality of interstate commerce in connection with his or its business as an investment adviser is subject to the registration, antifraud, and other provisions of the Advisers Act, unless the adviser is excepted from registration under Section 203(b) of the Advisers Act (15 U.S.C. 80b-3(b)). An adviser excepted from registration under the Advisers Act remains subject to its antifraud provisions.

I. BACKGROUND

Financial planning typically involves the provision of a variety of services, principally advisory in nature, to individuals or families with respect to management of financial resources based upon an analysis of individual client needs. Generally, financial planning services involve the preparation of a financial program for a client based upon information elicited from the client as to the client's financial circumstances and objectives. Such information normally would cover present and anticipated assets and liabilities, including insurance, savings, investments, and anticipated retirement or other benefits. The program developed for the client typically includes general recommendations for a course of activity, or specific actions, to be taken by the client. For example, recommendations may be made that the client obtain insurance or revise existing coverage, establish an individual retirement account, increase or decrease funds held in savings accounts, or invest funds in securities. A financial planner may develop tax or estate plans for the client or may refer the client to an accountant or attorney for these services. The provider of such financial planning services typically assists the client in implementing the recommended program by, among other things, making specific recommendations to carry out the general recommendations of the program, or by selling to the client insurance products, securities, or other investments. The financial planner may also review the client's program periodically and recommend revisions. Persons providing such financial planning services use various compensation arrangements. Some financial planners charge clients an overall fee for the development of an individual client program while others charge clients an hourly fee. In some instances financial planners are compensated, in whole or in part, through the receipt of sales commissions upon the sale to the client of insurance products, mutual fund shares, interests in real estate, or other investments.

A second common form of service relating to financial matters is that provided by "pension consultants" who typically offer, in addition to administrative services, a variety of advisory services to employee benefit plans and their fiduciaries based upon an analysis of the needs of the individual plan. Such advisory services may include advice as to the types of funding media available to provide plan benefits, general recommendations as to what portion of plan assets should be invested in various investment media, including securities, and, in some cases, recommendations regarding investment in specific securities or other investments. Pension consultants may also assist plan fiduciaries in determining plan investment objectives and policies and in designing funding media for the plan. They may also provide general or specific advice to plan fiduciaries as to the selection or retention of persons to manage the assets of the plan.[1] Persons providing such services to plans are customarily compensated for the provision of their services through the receipt of fees paid by the plan, its sponsor, or other persons; by means of sales commissions on the sale of insurance products or investments to the plan; or through a combination of fees and commissions.

---

[1]The authority to manage all or a portion of a plan's assets often is delegated to a person who qualifies as an "investment manager" under the Employee Retirement Income Security Act of 1974 (29 U.S.C. 1001 *et seq.*). Under that statute, which is applicable to private sector pension and welfare benefit plans, an "investment manager" must be a registered investment adviser under the Advisers Act, a bank as defined in the Advisers Act, or an insurance company which is qualified to perform services as an investment manager under the laws of more than one state.

Another form of financial advisory service is that provided by persons offering a variety of financially related services to entertainers or athletes based upon the needs of the individual client. Such persons, who often use the designation "sports representative" or "entertainment representative," typically offer a number of services to clients, including the negotiation of employment contracts and development of promotional opportunities for the client, as well as advisory services related to investments, tax planning, or budget and money management. Some persons providing these services to clients may assume discretion over all or a portion of a client's funds by collecting income, paying bills and making investments for the client. Sports or entertainment representatives are customarily compensated for the provision of their services primarily through fees charged for negotiation of employment contracts but may also receive compensation in the form of fixed charges or hourly fees for other services, including investment advisory services, which they provide.

There are other persons who, while not falling precisely into one of the foregoing categories, provide financial advisory services. As discussed below, financial planners, pension consultants, sports or entertainment representatives, or other persons providing financial advisory services, may be investment advisers within the meaning of the Advisers Act.

II. STATUS AS AN INVESTMENT ADVISER

A. *Definition of Investment Adviser*

Section 202 (a)(11) of the Advisers Act defines the term "investment adviser" to mean:

> . . . any person who, for compensation, engages in the business of advising others, either directly or through publications or writings, as to the value of securities or as to the advisability of investing in, purchasing, or selling securities, or who, for compensation and as part of a regular business, issues or promulgates analyses or reports concerning securities. . . .

Whether a person providing financially related services of the type discussed in this release would be an investment adviser within the meaning of the Advisers Act would depend upon all the relevant facts and circumstances. As a general matter, however, if the activities of any person providing such integrated advisory services satisfy each element of either part of the foregoing two part definition, such person would be an investment adviser within the meaning of the Advisers Act, unless entitled to rely on one of the exceptions from the definition of investment adviser in clauses (A) to (F) of Section 202(a)(11).[2] Accordingly, a determination as to whether a person providing

---

[2]See discussion of Section 202(a)(11)(A) to (F) in Section II B, *infra*.

financial planning, pension consulting, or other integrated advisory services is an investment adviser will depend upon whether such person: (1) provides advice, or issues reports or analyses, regarding securities; (2) whether he is in the business of providing such services; and (3) whether he provides such services for compensation. These three elements are discussed below.

1. *ADVICE OR ANALYSES CONCERNING SECURITIES.* It would seem apparent that a person who gives advice or makes recommendations or issues reports or analyses with respect to specific securities is an investment adviser under Section 202(a)(11), assuming the other elements of the definition of investment adviser are met, i.e., that such services are performed as part of a business and for compensation. However, it has been asked on a number of occasions whether advice, recommendations or reports that do not pertain to specific securities satisfy this element of the definition. In the view of the staff, a person who provides advice, or issues or promulgates reports or analyses, which concern securities, but which do not relate to specific securities, would generally be an investment adviser under Section 202(a)(11), assuming such services are performed as part of a business[3] and for compensation. The staff has interpreted the definition of investment adviser to include persons who advise clients either directly or through publications or writings concerning the relative advantages and disadvantages of investing in securities in general as compared to other investment media.[4] A person who, in the course of developing a financial program for a client, advises a client as to the desirability of investing in securities as opposed to, or in relation to, stamps, coins, direct ownership of commodities, or any other investment vehicle would also be "advising" others within the meaning of Section 202(a)(11).[5] Similarly, a person who advises employee benefit plans on funding plan benefits by investing in securities, as opposed to, or in addition to, insurance products, real estate or other funding media, would be "advising" others within the meaning of Section 202(a)(11). A person providing advice to a client as to the selection or retention of an investment manager or managers also would, under certain circumstances, be deemed to be "advising" others within the meaning of Section 202(a)(11).[6]

---

[3]In this regard, as discussed in detail below, it is the staff's view that a person who gives advice or prepares analyses concerning securities generally may, nevertheless, not be "in the business" of doing so and, therefore, will not be considered an "investment adviser" as that term is used in Section 202(a)(11).

[4]*See, e.g.,* Richard K. May (avail. Dec. 11, 1979); Hayes Martin (avail. Feb. 15, 1980); Pauline Wang (avail. Mar. 21, 1980).

[5]*See, e.g.,* Thomas Beard (avail. May 8, 1975); Sinclair-deMarinis Inc. (avail. May 1, 1981).

[6]*See, e.g.,* FPC Securities Corp. (avail. Dec. 1, 1974) (program to assist client in selection and retention of investment manager by, among other things, recommending investment managers to clients, monitoring and evaluating the performance of a client's investment manager, and advising client as to the retention of such manager); William Bye Co. (avail. Apr. 26, 1973) (program involving recommendations to client as to selection and retention of investment manager based upon client's investment objectives and periodic monitoring and evaluation of investment manager's performance). On occasion in the past the staff has taken no-action posi-

2. THE "BUSINESS" STANDARD. In order to come within the definition of an investment adviser, a person must engage for compensation in the business of advising others as to the value of securities or as to the advisability of investing in, purchasing, or selling securities or issue or promulgate reports or analyses concerning securities as part of a regular business. Under this definition, the giving of advice or issuing of reports or analyses concerning securities for compensation need not constitute the principal business activity or any particular portion of the business activities of a person in order for the person to be an investment adviser under Section 202(a)(11). However, a person who provides investment advice for compensation but is not *in the business* of advising others as to the value of securities or the advisability of investing in securities, or does not issue reports or analyses concerning securities as part of a *regular business*, does not come within the Advisers Act's definition of an investment adviser.

Whether or not a person's activities constitute being engaged in the business of advising others as to the value of securities or the advisability of investing in securities or issuing reports or analyses concerning securities as part of a regular business will depend on (1) whether the investment advice being provided is solely incidental to a non-investment advisory, primary business of the person providing the advice; (2) the specificity of the advice being given; and (3) whether the provider of the advice is receiving, directly or indirectly, any special compensation therefor.[7] As a general matter, the staff would take the position that a person who provides financial services including investment advice for compensation is *in the business* of providing investment advice within the meaning of Section 202(a)(11) unless the advice being provided by such person is solely incidental to a non-investment advisory business of the person, is non-specific, and is not rewarded by special compensation for such investment advice.

If a person holds himself out as an investment adviser or as one who provides investment advice, he would be considered to be in the business of providing investment advice. However, a person whose principal business is providing financial services other than investment advice would not be regarded as being *in the business* of giving investment advice if, as part of his service, he merely discusses in general terms the advisability of investing in securities in the context of, for example, a discussion of economic matters or

tions with respect to certain situations involving persons providing advice to clients as to the selection or retention of investment managers. *See, e.g.,* Sebastian Associates, Ltd. (avail. Aug 7, 1975) (provision of assistance to clients in obtaining and coordinating the services of various professionals such as tax attorneys and investment advisers, including referring clients to such professionals, in connection with business as agent for clients with respect to negotiation of employment and promotional contracts); Hudson Valley Planning Inc. (avail. Feb. 25, 1978) (provision of names of several investment managers to client upon request, without recommendation, in connection with business of providing administrative services to employee benefit plans).

[7] These criteria were developed as part of the staff's on-going review of prior staff interpretive letters and have not previously been articulated.

the role of investments in securities in a client's overall financial plan. The staff would, however, take the position that such a person is in the business of providing investment advice if, on anything other than rare and isolated instances, he discusses the advisability of investing in, or issues reports or analyses as to, specific securities or specific categories of securities (e.g., bonds, mutual funds, technology stocks, etc.).[8] In addition, a person who provides market timing services would be viewed as being in the business of giving investment advice. Finally, as previously indicated, a person will be regarded as being in the business of providing such advice if he receives any special compensation therefor or receives any direct or indirect remuneration in connection with a client's purchase or sale of securities. A person would generally not be considered to be receiving special compensation for the provision of advisory services if he makes no charge for the advisory portion of his services or if he charges an overall fee for financial advisory services of which the investment advice is an incidental part.

3. COMPENSATION.   The definition of investment adviser applies to persons who give investment advice and receive compensation therefor. This compensation element is satisfied by the receipt of any economic benefit, whether in the form of an advisory fee, some other fee relating to the total services rendered, commissions, or some combination of the foregoing. It is not necessary that a person who provides investment advisory and other services to a client charge a separate fee for the investment advisory portion of the total services. The compensation element would be satisfied if a single fee were charged for the provision of a number of different services, which services included the giving of investment advice or the issuing of reports or analyses concerning securities within the meaning of the Advisers Act.[9] As discussed above, however, the fact that no separate fee is charged for the investment advisory portion of the service could be relevant to whether the person is "in the business" of giving investment advice.

It is not necessary that an adviser's compensation should be paid directly by the person receiving investment advisory services, but only that the investment adviser receive compensation from some source for his services.[10] Accordingly, a person providing a variety of services to a client, including investment advisory services, for which the person receives any economic benefit, for example, by receipt of a single fee or commissions upon the sale to the client of insurance products or investments, would be performing such advisory services "for compensation" within the meaning of Section 202(a)(11) of the Advisers Act.[11]

---

[8]*Compare, Zinn* v. *Parrish*, 644 F.2d 360 (7th Cir. 1981), CCH Sec. L. Rep. para. 97,920.

[9]*See, e.g.,* FINESCO (avail. Dec. 11, 1979).

[10]*See, e.g.,* Warren H. Livingston (avail. Mar. 8, 1980).

[11]Section 202(a)(11)(C) of the Advisers Act excepts from the definition of investment adviser a broker or dealer who performs investment advisory services which are incidental to the conduct of its broker-dealer business and who receives no special compensation therefor. See discussion of Section 202(a)(11)(C) *infra*.

B. *Exceptions from Definition of Investment Adviser*

Clauses (A) to (E) of Section 202(a)(11) of the Advisers Act set forth limited exceptions from the definition of investment adviser available to certain persons.[12] Whether an exception from the definition of investment adviser is available to any financial planner, pension consultant, or other person, providing investment advisory services within the meaning of Section 202(a)(11), will depend upon the relevant facts and circumstances.

A person relying on an exception from the definition of investment adviser must meet all of the requirements of such exception. It is the view of the staff that the exception contained in Section 202(a)(11)(B) would not be available, for example, to a lawyer or accountant who holds himself out to the public as providing financial planning, pension consulting, or other financial advisory services. In such a case it would appear that the performance of investment advisory services by such person would be incidental to the practice of his financial planning or pension consulting profession and not incidental to his practice as a lawyer or accountant.[13] Similarly the exception for brokers or dealers contained in Section 202(a)(11)(C) would not be available to a broker or dealer, or associated person of a broker or dealer, acting within the scope of its business as broker or dealer, if such person receives any special compen-

---

[12]Section 202(a)(11) provides that the definition of investment adviser does not include:

- **(A)** a bank, or any bank holding company as defined in the Bank Holding Company Act fo 1956, which is not an investment company;
- **(B)** any lawyer, accountant, engineer, or teacher whose performance of such (advisory) services is solely incidental to the practice of his profession;
- **(C)** any broker or dealer whose performance of such (advisory) services is solely incidental to the conduct of his business as a broker or dealer and who receives no special compensation therefor;
- **(D)** the publisher of any bona fide newspaper, news magazine or business or financial publication of general and regular circulation;
- **(E)** any person whose advice, analyses, or reports relate to no securities other than securities which are direct obligations of or obligations guaranteed as to principal or interest by the United States, or securities issued or guaranteed by corporations in which the United States has a direct or indirect interest which shall be designated by the Secretary of the Treasury, pursuant to Section 3(a)(12) of the Securities Exchange Act of 1934, as exempted securities for the purposes of that Act. . . .

Section 202 (a)(11)(F) excepts from the definition of investment adviser "such other persons not within the intent of this paragraph, as the Commission may designate by rules and regulations or order."

[13]*See, e.g.,* Mortimer M. Lerner (avail. Feb. 15, 1980). The "professional" exception provided in Section 202(a)(11)(B) by its terms is only available to lawyers, accountants, engineers, and teachers. A person engaged in a profession other than one of those enumerated in Section 202(a)(11)(B) who performs investment advisory services would be an investment adviser within the meaning of Section 202(a)(11) whether or nor the performance of investment advisory services is incidental to the practice of such profession. Unless another basis for excepting such person from the definition of investment adviser is available, such person would be subject to the Advisers Act.

sation for the provision of investment advisory services.[14] Moreover, the exception from the definition of investment adviser contained in Section 202(a)(11)(C) would not be available to an associated person of a broker-dealer or "registered representative" who provides investment advisory services to clients outside of the scope of such person's employment with the broker-dealer.[15]

III. REGISTRATION AS AN INVESTMENT ADVISER

Any person who is an investment adviser within the meaning of Section 202(a)(11) of the Advisers Act, who is not excepted from the definition of investment adviser by virtue of one of the exceptions in Section 202(a)(11)(A) to (F), and who makes use of the mails or any instrumentality of interstate commerce in connection with such person's business as an investment adviser, is required by Section 203(a) of the Advisers Act to register with the Commission as an investment adviser unless specifically excepted from registration by Section 203(b) of the Advisers Act.[16] The materials necessary for registering with the Commission as an investment adviser can be obtained by writing Publications Unit, Securities and Exchange Commission, Washington, DC 20549.

IV. APPLICATION OF ANTIFRAUD PROVISIONS

The antifraud provisions of Section 206 of the Advisers Act (15 U.S.C. 80b-6), and the rules adopted by the Commission thereunder, apply to any person who is an investment adviser as defined in the Advisers Act, whether or not such person is required to be registered with the Commission as an investment adviser. Sections 206(1) and (2) make it unlawful for an investment adviser, directly or indirectly, to "employ any device, scheme, or artifice to defraud

[14]*See, e.g.,* FINESCO, *supra.* For a general statement of the views of the staff regarding special compensation under Section 202(a)(11)(C), see Investment Advisers Act Release No. 640 (October 5, 1978).

[15]*See, e.g.,* George E. Bates (avail. Apr. 26, 1979).

[16]Section 203 (b) excepts from registration

(1) any investment adviser all of whose clients are residents of the State within which such investment adviser maintains his or its principal office and place of business, and who does not furnish advice or issue analyses or reports with respect to securities listed or admitted to unlisted trading privileges on any national securities exchange;

(2) any investment adviser whose only clients are insurance companies; or

(3) any investment adviser who during the course of the preceding twelve months has had fewer than fifteen clients and who neither holds himself out generally to the public as an investment adviser nor acts as an investment adviser to any investment company registered under the (Investment Company Act). . . .

any client or prospective client" or to "engage in any transaction, practice, or course of business which operates as a fraud or deceit upon any client or prospective client."[17] An investment adviser is a fiduciary who owes his clients "an affirmative duty of 'utmost good faith, and full and fair' disclosure of all material facts."[18] The Supreme Court has stated that a "(f)ailure to disclose material facts must be deemed fraud or deceit within its intended meaning, for, as the experience of the 1920s and 1930s amply reveals, the darkness and ignorance of commercial secrecy are the conditions under which predatory practices best thrive."[19] Accordingly, the duty of an investment adviser to refrain from fraudulent conduct includes an obligation to disclose material facts to his clients whenever the failure to do so would defraud or operate as a fraud or deceit upon any client or prospective client. In this connection the adviser's duty to disclose material facts is particularly pertinent whenever the adviser is in a situation involving a conflict, or potential conflict, or interest with a client.

The type of disclosure required by an investment adviser who has a potential conflict of interest with a client will depend upon all the facts and circumstances. As a general matter, an adviser must disclose to clients all material facts regarding the potential conflict of interest so that the client can make an informed decision as to whether to enter into or continue an advisory relationship with the adviser or whether to take some action to protect himself against the specific conflict of interest involved. The following examples, which have been selected from cases and staff interpretive and no-action letters, illustrate the scope of the duty to disclose material information to clients in certain common situations involving conflicts of interest.

An investment adviser who is also a registered representative of a broker-dealer and provides investment advisory services outside the scope of his employment with the broker-dealer must disclose to his advisory clients that his advisory activities are independent from his employment with the broker-dealer.[20] Additional disclosures would be required, depending on the circumstances, if the investment adviser recommends that his clients execute securities transactions through the broker-dealer with which the investment adviser is associated. For example, the investment adviser would be required to disclose fully the nature and extent of any interest the investment adviser

[17]In addition, Section 206(3) of the Advisers Act generally makes it unlawful for an investment adviser acting as principal for his own account knowingly to sell any security to or purchase any security from a client, or, acting as broker for a person other than such client, knowingly to effect any sale or purchase of any security for the account of such client, without disclosing to such client in writing before the completion of such transaction the capacity in which he is acting and obtaining the consent of the client to such transaction. The responsibilities of an investment adviser dealing with a client as principal or as agent for another person are discussed in Advisers Act Release Nos. 40 and 470 (February 5, 1945, and August 20, 1975, respectively).

[18]SEC v. Capital Gains Research Bureau, 375 U.S. 180, 194 (1963) quoting Prosser, Law of Torts (1955), 534–535.

[19]Id., at 200.

[20]David P. Aug. 1, 1977.

has in such recommendation, including any compensation the investment adviser would receive from his employer in connection with the transaction.[21] In addition, the investment adviser would be required to inform his clients of their ability to execute recommended transactions through other broker-dealers.[22] Finally, the Commission has stated that "an investment adviser must not effect transactions in which he has a personal interest in a manner that could result in preferring his own interest to that of his advisory clients."[23]

An investment adviser who structures his personal securities transactions to trade on the market impact caused by his recommendations to clients must disclose this practice to clients.[24] An investment adviser generally also must disclose if his personal securities transactions are inconsistent with the advice given to clients.[25] Finally, an investment adviser must disclose compensation received from the issuer of a security being recommended.[26]

Unlike other general antifraud provisions in the Federal securities laws which apply to conduct "in the offer or sale of any securities"[27] or "in connection with the purchase or sale of any security,"[28] the pertinent provisions of Section 206 do not refer to dealings in securities but are stated in terms of the effect or potential effect of prohibited conduct on the client. Specifically, Section 206(1) prohibits "any device, scheme, or artifice to defraud any client or prospective client," and Section 206(2) prohibits "any transaction, practice, or course of business which operates as a fraud or deceit upon any client or prospective client." In this regard, the Commission has applied Sections 206(1) and (2) in circumstances in which the fraudulent conduct arose out of the investment advisory relationship between an investment adviser and its clients, even though the conduct did not involve a securities transaction. For example, in an administrative proceeding brought by the Commission against an investment adviser, the respondent consented to a finding by the Commission that the respondent had violated Sections 206(1) and (2) by persuading its clients to guarantee its bank loans and ultimately to post their securities as collateral for its loans without disclosing the adviser's deteriorating financial condition, negative net worth, and other outstanding loans.[29] Moreover, the staff has

---

[21]*Ibid.*
[22]Don P. Matheson (avail. Sept. 1, 1976).
[23]Kidder, Peabody & Co., Inc., 43 S.E.C. 911, 916 (1968).
[24]*SEC* v. *Capital Gains Research Bureau, supra* at 197.
[25]*In the Matter of Dow Theory Letters et al.*, Advisers Act Release No. 571 (February 22, 1977).
[26]*In the Matter of Investment Controlled Research et al.*, Advisers Act Release No. 701 (September 17, 1979).
[27]Section 17(a) (15 U.S.C. 77q(a)) of the Securities Act of 1933 (15 U.S.C. 77a et seq.)
[28]Rule 10b-5 (15 CFR 240.10b-5) under the Securities Exchange Act of 1934 (15 U.S.C. 78a et seq.). *See also* Section 15(c) (15 U.S.C. 78o(c)) of the Securities Exchange Act of 1934.
[29]*In the Matter of Ronald B. Donati Inc. et al.*, Advisers Act Rel. Nos. 666 and 683 (February 8, 1979, and July 2, 1979, respectively). *See also Intersearch Technology, Inc.*, CCH Fed. Sec. L. Rep. 1974–1975 Trans. Binder para. 80, 139 (Feb. 28, 1979) at 85,189.

taken the position that an investment adviser who sells non-securities invest-ments to clients must, under Sections 206(1) and (2), disclose to clients and prospective clients all its interests in the sale to them of such non-securities investments.[30]

V. NEED FOR INTERPRETIVE ADVICE

The general interpretive guidance provided in this release should facilitate greater compliance with the Advisers Act. The staff will respond to routine requests for no-action or interpretive advice relating to the status of persons engaged in types of businesses described in this release by referring persons making such requests to the release, unless the requests present novel factual or interpretive issues such as material departures from the nature and type of services and compensation arrangements discussed above. Requests for no-action or interpretive advice from the staff should be submitted in accordance with the procedures set forth in Investment Advisers Act Release No. 281 (Jan. 25, 1971). Accordingly, Part 276 of Chapter II of Title 17 of the Code of Federal Regulations is amended by adding Investment Advisers Act Release No. IA-770, Statement of the staff as to the applicability of the Investment Advisers Act to financial planners, pension consultants, and other persons who provide invest-ment advisory services as an integral component of other financially related services; thereto.

By the Commission:

                                                            George A. Fitzsimmons
                                                            Secretary.

August 13, 1981.

---

[30]See, *Boston Advisory Group* (avail. Dec. 5, 1976).

INDEX